Courts, Jurisdictions, and Law in John Milton and His Contemporaries

Courts, Jurisdictions, and Law in John Milton and His Contemporaries

Alison A. Chapman

The University of Chicago Press   CHICAGO & LONDON

The University of Chicago Press, Chicago 60637
The University of Chicago Press, Ltd., London
© 2020 by The University of Chicago
All rights reserved. No part of this book may be used or reproduced in any manner whatsoever without written permission, except in the case of brief quotations in critical articles and reviews. For more information, contact the University of Chicago Press, 1427 East 60th Street, Chicago, IL 60637.
Published 2020

29 28 27 26 25 24 23 22 21 20   1 2 3 4 5

ISBN-13: 978-0-226-72915-2 (cloth)
ISBN-13: 978-0-226-72929-9 (paper)
ISBN-13: 978-0-226-72932-9 (e-book)
DOI: https://doi.org/10.7208/chicago/9780226729329.001.0001

Library of Congress Cataloging-in-Publication Data

Names: Chapman, Alison A., author.
Title: Courts, jurisdictions, and law in John Milton and his contemporaries / Alison A. Chapman.
Description: Chicago ; London : The University of Chicago Press, 2020. | Includes bibliographical references and index.
Identifiers: LCCN 2020001534 | ISBN 9780226729152 (cloth) | ISBN 9780226729299 (paperback) | ISBN 9780226729329 (ebook)
Subjects: LCSH: Milton, John, 1608–1674—Knowledge—Law. | English literature—17th century—History and criticism. | Law in literature. | Law and literature—England.
Classification: LCC PR3592.L3 C47 2020 | DDC 821/.4—dc23
LC record available at https://lccn.loc.gov/2020001534

In memory of Lee Barton Chapman

CONTENTS

A Note on Texts ix
List of Abbreviations xi
Preface: Making Sense of Many Laws xiii

1	Introduction	1
2	Defending One's Good Name: Free Speech in the Early Prose	23
3	Monstrous Books: *Areopagitica* and the Problem of Libel	50
4	Civil Law and Equity in the Divorce Tracts	78
5	Defending *Pro Se Defensio*	99
6	The Tithes of War: Paying God Back in *Paradise Lost*	131
7	"Justice in Thir Own Hands": Local Courts in the Late Prose	151
	Afterword: Justice in the Columbia Manuscript	170

Acknowledgments 183
Bibliography 185
Index 201

ON TEXTS

Throughout this book I have silently modernized typography when dealing with early modern printed books: e.g., "haue" appears as "have," "iustice" as "justice," and "lavv" as "law." Otherwise, I have preserved early modern spelling. I have expanded standard abbreviations and symbols: e.g., "&" has been converted to "and." I have followed modern conventions about capitalizing titles. I have converted italics to regular font only for long stretches of italics; incidental italicized words have been preserved as they appear in the original text.

When using documents from *Life Records* and *Milton in Chancery*, I have reproduced them as found there with two exceptions: (1) I have changed superscripts to standard-size font; (2) when encountering a "con" or "cōn" suffix where modern spelling would supply "cion," I have silently updated it (examples include changing "descripcon" to "descripcion" and "sequestracōn" to "sequestracion"). All translations are my own unless noted otherwise. When citing Milton's prose, I have done so by volume and page numbers. When citing Milton's poetry, I have done so by book number and line number(s), in the case of *Paradise Lost*, or, in the case of the shorter poems, simply by line number.

The conclusion of this book examines the Columbia Manuscript, an early modern notebook miscellany in which some of Milton's political writings appear. There, in addition to my standard practice of regularizing superscripts, I have also silently converted the character "þ" to "th." So, for instance, "þᵉ" appears in the text as "the." The person who transcribed the excerpts in the

Columbia Manuscript used a personal symbol to indicate the prefix "con," and I have also silently converted this. As with *Life Records* and *Milton in Chancery*, I have updated "con" and "cōn" suffixes. Otherwise, I have preserved his spellings and abbreviations, although when needed for clarity, I have marked expansions in brackets.

ABBREVIATIONS

CM, John Milton, "John Milton Letters, 1649–1659," a notebook known as the Columbia Manuscript. Columbia Rare Books Library X823M64 S62, Columbia University, New York.
CPEP, John Milton, *The Complete Poetry and Essential Prose of John Milton*, ed. William Kerrigan, John P. Rumrich, and Stephen M. Fallon. New York: Modern Library, 2007.
CPW, John Milton, *The Complete Prose Works of John Milton*, ed. Don Wolfe et al. 8 vols. New Haven: Yale University Press, 1953–82.
LR, Joseph Milton French, ed., *The Life Records of John Milton*. 5 vols. New Brunswick, NJ: Rutgers University Press, 1966.
MC, Joseph Milton French, *Milton in Chancery: New Chapters in the Lives of the Poet and His Father*. New York: Modern Language Association, 1939.
PSD, John Milton, *Joannis Miltoni Angli Pro Se Defensio*. London, 1655.

**PREFACE:
MAKING SENSE OF MANY LAWS**

One goal of this book is to introduce readers to an early modern world whose jurisprudence was much less standardized than our own. The entries below explain some of the principal kinds of law operative in seventeenth-century England and key terms that I use to discuss them.

Roman law. To understand the laws of Europe, both secular and sacred, we have to appreciate the foundational role that Roman law played in early modern legal thinking and practice. During the classical period and the early days of empire, Rome was regulated by a sprawling, heterogeneous collection of statutes, legal customs, and courtroom procedures. In the sixth century, this body of law assumed a more clearly defined shape when the emperor Justinian ordered the compilation of the *Corpus Juris Civilis*—literally, the "body of civil laws," those laws that govern the *civis*—thereby digesting all of the various laws that had regulated a vast, diverse society into a single authoritative body of texts.

Canon law. In the twelfth-century Bolognese Renaissance, church scholars discovered the *Corpus Juris Civilis* and realized that with some adaptation, Roman jurisprudence could serve as an effective foundation for the emerging canon law of the church. For example, the canonical *ius patronatus*, which regulated the transfer of gifts and property between a designated lay patron and the church, was modeled on the Roman laws of patronage. As the church extended its reach, the Roman-based jurisprudence of the canon law flowed with it and became a kind of universal connective tissue binding together laity and clergy in all of their complex interactions. The English Reformation did not lead to a radical change in the existing canon law. Naturally, after the 1540s thorny cases in Protestant England no longer traveled up a chain of appeal that ended at the Vatican, and there was a certain amount of jurisprudential drift between English canon law and Continental canon law. However, on balance the two bodies of canon law were similar enough that canonists in Protestant England continued to rely on the learning of their European counterparts. The jurisdiction of the canon law courts was substantially reduced in 1641 by the Long Parliament, although as recent scholarship has shown, certain areas, such as tithes and probate, remained vibrant.

Civil law (capital "C"). The unified, Roman-based jurisprudence of the church provided a model for the secular nation-states. Earlier in the medieval period, the interactions of various political orders was made even more difficult by the coexistence of various legal systems. Over the course of several centuries, most of the nation-states of Europe followed the lead of the Catholic Church and adopted the *Corpus Juris Civilis* as their basic jurisprudential scaffolding. The *Corpus Juris Civilis* was supplemented over time by hundreds of juridical commentaries in something of the same way that the Bible had been buttressed by theological commentaries. This collected body of texts came to be known as the "Civil law," the law that regulated most of the civil societies of the Continent. In this book, I echo early modern English practice and use the terms "Roman law" and "Civil law" more or less interchangeably.

Ius commune. The *ius commune* refers to the shared system of legal thought that spanned most of Europe, and it comprises the secular Civil law and the sacred canon law, both of them resting atop the *Corpus Juris Civilis*. (Legal historians sometimes use the related term "Romano-canon law.") Since *ius commune* in Latin means "common law," the catchphrase illustrates the degree to which Roman law was the jurisprudential glue holding together much of Europe. It also exemplifies the difficulties that modern readers can face when confronted with the early modern jural world since the "common law" of the Continent was strikingly different from the "common law" of England.

Common law. This was the official legal system of early modern England although as this book argues, it was by no means the only one. For example, the common law landscape was dotted with Civil law courts such as the two university courts of Oxford and Cambridge and the court of the Admiralty. Common law was uncodified in the sense that it was not officially fixed by a single body of texts such as the *Corpus Juris Civilis* of the Continent. Instead, common law was based on case law, meaning that it had accreted over centuries on the basis of courtroom decisions, and while many of these decisions had been recorded in law reports written by individual jurists such as Sir Edward Coke, these reports were not themselves formal expressions of what the law said. Some scholars use the term "common law" in a restrictive way to exclude the growing body of statutes. However, because early modern common lawyers and judges frequently cited statutes in their writings and because most MPs thought of their legislative acts as contributions to the corpus of the common law, I use "common law" to encompass both case law and statutory law.

Natural law. Despite its name, natural law is not an actual legal system. It is instead the belief that God created the universe in accordance with certain fundamental principles—i.e., that there is a "law" that regulates all of "nature"—and that these principles are discoverable by human reason. Natural law assumed new jurisprudential relevance in the seventeenth century as jurists such as Hugo Grotius and John Selden used it as a conceptual yardstick for measuring the validity of purely human and applied laws. Thus natural law was behind the emergence of an early modern discourse of inalienable human rights and the development of international law, since both human rights and international law presumed a legal order that transcended the dictates of any one national code.

Positive law. Positive law literally means law that is "posited" by a human institution. The English Parliament added to the nation's body of positive law each time it created a statute, as did judges each time they issued a ruling in a case that could then serve as a precedent. At least in theory, positive law is different from natural law since while positive law is the result of localized human enactments, natural law is an expression of cosmic natural principles.

civil law (lowercase "c"). At various points in this book, I will be concerned with matters that did not rise to the level of criminal offenses. In these cases, I use the term "civil law" to indicate private matters that were prosecuted by individuals, as opposed to criminal threats to the commonwealth that were prosecuted by the state. This lowercase "civil law" must not be equated with uppercase "Civil law," the collected legal traditions of the European states. I risk this confusion only because the civil/criminal division is such a standard part of our modern lexicon that it offers the best means to talk about different categories of offenses.

Equity. As I have wrestled with the terminological predicaments of *ius commune*/common law and civil law/Civil law, I have often wished that early modern jurisprudence offered more available labels to choose from when discussing its different aspects. "Equity" provides another case in point. "Equity" in early modern English contexts could mean the specific approaches and remedies available only to judges in courts of equitable jurisdiction such as Chancery or the Court of Requests. But "equity" could also refer to those broad ideas of fairness and justice that were shared by all legal systems. In the chapters below, I take up both forms of equity, and I have worked to make it clear from the context which kind I have in mind.

CHAPTER 1

Introduction

One of the greatest obstacles that modern readers face when trying to understand early modern English courts and law is our tendency to project backward an idea of law as a unified fabric of norms with a relatively well organized and consistent judicial apparatus. While law in the modern world has its share of internal contradictions and jurisdictional struggles (e.g., tussles between different US courts or federal agencies), these are far less pronounced than the realities that early modern men and women took for granted. A comparison of two seventeenth-century English courts—the Court of the Admiralty, which followed the procedures of the Civil (or Roman) law, and King's Bench, a top common law court—throws these realities into high relief. In the Civilian Admiralty, clerks compiled a dossier of evidentiary documents written in English; the defendant could testify under oath on his own behalf; witnesses could be compelled with subpoenas; and the verdict was given by a judge who could order what we would call specific performance or an injunction (respectively, orders that someone either do something or quit doing it) but who could not ordinarily award monetary damages or apply capital punishment. King's Bench differed in each respect. Evidence was strictly oral and, at least at the beginning of the early modern period, apt to be conducted in law French; the defendant himself could not testify, owing to concerns about self-incrimination; there was no judicial means to compel witness testimony; the verdict was given by a lay jury; and while the judge could sentence offenders to pay damages or send them to prison or the gallows, he did not have injunctive powers. In London, these wildly different procedures could occur at the same time in courtrooms just a few miles apart.[1] Moreover, these differences in legal procedure were matched by differences in legal substance, meaning that the "contents" of the Civil law, or what it said, could be as unfamiliar to common lawyers as the procedural methods by which those "contents" were applied.

As this example indicates, the jural world of seventeenth-century England was a complex jurisdictional patchwork in which multiple legal systems (e.g., common law, Civil law, canon law, equity, forest law, merchants' law, etc.) were administered by various judicatures (e.g., Chancery, King's Bench, Admiralty, manorial courts, franchise courts, etc.). And the relationships between these legal systems and their associated courts constantly shifted as each one struggled to protect or enlarge its own remit, usually at the expense of others. The common law courts were acquiring greater control over adjudication, but this steady shift in the balance of judicial power only heightened everyone's sensitivity to the boundary lines between different courts and different legal systems. Eyeing the period's variegated legal terrain, historian Charles Gray observes that law in sixteenth- and seventeenth-century England was unique because it was "more deeply federalistic than [in] earlier and later periods." As a result, "jurisdiction was taken more seriously, its problems handled more delicately, because the mixed nature of the system was perceived as an essential and legitimate feature of it."[2] Building on Gray's work, Bradin Cormack has argued that many literary works written between 1509 and 1625, including ones by More, Spenser, and Shakespeare, are animated by contemporary jurisdictional struggles and in turn helped to reinforce them. Cormack makes a powerful case that thinking productively about literature and law in the early modern period requires thinking about literature and many different *kinds* of law.[3]

As this book argues, one of the best ways for modern readers to understand the jurisdictional variety of seventeenth-century England—and the challenges and opportunities this variety presented for those committed to justice and to social, religious, and political change—is to read the works of John Milton. In each of the chapters that follow, I take up one or more of Milton's

---

1. In a city such as Durham, various courts could even sit side by side. See A. Green, "Law and Architecture."

2. Gray, *Writ of Prohibition*, xv. See also Dawson, *History of Lay Judges*, 2–3. On the problems this variety presented to early modern state formation, see Lemmings, *Law and Government*.

3. Cormack, *Power to Do Justice*.

works—focusing primarily on his prose—to show how he gives careful attention to the different systems of law he saw around him and how he uses their terms and assumptions to structure his thinking.[4] The nature of my rhetorical project will become clearer if I imaginatively posit and then answer a series of follow-up "Why?" questions. First, "Why was Milton so predisposed to think about different legal systems?" His biography offers a partial answer. Partly by happenstance and partly by predilection, Milton had a remarkably varied exposure to different forms of law. Many of his family and friends had been educated at the Inns of Court and then practiced at common law; he, his father, and brother all pursued cases in the equity court of Chancery; his early patron and neighbor, the earl of Bridgewater, was the president of a prerogative court; as Latin Secretary, he wrote about events that raised questions of international law and maritime law; his defenses of the English people and his work as a licenser for the Commonwealth government all required a deep familiarity with statute law; and his writings attest to his deep reading in the major texts of Roman law and canon law.[5] Because of this exceptionally well-stocked jurisdictional toolkit, Milton was able to bring many vocabularies of law to bear on the problems before him. However, this is not a complete answer to the "Why?" question posed above, for simply asserting that Milton understood many kinds of law does not explain why he felt compelled to use them. I will return to this issue in more detail below; for now, the placeholder answer is that, somewhat paradoxically, different systems of law provided Milton with highly flexible ways to think about different questions of liberty, a subject that occupied him intensely throughout his lifetime.

Another, related "Why?" question is "Why Milton?" In other words, why have I chosen to zero in on this particular author, out of all the early modern writers who had a pronounced interest and competence in legal matters (Shakespeare, Donne, and Jonson spring immediately to mind in this

---

4. Despite gains in recent years, the body of criticism on Milton's extensive interests in law still remains small. While I signal specific critical debts in the chapters that follow, I here acknowledge more general debts to the following: Greenberg, "Law"; Kahn, *Wayward Contracts*; Rosenblatt, *Torah and Law in Paradise Lost*; Shawcross, *Development*; and Jenkins, *Inheritance Law*.

5. Milton's legal biography is explored in more detail in Chapman, *Legal Epic*, 16–25. Christopher N. Warren has demonstrated Milton's sensitivity to questions of international law in his *Literature and the Law of Nations*. On his experiences suing in England's equity courts, see French, *Milton in Chancery*, and Chapman, "Lay Reader's Guide." In subsequent chapters, I take up his exposure to laws relating to censorship/licensing and to the corpuses of Roman and canon law.

regard)?[6] To this, I make three answers. First, while this book is focused on Milton, it is not only about Milton. To give some examples, in the next chapter, I compare Milton's ideas of defamation with George Herbert's and John Donne's; in chapter 5, I contrast his use of Roman law in his third Latin defense, *Pro Se Defensio*, to the trial scene in Jonson's *Poetaster*; and in chapter 7, I use the 1661 conviction of John Bunyan to show the advantages and risks inherent in Milton's ideas for restructuring England's courts. Second, Milton is my primary subject of study because he simply had an outsized interest in the way that different systems compared with one another. Arguably more than any other major figure of the seventeenth century, he thought a lot about questions of jurisdiction, about the boundary lines that divided different spheres of influence and collections of legal norms. Third, Milton lived through exceptionally tumultuous times, and as a politically engaged citizen and then as an employee of the Interregnum government, he left behind a huge volume of treatises probing the relative rights of individuals, church, and state. As a result, a critic such as myself interested in his views of civil justice and jurisdiction has a deep and wide archive in which to search.

A final question is "Why Milton's prose?" Since with the possible exception of *Areopagitica*, Milton's poetry has had a more enduring appeal than his prose, why have I chosen to omit from consideration works such as *Samson Agonistes* and *Paradise Regained*? (My focus on the prose is not absolute, for *Paradise Lost* figures in chapter 6. It offers, I argue, one of his most nuanced reflections on the canon law of tithes.) This book concentrates on Milton's prose because his jurisdictional interests are, on the whole, more visible there than in his poetry. Milton aims his prose tracts at what he regarded as urgent social issues, and when he is thinking in this vein, he often uses the varying assumptions and vocabularies of different legal systems to help him build his arguments. My focus on the prose also distinguishes this book from my previous one, *The Legal Epic: Paradise Lost and the Early Modern Law*. There my main interest was in the way that Milton uses law in his epic poem to help justify the ways of God to men. As a result, I cast prose works only in the oc-

---

6. While the body of works on Shakespeare's legal involvements is too large to do justice to in a single note, readers can profitably start with Hutson, *Invention of Suspicion*; Maus, *Being and Having*; and Mukherji, *Law and Representation in Early Modern Drama*. See also the essays collected in Strier, *Shakespeare and the Law* and Hutson, *Oxford Handbook*. For discussions of Donne's jurisdictional awareness, see Kneidel, *John Donne*. I open chapter 5 with a consideration of the trial scene in Jonson's *Poetaster* and note there existing studies of Jonson's familiarity with both English and Roman law.

casional supporting role, often with an uneasy awareness that I was not giving them the attention they deserved. For example, in *The Legal Epic*, I mentioned Milton's neglected early treatise *Apology against a Pamphlet* only in passing as an example of how he often installs legal metaphors at the beginning of works, as if to help him think his way into his subject. However, this glancing treatment did not do justice to the way that legal reasoning informs the treatise's argument at a very deep level, a subject I explore in the next chapter. Similarly, in *The Legal Epic* I focused more on the role that law as a whole plays in his theodicy and less on his awareness of jurisdictional differences, my primary quarry here. A shift in terminology exemplifies the different arguments of these two books. In *The Legal Epic*, I used the catchall term "Romano-canon law" to refer to the consolidated sacred/secular law of the Continent because I was interested in this network of legal ideas as a whole. However, here I turn to what Milton saw as the tensions internal to this network, and so I talk about "Roman law" on the one hand and "canon law" on the other.

TWO BRIEF EXAMPLES

At this point, a pair of examples can usefully illustrate the phenomenon explored in this book. Excerpts from Milton's least-studied divorce tracts, *The Judgment of Martin Bucer* and *Colasterion*, demonstrate both his jurisdictional turn of mind and the particularly technical way in which it is often expressed. In both cases, Milton is complaining about the hostile reception given to his earlier divorce tract, *Doctrine and Discipline of Divorce*. In the preface to *Bucer*, having first detoured through a complex legal metaphor involving "bail," "endightment," and "attaintures," he claims that the present work, his translation of the prominent Reformer Martin Bucer's argument in support of divorce, might allow him "to get [his] appeachment"—i.e., the metaphorical crime of *Doctrine and Discipline*—"new drawn," or rewritten, as "a Writ of Error" (*CPW* 2:440). A writ of error was a form of appeal in which a complainant argued that errors of fact or law had invalidated the original judgment and that the records of the case should be sent to a higher court. In cases where a major Westminster court such as King's Bench or the Court of Common Pleas was the court of first instance, the writ of error sent the case to Parliament. The title page of *Bucer* addresses the treatise "*To the Parlament of England*" (*CPW* 2:421), so in the playful fiction of this passage, Milton says that he has been mistakenly convicted in a lower court (i.e., the court of public opinion that had condemned *Doctrine and Discipline*), and on the basis of Bucer's testimony presented here in *The Judgment of Martin*

Bucer, the case should now go to the nation's highest judicature on appeal.[7] The technical reasoning in this passage indicates why Milton's many jurisdictional references have gone previously unnoticed. The writ of error is no longer a functional part of American or British law, having been obviated or replaced by changes to civil procedure or appellate rules. As a result, while modern readers of Milton's divorce tracts may recognize the broadly legal tilt of a passage that refers to "attaintures" and "endightment," without a specific background in early modern legal history, they are unlikely to know that when he refers to a writ of error, Milton is not simply appealing to a single normative system that we would think of as "the law." Instead, he asks readers to think with him about the way in which different judicial venues might produce more or less just outcomes.

Milton's treatise *Colasterion* provides a similar example. *Doctrine and Discipline* had been attacked from two directions, by the Puritan minister William Prynne—a champion in the fight to reform the Church of England—and by the anonymous author of *An Answer to a Book, Intituled, The Doctrine and Discipline of Divorce*. In his response, *Colasterion*, Milton faces a dilemma: he does not want to ignore Prynne's attack, but neither does he want to castigate Prynne in the same way as the Answerer, whose bungled arguments he despises. Milton's solution is to charge Prynne and the Answerer with offenses from different legal systems. Prynne, he says, has committed a "rash and heedless calumny of his neighbour" (*CPW* 2:723). In context, Milton is administering only a hand-slapping. Calumny was the canon law's version of what we would call slander, and it was not a criminal offense. Canon law courts were also highly attuned to motive so a judge in a diocesan court faced with a defendant, such as Prynne, who had uttered a "rash and heedless"—as opposed to a premeditated—calumny would probably have ordered him to make a public apology. (Moreover, by the time Milton was writing *Colasterion*, the canon law courts had been stripped of much of their jurisdiction, so Milton is charging the Answerer with an offense that was unenforceable.) Milton is not nearly so gentle with the Answerer, whom he accuses of "*Champarty*" (*CPW* 2:727). The early modern period had a deep-seated fear of corrupt legal practices, and prominent among these was the crime of maintenance, which was encouraging or being involved in a lawsuit without just cause.[8] Champerty was an aggravated form of maintenance, and the common law writer

---

7. The early modern Parliament combined both legislative and judicial functions in a way that is largely alien to the modern world. See McIlwain, *High Court of Parliament*.

8. Strain, "Legal Reform and *2 Henry IV*," 280–81.

Thomas Blount calls it "an ancient grievance in our Nation."[9] Someone committed champerty when he abetted someone else's lawsuit for personal gain.[10] Milton alleges that the semiliterate Answerer has combined with a better-informed backer—a "stripling Divine" who has furnished scraps of theological knowledge—and also with the licenser/judge who has brought "his chair into the Title leaf; there sits and judges up or judges down." All of them are in cahoots for "round fees" (*CPW* 2:727). Unlike calumny, champerty was a serious offense. It had been prosecuted fiercely by Star Chamber before that court's dissolution in 1641, at which point cognizance transferred over to the common law courts.[11] So whereas Prynne has committed an offense hardly at the level of a misdemeanor, the Answerer has committed something akin to a felony.

These two excerpts are typical of this book's focus on civil, or private, law, with my discussion of champerty being the exception that proves the rule. The early modern period was so committed to the integrity and just operations of civil law—that is, to the idea that people with grievances against one another should have an impartial legal forum within which to seek redress—that any underhanded manipulation of these operations in the form of maintenance or champerty was punished as a crime. While early modern England, especially in the area of the common law, did not draw a crisp or consistent theoretical line between private law and public law in the way that we might expect, we can still usefully distinguish between those civil matters that concerned individuals and those that concerned the state as a whole. Into this latter category we can put offenses such as robbery, murder, treason, etc. (i.e., the corpus of the criminal law); the rights and obligations of soldiers vis-à-vis civilians (i.e., martial law); the efforts of England's courts and rulers to regulate the complex political, economic, mercantile, and military relationships between different

---

9. Blount, *Nomo-Lexicon*, s.v. "Champarti." As Samuel Thorne shows, Sir Edward Coke completely misunderstood a feudal statute about land ownership because he projected onto it his own century's anxieties about those who colluded in the crime of maintenance: Thorne, "Sir Edward Coke: 1552–1952," 11–12.

10. For example, a rich man eager to sabotage a neighbor might find a poor man who had a legal grievance against this same neighbor and agree to pay all his legal fees. This could work for the rich man in various ways. For example, he and the poor man might agree to split any damages awarded. The rich man might be hoping that a judgment would materially benefit him indirectly (hypothetically, the neighbor could be ordered to vacate land that the rich man could then acquire). Or, if he had a concurrent lawsuit of his own against the neighbor, the rich man might be trying to exhaust his neighbor's time and money.

11. On Star Chamber's efforts to punish maintenance, see Hudson, *Treatise*, 88–95.

nation-states (i.e., international law), and the extraordinarily vexed question of the rights of subjects vis-à-vis their rulers (i.e., constitutional law). In this book, I will track Milton's thinking as he explores various issues in private law. I restrict my focus in this way for two reasons. First, I am trying to bring into view a form of legal thinking that has often been neglected and thereby to compensate for a lopsidedness in the critical landscape. (For example, far more scholars know Milton's thoughts on the legality of regicide than his views of debt composition.) Second, for reasons that I explore further below, private law for Milton raised complex questions of individual choice and human liberty.

THE BRIDGE TO ALTERNITY

The first step toward understanding how and why Milton moves in and out of different legal systems is to shift away from a narrow idea of law as synonymous with positive law—i.e., as being only a top-down imposition of the secular nation-state. The work of the jurist and legal theorist Robert Cover can help make this shift. In his essays, Cover argues that law should not be understood simply as a given society's system of rules for control. Instead, law is embedded inside a larger constellation of narratives from which law takes its meaning: "We inhabit a *nomos*—a normative universe. We constantly create and maintain a world of right and wrong, of lawful and unlawful, of valid and void." The formal procedures and institutions of the law are only "a small part of the normative universe" since "no set of legal institutions or prescriptions exists apart from the narratives that locate it and give it meaning. For every constitution there is an epic, for each decalogue a scripture."[12] Cover's theory is useful because it expands the jural field beyond the boundaries of institutional law per se. When we widen our aperture to take in this larger field, Milton comes into view. Not an institutional servant of the corpus juris, he was nevertheless preoccupied by what Cover sees as the central concerns of the *nomos*: "right and wrong, lawful and unlawful, valid and void." In fact, Milton was arguably one of the chief activists of the early modern *nomos*.

Areopagitica provides a good example of Milton's deep involvement in the seventeenth-century *nomos*. At one level, *Areopagitica* is an antilaw argument in that Milton wants to put books and reading beyond the reach of England's

---

12. Cover, *Narrative*, 95–96. See also legal historian Robert W. Gordon's argument that any law/society divide is meaningless since law constitutes the terms upon which people think about their relationships to other people: "Critical Legal Histories."

legal authorities. In this sense, John Leonard is correct when he writes, "Milton throughout his career had little faith in laws."[13] However, Milton is not simply standing outside an institutional structure called "law" and hurling stones of protest. His whole approach is deeply juridical in that his argument fundamentally depends upon the same jural systems that he critiques. For example, on the title page of *Areopagitica* Milton addresses "the Parliament of ENGLAND" (*CPW* 2:485), and throughout the treatise he presses the MPs to repeal some provisions of an earlier licensing statute but to leave other provisions intact, such as those protecting copyright. As Nigel Smith reminds us, while earlier in the period, law typically appears mimetically in literature as "part of the architecture of plays or poems," much of the literature of the 1640s and 1650s "is literally a plea in the name of a desired legal practice."[14] *Areopagitica* is precisely such a legal plea. In the course of his argument, Milton weighs out the respective authority of Parliament vis-à-vis the "Jury" of readers (*CPW* 2:505), and by urging legislative action, he touches on the proper relationship between statutory law, custom, and case law. As I explore further in chapter 3, Milton is also keenly aware in *Areopagitica* of the way that different contemporary judicatures prosecuted transgressive words, and he uses references to debt imprisonment and sureties (both common law processes) to build his antilicensing argument. While Milton wants to exempt reading from all juridical controls, *Areopagitica* is simultaneously and paradoxically steeped in juridical ways of thinking.

Milton's two major divorce tracts, *Doctrine and Discipline of Divorce* and *Tetrachordon*, are similarly built around a legal scaffolding. Like *Areopagitica*, they are addressed to Parliament, and Milton urges a specific legislative change: he wants the MPs to strip jurisdiction over divorce away from the canon law, much as they had done for usury in 1571 and would do again for frauds in 1677. However, the example of usury also illustrates what Milton saw as the danger of such legislation, for when Parliament set a legal rate for usury, it thereby made violations of usury enforceable in the common law courts. Especially on the subject of divorce, Milton was not an Erastian, meaning that he did not want secular judges to don the robes of their ecclesiastical colleagues and begin hearing cases about the validity of marriage.[15] In effect, Milton wants Parliament to pass a law that says to the ecclesiastical courts, "you may not litigate the issue of divorce," but that also says, "we will not

---

13. Leonard, *Value of Milton*, 4.
14. N. Smith, "Legal Agency," 605.
15. On Milton's anti-Erastian stance, see Gregory, "Did Milton Have?"

litigate this issue either." Martin Dzelzainis argues that for Milton, to be free means to be *sui juris*, under one's own jurisdiction instead of subject to the jural power of another, and this impulse is especially visible in the divorce tracts, where he claims that each man should be "a Law in this matter to himself" (*Doctrine and Discipline of Divorce, CPW* 2:347).[16] However, Milton's *sui juris* claims appear embedded in works whose fundamental logical warrant is that each man is also *sub juris*, under the authority of another. After all, if men and women were not, in fact, *sub juris*, there would be no reason to mount a legally informed argument to Parliament in the first place. Exploring Milton's repeated recourse to Roman law, Dzelzainis pinpoints the seeming contradictions in Milton's thinking: "The paradox which we need to grasp therefore is that, in the very act of defining Christian liberty as freedom from the law, Milton falls back on the conceptual framework of the Roman law of persons."[17] While Dzelzainis is arguing that Roman law in particular matched Milton's interests, in fact Milton reaches for many other kinds of laws as well when he wants to think about liberty and righteousness, and so Dzelzainis's point about the complex and conflicted role of law in Milton's thinking has a greater purchase than he allows.

Cover's idea of the role of law in the larger *nomos* helps us see why law was such a source of combined frustration and fascination for Milton. Law has often been regarded reductively as the "mask of privilege" or the ventriloquized voice of state power. However, Cover argues that it is more usefully seen as "a system of tension or a bridge linking the concept of a reality to an imagined alternative."[18] Each community builds a legal "bridge to the future" using "the materials of sacred narrative that take as their subject much more than what is commonly conceived as 'the legal.'"[19] Arguably more than any other English writer, Milton liked to imagine connections between "the concept of a reality" and "an imagined alternative." The bridge connecting Earth and Hell and the ladder connecting Earth and Heaven in *Paradise Lost* are only the most obvious instances. We could also adduce *A Masque*'s vision of the "due steps" that lead some mortals to "the palace of eternity" (*CPEP* 7, 14); sonnet 7's focus on "Time" and the "will of Heav'n" guiding Milton toward his assigned "lot" (*CPEP* 12, 11); and the "rousing motions" that stir Samson into violent action (*CPEP* 1382). In these and other examples, Milton is thinking theologi-

---

16. Dzelzainis, "Republicanism," 301–4.
17. Dzelzainis, "Liberty and the Law," 61.
18. Cover, *Narrative*, 175, 101.
19. Cover, *Narrative*, 177.

cally about the pathways by which people can move closer to or further from God. Law provides a similar pathway at a societal level. It endlessly makes a utopian promise to lead people into a more just world. However, it also endlessly breaks that promise. Bridges exist to connect Point A to Point B, and when those two points are the configurations of the "now" and the hoped-for alternative of the "not yet," the bridge must change constantly as its termini do. But systems of law have a tendency to harden in place, and so instead of being a mere pathway to justice, law often demands obedience for its own sake. Especially within an early modern framework that saw human legal systems as to some degree reflections of God's will for humanity, law endlessly points beyond itself to a higher, greater principle. As John Donne put it in one of his sermons, "no Law can be so meerely a Humane Law, but there is in it a Divine part," and "there is a certain Divine soul, and spark of Gods power, which goes through all Laws, and inanimates them."[20] And yet law endlessly betrays its deepest function by making itself into its own *telos*. This paradoxical dynamic explains why Milton is so repeatedly drawn to systems of law and why he so ceaselessly refuses to accept any one of them.

MANY KINDS OF LAW

Above I glanced at the breadth of Milton's exposure to different forms of law, and it is worth dwelling here on the fact that just his and his family's experience with litigation would have taken them in and out of multiple courtrooms. The 1624 *Milton v. Ayloffe* suit provides a good example. When John Milton Sr. and James Ayloffe disagreed about a £50 bond, they first took their differences to the Lord Mayor's Court, a small urban judicature that both parties had initially agreed upon because proceedings there were relatively swift and inexpensive. However, the Lord Mayor's Court did not produce what Milton Sr. regarded as a fair verdict, so he took his case to the common law Court of Common Pleas. Aware of Milton Sr.'s recourse to Common Pleas, Ayloffe filed a countermotion in Chancery, the nation's primary court of equity (*MC* 21–26).[21] Similarly, Milton Jr.'s suit against Sir John Cope started in 1638 in a

---

20. Donne, "Preached at Lincoln's Inne," 10. For further discussion of the early modern imbrication of law and religion, see Chapman, *Legal Epic*, 35–64; Shuger, *Censorship*; Berman, *Law and Revolution II*; Berman, *Faith and Order*; Witte, *God's Joust*.

21. This leapfrogging was a customary feature of many early modern lawsuits. For a remarkable example of how litigants could use multiple jurisdictions to their advantage, see Jenks, "Picking Up the Pieces."

common law court (perhaps with a writ of latitat in King's Bench, although the records have been lost), but by 1654, Milton was in Chancery asking for subpoenas. Likewise, the remarkably complicated legal battle over the Forest Hill property that involved both Milton and his father-in-law, Richard Powell, included hearings and filings in the Court of Common Pleas, Chancery, the Chancellor's Court of the University of Oxford, and the Court of the Exchequer.[22] As I will discuss further in chapter 7, Milton also appeared several times in the Court of the Goldsmiths in regard to real estate issues, and whereas we moderns would classify this panel as an administrative body rather than a legal one, the early modern period regarded such private courts as legitimate centers of adjudication.

We can begin to see how unproductive it is to think of early modern law as a unified conglomeration of mandates and procedures, and yet this is how law has often figured in the work of critics. For example, Stanley Fish writes that for Milton "the idea of positive law, with its list of fixed eternal prohibitions, becomes untenable."[23] Fish is correct in the sense that Milton distrusted monopolies of all kinds, including legal ones, and so when he is thinking at the broadest conceptual level about "the law" as a whole, he indeed rebels at the idea of its constraints. But Fish's assertion also erects an inadvertent straw man since when Milton looked out at the legal world around him, he did not see anything like a unified system of positive law. Writing in 1762 in *the Critical Review*, Tobias Smollett describes the "vast chaos" created by the aggregation of "the common law, the statute law, the provincial customs, the crown law, the law custom of parliament, the reasonable customs, the canon law, the civil law, the forest law, the law of marquee and reprisals, the commercial laws, [and] the martial laws." When an observer considers the "immense variety," "the number and variety of laws," and "the flat contradiction which frequently occurs between law and equity," he "shall find little cause to be astonished at the difficulty of obtaining justice."[24] Milton was fascinated by what Fish calls the "idea of positive law" not because he could look around at his contemporary world and see some single body of well-integrated law but because he *could not*. While at a personal level Milton might have empathized with Smollett's complaint, these various legal systems also presented him with various ways of thinking about problems of justice. That is, whatever his frustration

---

22. On the intricacies of the Forest Hill case, see *MC* 124–45, 71–110. For a description of Milton's legal battle against the Copes, see Chapman, "Lay Reader's Guide."

23. Fish, *How Milton Works*, 353.

24. Smollett, "Frederician Code," 3. See also A. Parker, "Tobias Smollett and the Law."

with having to use different jurisdictions to settle his own legal affairs, these same jurisdictions offered him a rich trove of terms, ideas, procedures, and substantive norms for representing questions of right and wrong. They also provided him with a tool for thinking about the Bible. Milton and his contemporaries saw systems of temporal law as—in theory, at least—extensions of divine law. For some, this relationship meant that English common law could be regarded almost literally as "the law of God,"[25] but Milton used the law/Law homology in a variety of ways. Sometimes he reads "downward," by which I mean he pulls down divine precepts from above and says that human laws must conform to them. But as chapter 4 suggests, sometimes he reads "upward" as when he argues that God's statutes about marriage should be read in a way that conforms to the flexibility and interpretive discretion he finds in Roman law.

At various points in this book we will see Milton alluding to the jury trial, and this pattern of allusions shows both how he moves adroitly in and out of different legal systems and how easy it is to mistake the operations of one legal system for the workings of "the law" as a whole. My argument is deeply indebted to the work of Sharon Achinstein and Elizabeth Sauer, who have shown how Milton depends upon and tries to fashion a body of engaged readers, and both of them convincingly connect the emergence of a more active early modern readership to contemporary juridical changes. For example, Sauer observes that while the "identification of writers and readers as judges and juries" had a long-standing history, this identification had a stronger punch in Milton's day because of recent judicial changes.[26] In support, she points to the changing role of the jury. In previous centuries, juries had been self-informing, meaning that as men of the neighborhood, they presumably walked into the courtroom already familiar with the characters of those involved and thus with a reasonably accurate sense of where guilt and innocence lay. But during the early modern period, juries acquired the role we are accustomed to today: they served as disinterested and objective assessors of the evidence presented to them. Sauer is correct about the changing role of the jury and correct too in connecting it to the increasingly alert and discriminating habits of English readers. The only hitch in her insightful discussion is that

---

25. Judge Jermyn claimed this at John Lilburne's trial in 1649. Quoted and discussed in T. A. Green, *Verdict according to Conscience*, 171.

26. Sauer, "*Paper-Contestations*," 21. Achinstein explores John Lilburne's ideas of the jury and then argues that these inform Milton's conception of his readers in *Areopagitica*: Achinstein, *Milton and the Revolutionary Reader*, 46–70.

she equates the work of the jury with "the English legal system" and "the law as a whole."[27] However, juries were unique to common law courts, and other English courtrooms had different methods for adjudicating. For example, in a court of equity jurisdiction such as the Court of Requests (where Milton's father appeared as a defendant in *Cotton v. Milton*),[28] a single judge passed a verdict, but in a prerogative court such as Star Chamber or the Council of Wales and the Marches, rulings came from a panel of judges. Even within the common law system, there were variations from the jury trial norm, as with the rise of summary procedure, which allowed justices of the peace and judges in quarter sessions simply to pronounce a verdict. My intent is not to nitpick Sauer's argument, which remains one of relatively few that have taken seriously the role that law and legal procedures play in Milton's thinking. Rather, I use it to indicate how easily procedures specific to one early modern legal system can be seen as straightforward synecdoches for "the law" writ large. When we adopt an overly homogenized idea of "the law" as it existed in early modern England, we perforce cannot see the way that Milton mixes and matches elements from different legal systems. For example, as I show in the following chapters, every time that Milton refers to the jury, he is weighing out the relative advantages of one kind of legal system vis-à-vis another and thus reflecting on which one provides the most direct route to justice.

Milton's varied jurisdictional interests have also been occluded by the allure of crime. For the most part, critics who have looked at law in relationship to Milton's works have focused on criminal law. To give three examples, critics have debated whether or not the earl of Castlehaven's trial for rape and sodomy has any bearing on Milton's *Masque Performed at Ludlow Castle*; Lynne Greenberg has argued for the role of criminal speech in *Samson Agonistes*; and jurists Jillisa Brittan and Richard Posner have applied principles of modern penal theory to *Paradise Lost*.[29] However, the critical field is lopsided since these arguments are not counterbalanced by comparable ones about civil mat-

27. Sauer, *"Paper-Contestations,"* 20.
28. French provides a description of this case in *MC* 51–61.
29. Barbara Breasted argues for the importance of this trial as a context for the masque: see her *"Comus* and the Castlehaven Scandal." John Creaser offers a rebuttal in "Milton's *Comus.*" For an argument that *A Masque* is preoccupied with a different criminal case, see Marcus, "Milieu." For other discussions of criminal law in Milton's works, see Greenberg, "'Peal of Words'"; Greenberg, "Dalila's 'Feminine Assaults'"; Brittan and Posner, "Penal Theory in *Paradise Lost.*"

ters.[30] To cite only one obvious lacuna, no one has examined Milton's various suits in Chancery for what they suggest about his understanding of debt, obligations, and trust. I am not suggesting that an interest in crime is misguided; to the contrary, given the complex ties between crime and sin in early modern thinking, criminal law provides an important context for Milton's thinking. Rather, my point is that focusing only on criminal law brings with it attendant risks. Legal action in early modern England overwhelmingly meant *civil* legal action, and most of the extraordinary innovations of the period occurred in this area of the law. Thus criminal law was only one small and relatively static corner in a bustling forum of legal ideas. For the purposes of this book, the greatest problem with focusing on crime is that it tips us toward the idea that England had only one legal system. Because almost all offenses at or above the level of felony were handled by the common law courts, scholars interested in crime have few reasons to explore other judicatures.[31] In contrast, as we saw just above with Milton's own litigation experiences, civil cases often traveled complex paths through various courts where they were subject to different procedures, different evidentiary standards, and different options for remedy and enforcement.

As the chapters that follow will indicate, Milton is primarily interested in civil law because it allowed more scope for individual choice.[32] While the early modern period gave private individuals more control over criminal prosecutions than we moderns are accustomed to, the principals in a criminal action still had much less agency than those in a civil one. Consider the likely outcome had Milton been excluded from the 1660 Act of Oblivion. He would have been arrested and imprisoned. He then would have been put on trial for treason. He would not have seen the evidence against him ahead of time, and since criminal trials at the time did not include defense attorneys, he would have had few ways to fend off the full brunt of the state's arguments. He would have listened to a verdict rendered by the jury and then a sentence read by

---

30. There are some noteworthy exceptions, such as Todd Butler's argument that Milton's divorce tracts contribute to changes in the legal idea of spousal privileges. See his "Milton, Deliberative Liberty."

31. Although as Greenberg points out in "Milton's Figure of the Whore," the crime of prostitution was exceptional in that it was variously prosecuted by different jurisdictions. I am grateful to Prof. Greenberg for the chance to read this work in manuscript.

32. My emphasis on civil law as an expression of individual agency is broadly indebted to Christopher W. Brooks's groundbreaking work on legal activity in early modern England. See in particular his *Lawyers, Litigation* and *Pettyfoggers and Vipers.*

the judge. And then he would have waited either to be pardoned or to be hauled to the scaffold to be hanged, drawn, and quartered or, if his sentence was softened, to be beheaded. Throughout the process, he would have been a passive pawn in the hands of the state. In contrast, reading the documents in a civil case such as *Milton v. Cope*—in which the issue was the Copes' refusal to pay money owed on a bond—shows a quite different situation. We see instead a chess match between individuals, and at each point, we can sense Milton asking himself questions about what to do next: What writ should he bring at common law? Should he drop the case? Should he transfer it to Chancery? Who should he ask to have subpoenaed? What questions should be in the interrogatories? How should these questions be framed to elicit the facts he needs? Should he offer to settle out of court?[33] If we think of the criminal law as instantiating a "vertical" relationship between the people and the state, then the civil law both regulated and expressed the complex "horizontal" relationships between private individuals, what Milton in *A Readie and Easie Way* calls justice "between man and man" (*CPW* 7:383). The state provided the mechanisms of adjudication (statutes, judges, courtrooms, clerks, bailiffs, etc.), but it was up to private individuals to use them. Because the civil law was one aspect or expression of the perennial frictions between private individuals, Milton could use it to explore different questions of just relations in the early modern social world.

NATURAL LAW

Another way to describe this book is to say that it studies Milton's commitment to natural law as that commitment plays out across the jural field. Natural law was not a legal system, meaning that there was no corpus of natural law statutes and no court handing out natural law verdicts anywhere in England or on the Continent. It was instead a set of theological and philosophical convictions. Natural law held that God had coded fundamental principles into the cosmos and that these principles were discoverable by the proper application of human reason. First woven into the Christian tradition by Aquinas and then later elaborated by Jean Gerson, this idea took on new jurisprudential implications in the seventeenth century. Those who believed in natural law were committed to the idea that actual human laws—whether those came from the systems of canon law, common law, Civil law, *Brehon* law, Scots law, etc.—should conform as closely as possible to larger rational principles. Jurists such

---

33. Further discussion of this case can be found in Chapman, "Lay Reader's Guide."

as Alberico Gentili and Hugo Grotius used the theory of natural law to argue for overarching systems of international law that bound all peoples and all nations. Milton's commitment to natural law is unmistakable. For example, in *Doctrine and Discipline of Divorce*, he attacks the canon law on the grounds that "to command love and *sympathy*, to forbid dislike against the guiltles instinct of nature, is not within the province of any law to reach" (*CPW* 2:346). In support, he cites the "high principles" of Plato's *Gorgias* in which Plato argues that justice is inherent in the nature of things and not merely an applied convention (*CPW* 2:346).[34] However, arguing for natural law is a bit like arguing for fairness: people who might agree with one another on principle can have wildly diverging views about specific applications. For example, the canonists saw their law as supremely compliant with natural law.[35] In contrast, Milton argues in his divorce tracts that the canon law is a supreme corruption of it. Thus simply asserting a commitment to natural law does not necessarily take one very far toward determining what actual laws and legal configurations are most reasonable.

Milton's dissatisfied fascination with different forms of law results from the convergence of three different beliefs or inclinations. First, we can see in his writings evidence of what legal historian Paul Halliday sees as widespread "lay longings for a righteous law."[36] In his first Latin defense, *Pro Populo Anglicano Defensio*, Milton yearns for a nation that will "administer incorruptible justice to the people," one where law functions "to help those cruelly harassed and oppressed, and to render to each man promptly his own deserts" (*CPW* 4:681). To paraphrase the preamble to the US Constitution, he desperately wanted the English to form a more perfect union. This desire coexisted comfortably with a second one. He believed that laws should be conformable to reason and that there were larger principles of justice that all human legal systems should embody. As he argues in *Pro Populo*, "should any law or custom conflict with divine or natural law or reason, it is not to be considered a valid law" (*CPW* 4:486). The goal of all nations is to create laws that align with "divine or natural law or reason" and to discard those laws that do not. However, these two complementary convictions collide with a

---

34. On Milton's commitment to natural law, see White, *Natural Law*, 216-51; Fulton, *Historical Milton*, 99-101, 143-73; N. Smith, "*Areopagitica*: Voicing Contexts," 105-11; Sauer, *Milton, Toleration, and Nationhood*, 74-94. For general discussions of natural law, see Tuck, *Natural Rights Theories*; Oakley, *Natural Law*; Bobbio, *Thomas Hobbes*.

35. Kuttner, "Natural Law and Canon Law."

36. Halliday, "Birthrights," 588.

third: Milton was skeptical about collections of normative rules because they limit the liberty of the individual to make his or her own choices and because they can encourage idolatrous veneration of the letter of the law by snuffing out the gentle breath of its spirit. Milton thus found himself in the vice grip of a dilemma. On the one hand, he believed that the nation urgently needed a righteous body of law and that human reason was capable of creating laws that aligned with the divine will. On the other hand, he believed that all legal systems by their very nature constrain individual liberty and, as external formalizations, can never fully express God's higher justice. This is the juridical version of the predicament that Arthur Barker traces in Milton's thinking about the church.[37] Barker argues that Milton both wanted church discipline and yet recognized that discipline impinged on personal choice. While in his earlier pamphlets he tried to find an ecclesiastical middle ground, Milton later moved toward the pole of liberty and rejected both church discipline and the institutional structures it served. But there is a crucial difference between resisting the uniformity and consistency of a national church and resisting the uniformity and consistency that result from the rule of law. Doing the latter brings a higher risk of anarchy, and Milton was committed to the idea of a stable and orderly civil society. Thus in some ways, articulating his vision of the proper scope of law proved to be a more intractable problem than articulating his vision of the church.

The pressure of Milton's contradictory beliefs about law and justice drives the impulse traced in the following chapters. He refuses to make his bed inside any one legal system, as if that particular set of rules provides "the way" to encourage virtue and foster peace and justice. Instead, he moves through different systems in something of a dizzying fashion, testing them under varying conditions. On the subject of injurious words, he supports the common law courts against the prerogative ones. However, the vision of localized courts he offers in the late political prose tracts rejects the common law model. While he uses common law in the first two defenses for its constitutional implications, he turns instead to Civil law in his third defense, and Civil law jurisprudence also supports his argument for divorce. On the subject of tithes, he opposes all legal regulations, whether those come from the mouths of ecclesiastical or common law judges. This juridical kaleidoscope means that unlike his brother Christopher, John Milton would have made a poor judge since judges cannot rummage around among various normative rules and select the ones

---

37. Barker, *Milton and the Puritan Dilemma*.

that they would like to apply.[38] But Milton never set out to create a coherent system of jurisprudence. He was a poet and polemicist, and what his jurisdictional thinking lacks in orderly coherence, it makes up in kinetic energy. Ultimately, Milton's quest for justice has the same restless striving that he associates in *Areopagitica* with the quest for truth. Like the god Osiris, Truth was "hewd . . . into a thousand peeces, and scatter'd . . . to the four winds." Ever since, those who love truth—like those who love justice—must go "up and down gathering up limb by limb still as they [can] find them." While this assembling of both will not be complete until the "Masters second coming" (*CPW* 2:549), the highest calling of people such as Milton is to piece together truth and justice from shards uncovered here and there in a fallen world.

CHAPTER SUMMARIES

One of the subarguments of this book is that Milton was preoccupied with the dark power of injurious words, and so I open with a pair of chapters that explores his views of libel. In chapter 2, I focus on his early prose works *Animadversions* and *An Apology against a Pamphlet*, treatises that have been relatively neglected in Milton criticism. Milton wrote both in response to printed attacks, and in these treatises he first begins reflecting on the nature of free speech: When should one speak up in one's own defense? Can true words be defamatory? What makes certain words legally actionable? Milton answers these and similar questions by contrasting two contemporary legal constructions: the crime of seditious libel as applied by Star Chamber and the tort of defamation as applied by the common law. Over the course of these treatises, he increasingly inclines toward the common law construction. He argues that defamation should be a private civil matter between individuals, not a subject for state prosecution, and that people have a right to speak the truth, even if that truth is damaging. This position allows him to imagine a greater "permission of free writing" (*Animadversions, CPW* 1:670) while still providing protections against egregiously vicious and untrue attacks. In order to illuminate what is original about Milton's arguments, this chapter compares his views with works by his contemporaries John Donne and George Herbert in which they similarly consider the best response to injurious words.

In chapter 3, I argue that Milton carries the ideas developed in *Animadversions* and *An Apology against a Pamphlet* forward into *Areopagitica*, written

---

38. Christopher Milton served as a baron of the Exchequer and then a judge in the Court of Common Pleas. For more details, see Campbell, "Milton, Sir Christopher."

about two years later. Critics have long puzzled over this treatise's apparent logical reversals, as when Milton argues, "as good almost kill a Man as kill a good Book," yet also says that some books should be "justly burnt, or sunk into the Sea" (*CPW* 2:492, 505). This chapter claims that a concern with defamation lies at the heart of *Areopagitica*'s most contradictory passages. Milton regards personally injurious words as the line in the sand, the point at which free speech goes too far and should be subject to prosecution. Conversely, other forms of transgressive speech are best ignored or tolerated. As in *Animadversions* and *An Apology*, he also suggests that the nation's common law courts offer the proper means of policing injurious words. When lapses in civility rise to the level of defamation, people have the right to take legal action against one another. This takes the problem of controlling transgressive speech out of the hands of the state and puts it in the hands of people themselves. In order to put the juridical argument of *Areopagitica* in a wider context, I compare it both with John March's *Actions for Slaunder*, the first book on the jurisprudence of defamation, and with Milton's treatment of blasphemy in his 1659 *Treatise of Civil Power*.

Milton's interest in different jurisdictions appears in sharp relief when we compare chapters 2 and 3, where he throws his intellectual weight behind the common law, with chapters 4 and 5, where we see him turning to the Civil law. This was the dominant legal system on the Continent, one that was based on Roman law as codified in Justinian's massive *Corpus Juris Civilis*. As chapter 4 demonstrates, Milton relies crucially on Civil law in his two main divorce tracts, *Doctrine and Discipline of Divorce* and *Tetrachordon*, not only because divorce was allowed under Civil law but also because Civil law provided him with an invaluable hermeneutic approach. Faced with the task of applying statutes to widely varying sets of circumstances, Civilian judges used the interpretive principle known as equity. In his divorce treatises, Milton argues that God's statutes should be read in a similarly equitable way, with an eye to the intention of the lawgiver rather than to the literal words of the law, and by championing the Civilian understanding of equity, he simultaneously rejects the equity of the canon law. Ultimately, Milton's argument about how to read the Bible properly is made possible by a long tradition of statutory interpretation that he finds in the texts of Roman law.

In the same vein as chapter 4, chapter 5 also studies Milton's use of Civil law, although whereas the divorce tracts show his interest in substantive aspects of Civil jurisprudence, this chapter shows him engaging more with the Civil law's procedural side. *Pro Se Defensio* is the third of three Latin defenses that Milton wrote in the 1650s, and as this chapter argues, it is also his most misunderstood work. Because modern translations do not capture the legal meanings of key Latin words such as *fama* and *iniuria*, modern readers have not recognized that Milton is using foundational ideas from the Civil law to mount a defense of himself. He had been attacked in print by an anonymous author whom Milton believed to be the priest Alexander More, a resident of the Low Countries. Milton uses the same Continental legal system to which More was subject to show that he, Milton, has been unjustly accused and that More is guilty of libel. With its focus on the law of *iniuria* as understood and applied in the European *ius commune*, this chapter complements my discussion in chapters 2 and 3 of how Milton looks to the English common law of defamation as a corrective to homegrown libels.

Not an unquestioning partisan of any one legal system, Milton was instead committed to the idea that all of them have both virtues and liabilities. All of them, that is, except one: he was implacably hostile toward the canon law in part because it presupposed a hierarchical and national church, an ecclesiastical model he rejected. Chapter 6 turns to the role canon law plays in Milton's thinking, looking first at his anti-tithe arguments in *Considerations Touching the Likeliest Means to Remove Hirelings out of the Church* and then at his great epic poem, *Paradise Lost*, which he wrote around the same time. Readers of book 6 have long noted the series of puns that Satan uses to taunt the good angels during the War in Heaven. This chapter explores the financial and legal meanings that weave through these puns. Satan construes his war against God as a financial transaction, one in which he uses a material currency (i.e., ammunition) to repay the "debt . . . of gratitude" that he finds so famously oppressive during an earlier soliloquy (*CPEP* 4.52). Satan calls his martial repayment a form of "composition" (*CPEP* 6.613), a term commonly used in canon law tithing arrangements. Milton uses the War in Heaven to show how the canon law of tithes and its associated legal practices corrupt the proper relationship between God and his creations.

A similar interest in how law can help foster or undermine just communities is evident in the six prose treatises Milton wrote in 1659 and 1660 as he was contemplating the nation's impending return to monarchy. Chapter 7 explores the fact that in five of these treatises, Milton offers suggestions for restructuring England's judicial system. He bucks the growing monopoly of the common law and advocates instead for a network of autonomous local courts, each one empowered to do justice in its locality, and this chapter compares his reflections with those of common law jurists such as Edward Coke and Matthew Hale. Milton's discussions of local courts suggest his growing skepticism about the common law model of the jury. As chapters 2 and 3 demonstrate, in his earlier works Milton uses the jury as a symbol of the English people's powers of discernment and their ability to participate effectively in their own governance. However, as the Restoration approached, his view of the English darkened, and in these five treatises, he inclines toward a Civilian model in which cases were heard and decided by a judge alone. This chapter concludes by comparing Milton's imagined judicial system with one of the most famous trials of the early Restoration years: the conviction and imprisonment of Milton's fellow dissenter John Bunyan.

In the afterword, I turn from a direct examination of Milton's works and look instead at the textual company they keep in one seventeenth-century manuscript miscellany. The Columbia Manuscript is important in Milton studies because it includes transcripts of two of the political treatises discussed in chapter 7 as well as all of his state letters, some known from no other source. While scholars compiling editions of Milton's prose have studied those portions of the Columbia Manuscript that are by Milton, no one has examined the whole notebook. This final chapter shows that Milton's works in the Columbia Manuscript are nestled in a jurisdictional framework, for whoever compiled the notebook paired Milton's treatise with works such as an index of topics in Civil law, a defense of the Court of Requests, a discussion of the legal status of ambassadors, and a description of the relationship between equity and law. Collectively, these works suggest that the compiler supported the minor jurisprudences of early modern England.[39] The fact that he also copied out Milton's arguments for local courts as found in *A Letter to a Friend* and *Proposalls of Certaine Expedients* suggests that he saw in them a like-minded commitment. In *Areopagitica*, Milton argues that English society will be healthiest when it accommodates a range of "brotherly dissimilitudes" (*CPW* 2:555). Both he and the compiler of the Columbia Manuscript evidently felt the same way about the law. They both believed that justice was best served when the English judicial landscape was not homogenized and when it offered instead friendly jurisdictional dissimilitudes, each providing its own granular approach to doing right in a world of wrong.

39. On England's minor jurisprudences, see Goodrich, *Law in the Courts of Love*.

CHAPTER 2

Defending One's Good Name: Free Speech in the Early Prose

Throughout his lifetime, Milton worried about the ease with which people could turn words into weapons. For example, in the preface to *The Judgment of Martin Bucer*, he pauses for a moment to reflect on his decision to champion divorce and thereby to "put off into this wild and calumnious world," and he regrets the "world of disesteem" this decision has brought him (*CPW* 2:434). In sonnet 12, he similarly considers the hostile reception of his divorce arguments, and he complains about the "barbarous noise" that has beset him from all sides (*CPEP* 3). Related concerns crop up in later works. Sonnet 16 advises Cromwell to rise above the "detractions rude" of hostile, envious men, and several years later on the eve of the Restoration, he reflects in *A Readie and Easie Way* on the tide of "diabolical forerunning libels" that have poured "insolencies," "menaces," and insultings" on the heads of well-intentioned people such as himself (*CPEP* 2; *CPW* 7:452). On the problem of toxic language, Milton was part of a much larger chorus. In a 1641 speech before the House of Commons, Sir Edward Dering lamented, "this hath been a very accusative age," a comment that generally sums up the early modern sense that personal abuse was on the rise, fueled by the period's widening political, religious, and social rifts.[1] Modern scholars have amply supported Dering's point by drawing attention to the flood of printed and manuscript insults and the corresponding rise in prosecutions for injurious words.[2]

As this chapter argues, Milton first grapples with the power of abusive lan-

---

1. Dering, *Collection of Speeches*, 112.
2. For a sampling of critical studies of libel, see McRae, *Literature, Satire*; Bellany, *Politics*

guage in two of his early prose works: *Animadversions upon the Remonstrants Defense against Smectymnuus* (henceforth *Animadversions*) and *An Apology against a Pamphlet Called a Modest Confutation of the Animadversions upon the Remonstrant against Smectymnuus* (henceforth *An Apology*). These are respectively the third and fifth of his cluster of five antiprelatical tracts in which he attacks the Church of England and its hierarchies, and especially in comparison to the more famous treatises *The Reason of Church-Government* and *Of Reformation*, they have been widely overlooked. In all of his antiprelatical treatises, Milton joins the contemporary debate about church hierarchy. On one side, there were those—such as Puritans and Independents—who sought to abolish bishops and the associated trappings of episcopacy. On another, there were those—such as Church of England clerics—who argued that episcopacy was the will of God. As Milton discovered firsthand when he came to the defense of the anonymous Puritan ministers who wrote under the pseudonym "Smectymnuus," this debate included a remarkable amount of bitter, personal mudslinging. In the two treatises studied below, he reflects on the nature of such personal attacks and tries to work out when injurious words should be allowed in the interests of truth and when they should be banned.

This chapter seeks to make three main points. The first is simply that *Animadversions* and *An Apology* are deeply concerned with both the opportunities and the dangers of free speech. Milton argues for a "permission of free writing" because it crucially advanced what he regards as truth, but he is simultaneously wary of opening the gate to personal abuse in the process (*Animadversions, CPW* 1:670). My second point is that because of his concern with toxic language, Milton thinks about free speech more in a legal register than in a political one. Critics who have studied Milton's views of liberty of the press are usually thinking politically, meaning that they are interested in censorship as the top-down effort of state agents to control the dissemination of transgressive ideas.[3] However, as Debora Shuger argues, our modern preoccupation with censorship has led us to overlook the fact that "virtually all substantive law dealing with the regulation of language concerned

---

of Court Scandal; A. Gordon, "Act of Libel"; Croft, "Libels, Popular Literacy." Bellany and McRae have edited an online compendium of manuscript libels: "Early Stuart Libels."

3. Critics who have looked at legal contexts have primarily studied the statutes, proclamations, and executive actions that specifically targeted printers, compositors, booksellers, authors, etc. Joad Raymond provides the most nuanced and compelling example of this approach—and also an overview of relevant scholarship—in his "Censorship."

defamation."⁴ Milton's two tracts support Shuger's point, for he regards free speech primarily as a question of civility and Christian charity and only secondarily as a political right. My third point is a jurisdictional one: in advocating for certain legal ground rules that would control injurious words, Milton takes sides in a contemporary judicial tug of war. He rejects the jurisprudence of seditious libel as construed by Star Chamber and embraces instead the jurisprudence of defamation as applied by the common law courts.

In effect, *Animadversions* and *An Apology* take up some of the same questions that early modern judges, juries, plaintiffs, defendants, and lawyers struggled with: how to draw the line between legally actionable words and merely insulting ones and how to prevent injurious speech without silencing speech altogether. They thus provide an important bridge to Milton's thinking in *Areopagitica*, which I take up in the next chapter. The word "libel" and its variants ("libelous," "libeling," etc.) occur more in *Animadversions, An Apology*, and *Areopagitica* than in the rest of Milton's corpus combined, and in each case Milton brings to bear specific juridical concepts to reflect on the legal and societal problem of defamation. This problem occupies his attention because it threatened to tear his world apart. In book 4 of *Paradise Lost*, Satan says that "true reconcilement" can never grow "Where wounds of deadly hate have pierced so deep" (*CPEP* 4.98–99). In the two pamphlets studied here, Milton attempts to solve the contemporary problem of "deadly hate" as it poured from early modern pens and presses and to figure out how to be a just man or just woman in the wild and calumnious seventeenth century.

A STUDY OF TWO JURISDICTIONS: COMMON LAW AND PREROGATIVE COURTS

The first two strands of this chapter's argument—that *Animadversions* and *An Apology* are concerned with the problem of defamation and that Milton thinks about this problem within a legal as opposed to a purely political or ideological framework—will suffuse the discussions that follow and thus need no prefatory explanation here. However, the third strand—that Milton champions one particular judicial construction of injurious words—warrants more detailed consideration both because of the extreme slipperiness of the term "libel" and because most modern readers are unlikely to know how early modern judica-

---

4. Shuger, *Censorship*, 69.

tures differently defined and punished transgressive language.[5] Early modern men and women often used "libel" to refer to any distasteful book, whether or not it was actually defamatory. For example, as Philip Hamburger shows, many seventeenth-century prosecutions for the crime of "seditious libel" were for failures of licensing, meaning that there was nothing specifically libelous about the books at all.[6] In a more strictly legal context, "libel" could indicate either a crime or a civil offense (what we moderns would call a tort), meaning that simply calling something a "libel" did little to clarify the offense, its gravity, or the kind of court that should handle it. To make things more confusing, there was no consistent legal distinction made between slander and libel as, respectively, spoken versus written forms of defamation. For example, the title of *A Modest Confutation of a Slanderous and Scurrilous Libell* (a treatise that attacked Milton's third antiprelatical tract, *Animadversions*) confounds our modern common sense because a "libel," by definition, cannot also be "slanderous." Milton does not help matters, for he uses "libel" to refer to all forms of transgressive speech, whether politically dissident or personally injurious, spoken or written, crime or tort. So that readers can better navigate this maze of complexities, I have regularized my terminology in two main ways. First, because I am interested in libel in the sense of hurtful language instead of ideological dissidence, I use terms such as "defamation," "injury," and "injurious words" as often as possible in order to emphasize the way they damaged other people's reputations. Second, because my argument relies crucially on the distinction between criminal words and civil/tortious ones, I use "seditious libel" for the criminal form of libel and "civil defamation" for the tort. When quoting Milton's own references to something he calls a "libel" or "libelous," I have tried to make the construction he has in mind clear from the context.

Virtually all early modern jurisprudence about defamatory words derives from the Roman law of *iniuria* with its conjoined concerns with *contumelia* (insults to face, or that which brought shame and disrespect upon someone) and *calumnia* (false accusations, or that which brought someone into danger of the law). As Richard Helmholz shows, this Roman legal construction was absorbed into English canon law in the thirteenth century, which explains why

---

5. David Ibbetson points to the "fluidity of the law of libel in the early seventeenth century" as early modern courts shifted their legal constructions, expanded or contracted their jurisdictional range, or adjusted their sentencing and enforcement procedures. Because of this fluidity, no generalized description of the jurisprudence of libel can ever be absolutely accurate since exceptions can always be found. See Ibbetson, "Edward Coke, Roman Law," 502.

6. Hamburger, "Development."

during the medieval period, calling someone a liar (*contumelia*) or a thief (*calumnia*) was cognizable only in the ecclesiastical courts.[7] Beginning around the sixteenth century, these Romanist ideas of *iniuria* started to migrate from the canon law over into the English secular courts.[8] Common law jurists allowed litigants to bring an action on the case for defamation provided that one of two conditions was met: (1) the insulting words had to include the imputation of a secular crime, or (2) the words had to have resulted in material harm or loss. Unlike the church courts, which could only enforce penance, the common law courts could award damages, and this fact, combined with what Steve Hindle aptly terms the period's "obsession with personal credit" and its "almost instinctive" use of law to resolve grievances, led to an explosion in defamation suits.[9] Two aspects of common law defamation will be important in the pages that follow. First, truth was allowable as a defense because common law jurists felt that people should not be able to use a defamation lawsuit to benefit from their own evil actions. If the defendant could demonstrate that his allegations were true, then the plaintiff would likely lose his case, and the appeal to truth appears to have been one of the most distinctive features of common law defamation. Second, because the common law predominantly regarded defamation as a civil offense,[10] those convicted were usually ordered to pay damages and were not subject to criminal penalties such as imprisonment or blood sanctions (whipping, mutilation, branding, etc.). Given that he was the

---

7. The definitive discussions of defamation in the early modern ecclesiastical courts appear in Helmholz, *Roman Canon Law*, and Helmholz, *Select Cases*. See also Ingram, *Church Courts*, and Ingram, "Law, Litigants." For a more general discussion of how canon law forms the basis of English secular law, see Berman, *Law and Revolution*.

8. The following discussion of defamation in the common law courts and Star Chamber is based on the discussions found in Holdsworth, *History of English Law*, 5:205-12, 8:333-78; Plucknett, *Concise History*, 483-502; and Manning, "Origins of the Doctrine." For a case study of the conflict between common law and Star Chamber ideas of defamation/libel, see the description of Lewis Pickering's trial in Bellany, "Poem." See also Shuger's account of how common law and Star Chamber procedure differed in "Prison Diaries." On the ballooning volume of defamation suits, see Sharpe, *Defamation and Sexual Slander*, 3-4.

9. Hindle, *State and Social Change*, 81; March, *Actions for Slaunder*. The general litigiousness of the early modern English people has been studied by Christopher Brooks in *Lawyers, Litigation* and *Pettyfoggers and Vipers*.

10. There were two exceptions. The 1275 statute of *scandalum magnatum* made insults to peers or the royal family a common law crime. In general, however, this statute and its later legislative refinements were rarely enforced. In what were known as *qui tam* proceedings, a private individual could initiate a common law criminal lawsuit for words, although this action was also rare.

brother of a common lawyer and given, too, the remarkably widespread diffusion of common law knowledge into all levels of early modern English culture, Milton would have had ample knowledge of at least the broad outlines of defamation jurisprudence and probably also its more technical features.

However, the common law courts were not the only secular judicature where injurious words could be prosecuted. Private words could lead to public disorders. Sending an insulting letter could incite a man or his family to revenge and add to the growing problem of dueling. Insulting words about a public official could lead to riots and protests. Recognizing the potentially destabilizing social effects of insulting language, Star Chamber enforced the law of seditious libel, which targeted damaging words aimed at either a private individual or a public figure, although most prosecutions concerned the latter.[11] As Coke explains in his landmark report "The Case *de Libellis Famosis*," there can be no "greater scandal of government" than to allege that the king has appointed "corrupt or wicked Magistrates."[12] The scope of seditious libel was also extended to protect Church of England prelates who, like secular magistrates, were seen as pillars of the social order. As the jurist Robert Post writes, seditious libel was a "quintessentially political crime," and so prosecutions were aimed at protecting the "special veneration . . . due to those who rule."[13] The most famous seventeenth-century instance of prosecution for seditious libel was the Star Chamber trial of the Puritan writers William Prynne, John Bastwick, and Henry Burton for their attacks on episcopacy and the policies of Archbishop William Laud.[14]

The two characteristic features of common law defamation noted above did not apply in seditious libel cases. First, truth was no defense. In a sedi-

---

11. By the seventeenth century, seditious libel had become one of Star Chamber's signature actions, but it was technically a common law offense. Despite its notorious reputation as a court of extralegal prerogative, Star Chamber largely enforced existing common laws. For further discussion of how myths about Star Chamber differed from early modern realities, see Barnes, "Star Chamber Mythology."

12. Coke, *Selected Writings*, 1:146.

13. Post, "Reconciling Theory," 2359.

14. For Prynne's narration of the legal maneuvering involved, see Prynne, *New Discovery*. The fact that bishops could sit on both the High Commission and the Star Chamber bench meant that offenses that could not technically be prosecuted in one jurisdiction could be shunted to the other. See Scofield, *Study of the Court of Star Chamber*, 47-48. On the increase of bishops in Star Chamber during the Stuart years, see Phillips, "Last Years," 114. On the general bias of Civilian lawyers toward the ecclesiastical hierarchy, see Levack, *Civil Lawyers*, 158-95.

tious libel suit, the judges were interested only in whether the words had disrupted the peace, which true words could do as effectively as lying ones. As Coke puts it, "it is not material whether the Libel be true, or whether the party against whom the Libel is made, be of good or ill fame; for in a setled state of Government the party grieved ought to complain for every injury done him in an ordinary course of Law, and not by any means to revenge himself, either by the odious course of libelling, or otherwise."[15] Libelers were like duelists in that they had taken the law into their own hands, and as in a duel, the issue of fair/unfair provocation or the prior guilt/innocence of the two parties was legally beside the point. One of the most astute chroniclers of early modern Star Chamber proceedings, the lawyer William Hudson, points to the legal irrelevance of truth as one of the most distinctive features of seditious libel trials. Hudson argues that Star Chamber has reason to punish "not the matter but the manner" of toxic words on the grounds that "libeling against a common strumpet is as great an offense as against an honest woman, and perhaps more dangerous to the breach of the peace."[16] Second, seditious libel was generally treated as a crime and not, as in the common law, a civil wrong, a fact exemplified in the infamous punishments meted out to Prynne, Bastwick, and Burton. Depending on the perceived severity of the libel, offenders could be fined, imprisoned, pilloried, whipped, or subject to judicial mutilation such as branding or nose slitting.

JOSEPH HALL AND THE CRIME OF SEDITIOUS LIBEL

In the opening sentence of his 1640 *An Humble Remonstrance*—the work that triggered Milton's response *Animadversions*—Bishop Joseph Hall explains why he feels compelled to write against the five Puritan clergymen known as the Smectymnuans who had published attacks on English episcopacy: he feared "lest the world should think the Presse had of late forgot to speake any language other then Libellous."[17] Having opened with seditious libel,

---

15. Coke, *Selected Writings*, 1:146–47. Coke was the period's foremost apologist for the common law, but as attorney general, he also sat on the Star Chamber bench and in this capacity wrote the landmark report on seditious libel. His role in two courts illustrates the jurisdictional complexities of the period.

16. However, Hudson is also uneasy about this feature of seditious libel, for it strikes him as only just that "upon speaking of words, although they be against a great person, the defendant may justify them as true." Hudson, *Treatise*, 102–3, 104.

17. Joseph Hall, *Humble Remonstrance*, 1. As Bellany points out, by 1630 a number of major trials before Star Chamber—most notoriously, Pickering's Case—had led to a wide-

Hall returns repeatedly to this subject throughout his treatise. For example, he complains that while those who love episcopal hierarchy have remained quiet, their opponents "have burst forth into sclanderous Libels," and he reasons that "these Libellers" against the church are as disruptive as attacks on the state.[18] He is aghast that "ignorant or spightfull Sectaries" have been free in "their Libels" to attack the government of the English church.[19] So central is Hall's concern with libel in *An Humble Remonstrance* that he can sum up the main thrust of the work as follows: "one of the maine pieces of the substance of [this treatise] . . . was a too just complaint of the shamefull number of Libels, lately dropped from our lawlesse Presses."[20]

When he accuses his opponents of "libel," Hall is not using the word in its most capacious sense to mean a generally offensive or pugnacious book. Instead, he means that his opponents have committed the specific crime of seditious libel as construed by the court of Star Chamber. For example, he reasons that those who write "sclanderous libels" have "indeavoured, through the sides of some misliked persons, to wound . . . [England's] Government."[21] This is the logic of seditious libel whereby an attack on a private individual could be legally regarded as an attack on the commonwealth. The Smectymnuans have tried to pierce the heart of the state "through the sides" of their individual targets. The jurisprudence of seditious libel also explains Hall's primary emphasis on the dangerousness of the Smectymnuans. Although at places in his treatise Hall defends the truth of liturgy and episcopacy, *An Humble Remonstrance* opens by arguing not that the antiepiscopalians are wrong but that they are "wilde and lawlesse."[22] This is the Star Chamber idea that seditious libels are known more by their disruptive civic effects than by their inherent falsity. Finally, the doctrine of seditious libel also underpins Hall's claims that the Smectymnuans are "Libellers" for having generally attacked a group of people ("some great persons") and a collective entity ("that sacred Government" of the church).[23] Common law

---

spread association between Puritanism and libel. See Bellany, "Poem," and Bellany, "'Rayling Rymes,'" 294.

18. Joseph Hall, *Humble Remonstrance*, 7.

19. Joseph Hall, *Humble Remonstrance*, 34–35.

20. This is Hall writing in his next pamphlet—*A Defense of the Humble Remonstrance, against the Frivolous and False Exceptions of Smectymnuus* (London, 1641), 3—and summing up the previous one's central concern.

21. Joseph Hall, *Humble Remonstrance*, 7.

22. Joseph Hall, *Humble Remonstrance*, 8.

23. Joseph Hall, *Humble Remonstrance*, 8, 7.

defamation was a personal insult, and so generalized complaints about whole categories of people would have had no legal traction.[24] Star Chamber reasoned differently, and in that judicial context, Hall is correct to claim that it is an actionable "foul sclander" simply to "charge the name of Episcopacie" with wrongdoing.[25]

In his follow-up work, *A Defense of the Humble Remonstrance*, Hall similarly claims that his opponents have committed a crime and should be punished accordingly. He opens his preface by again "bemoaning the lawlesse frequence of seditious libels" perpetrated by his Puritan opponents.[26] He repeats his charge that the Smectymnuans are guilty of "slander" and "slanderous fiction" against the collective body of bishops, and he defends the right of bishops to sit legally as judges "in Court of Star-chamber."[27] In another passage, Hall describes the Root and Branch Petitioners as "libelling Separatists," and he says "it is an hard question" whether those "Libellers" or "these their mis-zealous Advocates"—by which he means the Smectymnuans—are "more justly to be branded for Incendiaries."[28] He would like to see them literally branded, one of the forms of judicial disfigurement that prerogative courts such as Star Chamber had at their disposal. He then asks "whether it were not most lawfull and just" to punish the Smectymnuans, who have "jeopard their eares," an allusion to the fact that those convicted of seditious libel often had their ears cut off or nailed to a post.[29] He then turns from the Smectymnuans and charges Milton himself. Milton wrote the "Postscript" to the Smectymnuan treatise *An Answer to a Booke Entituled An Humble Remonstrance*, and in it he provides a lurid genealogy of episcopacy through the centuries. Hall satirically calls the "Postscript" a "goodly *Pasquin*."[30] A "pasquin" (or "pasquinade" or "pasquil") referred to a scathing attack or lampoon, often one that had been posted in a public place, and it was used interchangeably with "libel" in the period.[31] In the case that formed the basis of Coke's report "The Case *de Libellis Famosis*," Star Chamber had tried the Puritan Lewis

---

24. In fact, among the weaknesses of the early modern common law were the facts that multiple defendants could not join together in a single writ nor could an entity like a corporation be sued for damages.
25. Joseph Hall, *Defense of the Humble Remonstrance*, 7.
26. Joseph Hall, *Defense of the Humble Remonstrance*, A3.
27. Joseph Hall, *Defense of the Humble Remonstrance*, 151, 152, 155.
28. Joseph Hall, *Humble Remonstrance*, 8.
29. Joseph Hall, *Defense of the Humble Remonstrance*, 158, 156.
30. Joseph Hall, *Defense of the Humble Remonstrance*, 159.
31. McRae, *Literature, Satire*, 27.

Pickering for pinning a pasquin to Archbishop Whitgift's hearse.[32] Pickering was sentenced to pay a £1,000 fine, spend a year in prison, and be pilloried in three cities. Hall thinks that the author of the "Postscript"—Milton—should suffer the same.

ANIMADVERSIONS AND THE FREEDOM TO WRITE

When he wrote *Animadversions* in answer to Hall's work, Milton began grappling for the first time with how to respond appropriately to verbal attacks. Along one axis, he meets Hall's accusations of libel with counteraccusations of his own. For example, quoting Hall's lament about the "shamfull number of Libells" that the Smectymnuans had written about the bishops, Milton retorts, "How long is it that you, and the Prelaticall troop have bin in such distast with Libells?" (*CPW* 1:667). In support of his claim that Hall is guilty of the very offense he complains most about, Milton points to the bishops' many "defaming invectives," and he cites Bacon's observation that while no one was allowed to insult the bishops without penalty, the bishops were allowed to insult the Puritans (*CPW* 1:668). But running in parallel with these tit-for-tat exchanges are broader arguments about what Milton calls "a permission of free writing" (*CPW* 1:670). Because he is primarily focused on the relationship between "free writing" and injurious language, Milton looks to the early modern jurisprudence of insult and civility rather than to a political framework concerned with liberty and obligations. He is not asking himself questions such as "What can people be allowed to say about their government?" and "Does the individual have a fundamental right to self-expression?" Instead, he asks himself legally oriented ones such as "What is the difference between merely insulting words and actionably injurious ones?" and "Are defamatory words a criminal or a civil offense?"

A concern with injurious words envelops most of *Animadversions*' references to free speech. For example, Milton contrasts the "defaming invectives" written by England's bishops with the fact that, according to the Roman historian Livy, Roman slaves once a year "might freely speake their minds," a reference to the day during Saturnalia when slaves put on their masters' clothes and were served by their masters at meals (*CPW* 1:669). Since even slaves had such freedoms in ancient Rome, Milton finds it unbearable that until recently "the free borne people of *England*" could not criticize the bishops without facing the "censure of Libelling" (*CPW* 1:669). In context, Milton is think-

---

32. Bellany, "Poem," 160.

ing about speech acts aimed at other people. While Livy's slaves might have publicly proclaimed their thoughts about politics and religion, the domestic framing—wearing their master's robes and hats, watching that master pour wine and carry plates, etc.—suggests that the main liberty slaves enjoyed was to speak their minds about their owners. Once a year, they had the freedom to offer personal criticisms without penalty. In a similar vein, Milton argues that Star Chamber's use of seditious libel against the Puritans has created "an injurious strangle of silence" (*CPW* 1:669). Although this can sound like a reference to free speech in a broadly political sense, Milton's adjective "injurious" points in a different direction. In the *ius commune*, the laws relating to *iniuria* formed an entire subcategory of jurisprudence, an indicator of the Civil law's abiding concern with affronts to honor and public standing.[33] These emphases had filtered over into English law and culture, and in early modern English usage, "injury" referred almost exclusively to direct personal harm, usually of the legally actionable variety. Libel was simply one variety of *iniuria*. When he complains about the "injurious strangle of silence" inflicted by the enforcement of seditious libel, Milton turns the bishops' preferred legal weapon back against them. Men such as Hall claimed that writers such as Milton had committed injury/libel against them; Milton counterclaims that the real injury/libel is to "those who were subjected to the 'strangle of silence.'" These strangled men could not defend their reputations by pointing out the failings of their clerical opponents. Thus rather than alleviating or deterring injury, the law of seditious libel has aggravated it. In *Animadversions*, Milton works his way toward an idea that repressing free speech hampers society as a whole and deters the spread of religious and political enfranchisement. But the immediate context in which his thoughts arise is the problem of direct personal injury and the kinds of stinging allegations that turned men into plaintiffs and their opponents into defendants in a court of law.

Milton's argument in *Animadversions* depends upon recent judicial changes. When he was refuting the Smectymnuans, Bishop Hall took seditious libel for granted. He assumed that libelous writings would be punished as a crime and that this crime would be handled by Star Chamber. But judicial realities changed in the narrow space between Hall's treatises and Milton's response. Hall wrote his treatises early in 1641 when Star Chamber was still active. A few months later, on July 5, 1641, the Long Parliament dissolved it because of the court's associations with Stuart absolutism. Milton wrote *Animadversions* roughly a month after that, perhaps in August 1641. So when he

---

33. Fraher, "Preventing Crime," 225.

published his treatise, seditious libel was newly an offense without an enforcement mechanism. Milton happily calls attention to this judicial situation.[34] For example, in response to Hall's earlier hope that Star Chamber will clip the Smectymnuans' ears, Milton responds, "the punishing of that which you call our presumption and disobedience lies not now within the execution of your fangs" (*CPW* 1:729). Because seditious libel was a crime, plaintiffs such as Hall had used it to sink their "fangs" into their opponents' flesh. Milton points out that the altered legal circumstances have offered him more freedom to write. Quoting Hall's complaint about "libelous" pamphlets, Milton replies that Hall himself is unversed in the "lawes of discreet *Rhethorique*" (*CPW* 1:667). Without a conciliar court enforcing the law of seditious libel, Milton can now twit Hall on his violation of a different set of laws. Hall had written, "I doe gladly fly to the barre," meaning he relies on the judicial bar of Star Chamber to pronounce his innocence and his opponents' guilt. Milton replies, "To the barre with him then"; since the juridical situation has changed, Hall himself is likely to be convicted (*CPW* 1:666). Milton is equally pleased that the top ecclesiastical court, the Court of High Commission, has also been abolished (this occurred a few months before Parliament abolished Star Chamber), and so people can no longer be "strappado'd with an Oath *Ex Officio*," a reference to that court's practice of swearing men to tell the truth without informing them of the charges against them (*CPW* 1:675). Milton argues that Christ never put a "piece of temporall judicature" into the hands of ministers (*CPW* 1:722). With the abolition of both the Court of High Commission and Star Chamber, prelates no longer sat on judicial benches, which, Milton says, is at it should be: "a Church-mans jurisdiction is no more but to watch over his flock," not to attend "Sessions, and Jayle-deliveries" (*CPW* 1:716, 721).

THE "ROUGHER ACCENT" OF *ANIMADVERSIONS*

The abolition of Star Chamber and the vacating of seditious libel have important stakes for our understanding of *Animadversions* since these changes give Milton the freedom to adopt a more pugnacious style. Before, "liberty of speaking" was "girded, and straight lac't" (*CPW* 1:669). However, "now"—Milton repeats the word twice in the same sentence to underscore how judicial realities "now" differ from those even a few months before—people are opening their mouths and lifting their pens. Milton here refers both to the

---

34. For discussion of the dating of *Animadversions*, see *CPW* 1:653.

relaxing of licensing regulations in the early years of the Long Parliament and also to the abolition of Star Chamber, which had jurisdiction over the press. When he refers to this "liberty of speaking," Milton does not primarily mean that new ideas are emerging, although that is a hoped-for consequence of these judicial changes. Instead, his immediate meaning is that this "liberty" will lead to a greater "efficacy of words" (*CPW* 1:669). In context, he is talking about the fact that people can now speak the truth about one another's wrongdoings.

This focus on interpersonal criticisms helps explain Milton's preface, which Thomas Kranidas calls "one of the most explicit rhetorical programs for a single piece in English Renaissance literature."[35] Milton devotes most of his preface to justifying his decision to "handle" Hall with a "rougher accent" than readers might be accustomed to. He will even indulge in "grim laughter" at Hall's expense (*CPW* 1:662, 663). While "tender and mild consciences" might wince at his approach, he is not using "levity or insolence" for its own sake (*CPW* 1:662, 663). Instead, Milton is trying to find a balance between two extremes. On the one hand, he wants authors to have the liberty to refute their opponents, and he is delighted that Star Chamber is no longer around to punish mudslinging. And yet on the other, he knows that the new freedom to write can degenerate into vicious attacks. In this acerbic preface, he calls attention to his attempt to occupy a rhetorical middle ground. He seems to be testing out how he can push back energetically against Hall without thereby straying into speech that would qualify as civil defamation. In a deeply juridical line of reasoning, Milton explains the "lawfull reason" for his combative approach. He allows that "private and personall" injuries should be met with meekness and forbearance, an echo of the contemporary idea that those with grievances should either turn the other cheek or offer a friendly correction to the offender in private (*CPW* 1:662).[36] But because Hall has been a "notorious enimie to truth," he poses a threat to the commonwealth, and public enemies should not be met with private correction. Instead, they deserve "detecting," a strongly legal word in the period that carried the sense of making crimes known to officials (*CPW* 1:662).[37] As William Ames explains, injurious words that seek either "the amendment of the offender" or "the prevention [of harm] to others" are allowed since by these means, "a growing evill is

---

35. Kranidas, "Style and Rectitude," 251.

36. Shuger discusses the widespread assumption that injuries should first be dealt with in private: Shuger, *Censorship*, 156.

37. *OED Online*, s.v. "detect," v., def. 2a.

some way represt and not promoted."[38] *Animadversions* follows this line of reasoning. Milton argues that because Hall and his episcopal followers have practiced "collusion" against the people of England, he and the Smectymnuans are right to "uncas[e]" their "false trade of deceiving" and their "grand imposture" (*CPW* 1:663), even if that means adopting an acerbic style. Early modern jurists knew that true allegations could be brought to satisfy personal spite, and so those who accused others had to demonstrate what the Roman jurist Bartolus called an *animus corrigendi*, the intention of improving or correcting, as opposed to an *animus iniurandi*, the intention of harming.[39] Thus Milton offers a legally informed defense when he explains that he and the Smectymnuans can be excused because they wrote "without all private and personall spleene" and "not without many hazards." He alludes to the role that paid informers played in the early modern court system when he says that he also wrote "without any thought of earthly reward" (*CPW* 1:663).[40] At a certain point, the sins of others had to be made known. The man who did so could be acquitted in both a moral register and a legal one, meaning that he had been neither uncharitable nor libelous.

Milton imagines books as active participants in the law enforcement process, and by doing so he strategically detours around a legal obstacle. As Shuger points out, *iniuria* law both in England and on the Continent rested on the assumption that accusations should be made in a courtroom, not in the extrajudicial venue of a book: "The fact that the libeler chose not to make his accusations in a court of law itself creates a strong presumption that his aim was not justice" but rather to shame his opponent, since "charging another with wrongdoing in such a way that the accused has no chance to speak in his own defense violates rather basic principles of fairness."[41] Milton's innovative solution is to imagine books themselves as courtrooms where offenses

---

38. Although strictly speaking this quote comes from a casuist work rather than a legal one, the principles Ames relies on were shared by early modern jurists, an indicator of the way that law and religion had many overlapping assumptions. Ames, *Conscience*, Tt4v. Shuger quotes and discusses Ames in *Censorship*, 128.

39. See Shuger, *Censorship*, 171–73. For the Bartolus quote, see his *Omnium Iuris*, sig R4v [also paginated as 132v]. On the role of malice in civil defamation, see Holdsworth, *History of English Law*, 8:342–45 and 372–73.

40. As Elizabeth Sauer points out, many of those who wrote pamphlets exposing wrongdoing had mercenary motives: Sauer, "Paper-Contestations," 22. For an example of the early modern attempt to control the proliferation of informers, see Dean, *Law-Making and Society*, 204–7.

41. Shuger, *Censorship*, 175.

can be made known, evidence heard, and verdicts rendered. This tactic first appears when he points to past times when wise rulers would "thrust themselves under disguise into a popular throng" or "stand the night long under the eaves of houses" in order to "hear every where the free utterances of private brests" (*CPW* 1:670). Milton applauds the impulse but points out that it brought risks such as being "cudgel[ed]" for eavesdropping or suffering the "over-head emptying" of a chamber pot (*CPW* 1:670). He rejoices that realities are different now. The new "permission of free writing" allows each author to produce "an Anatomie of the shiest, and tenderest particular truths" he sees, and so the ruler who wants to know what his people think can now simply open a book. When he refers to "free writing" about previously hidden "Truths," Milton is not talking about radical new political ideas. Instead, he means that books shine a light on the ugly wrongdoings of individuals (*CPW* 1:670). For example, he calls books "nettlers" and even "blabbs." A blab was a common term for a gossip, one who spread news about other people. When Milton tells his opponent, Hall, that these books will reveal "your fellows [i.e., the bishops'] feats," he means that they will drag the hitherto secret crimes of prelacy out into the open. Metaphorically deputizing the books written by "free-spoken and plaine harted men," Milton says that they will serve as the "eyes of their Country, and the prospective glasses of their Prince" (*CPW* 1:670). First contemplating in print the role that books should play in English society, Milton imagines them acting as the neighborhood watch and helping to stamp out wrongdoing.

As Milton reflects on how to have a greater "liberty of speaking" while still maintaining order and civility, he edges his way increasingly toward the common law's construction of defamation. To some degree, this drift seems almost inevitable. He does not like seditious libel, but neither does he want freedom of speech taken to the opposite extreme where anything goes. The common law of defamation offered a workable middle ground. It provided greater scope for speech than seditious libel did. However, it still put clear limits on speech, and an action on the case could be brought in the event that someone accused another of a secular crime or caused material harm. We see the logic of the common law peeking out at various points in *Animadversions*. Juries were a distinctive feature of common law courtrooms so when Milton says that a "Jury of Logicians" would convict Hall for his misuse of "Logicall maxims," he seems to be thinking about his dispute with Hall within a loosely common law framework (*CPW* 1:673). He moves from a metaphorical to a literal jury when he argues that a book "presents . . . lurking evill" to the notice of rulers and magistrates (*CPW* 1:670). His phrasing relies on the widespread early modern meaning of "to present" as to "bring or lay before a court [or] magistrate," a usage central to the common phrase "jury of presentment."[42] He gives authors a role analogous to that of the grand jury, a body of men who were to use their intimate knowledge of local events and persons to "present" crimes and other offenses to the legal system.[43] At other points in *Animadversions*, Milton seems to be relying on the common law idea of defamation. For example, he appeals to the logic of the common law when he defends himself against "the censure of Libelling" by claiming that he has simply spoken the truth. He argues that the "voyce of Truth" and "the aggreev'd and long persecuted Truth" must be heard, even if his treatment of his textual adversary strikes some readers as injurious (*CPW* 1:669). His biting sallies are "the speediest way to see the truth vindicated" (*CPW* 1:664). He is allowed a "well heated fervencie" because even his most pungent rhetoric comes from a "zeale of truth" (*CPW* 1:663). Milton's claim that truth protects him from a charge of injurious words was a standard gambit in common law suits. Throughout *Animadversions*, the logic of common law defamation allows him to walk the line between nonactionable insult and actionable injury. The following exchange provides a typical example: Hall had patronizingly referred to the Smectymnuans as "these brotherly Slanderers," and in *Animadversions*, Milton retorts, "a man had better be a hog then your Brother" (*CPW* 1:694).[44] While these words might have gotten Milton convicted of seditious libel, they would not qualify as defamation in a court of common law. Milton does not impute a crime to Hall, and it is hard to imagine how Hall could demonstrate that these words had caused him actual material harm, the two basic thresholds for a successful defamation suit.

Understanding the juridical situation can change how we think about the two men involved. Most critics who have discussed *Animadversions* have regretted Milton's vehemence and have expressed sympathy toward Hall. For

42. *OED Online*, s.v. "present," v., def. 3.

43. Milton's stress on the judgment of the jury echoes a contemporary appeal to the political judgment of the English people. Exploring the reasons that impelled the sudden emergence of English newsbooks in 1641, Joad Raymond links them to the Grand Remonstrance of that same year, which was addressed to the people of England. Newsbooks were made possible by a "symbolic leap in attitudes toward the polity" and an "expansion of the intellectual franchise to include a wider body of people." Raymond, *Invention*, 123.

44. Judging from the almost complete critical silence about *Animadversions*, most Milton scholars have tacitly agreed. Kranidas argues that Hall was being more insufferable than modern critics have recognized, although he does not explore the juridical workings of the two tracts.

example, in his preface to *Animadversions* in the *Complete Prose*, Rudolf Kirk shakes his head over Milton's insults and writes, "we can scarcely condone the language [Milton] initiated against a good man" (*CPW* 1:655). But Kirk misses the fact that Milton is fighting with a bated sword while Hall is not. "Slander" was another synonym for "libel," and so underneath the genteel veneer of "brotherly Slanderers," Hall is charging Milton with a criminal offense, one that could lead offenders through Star Chamber and then on to jail or to the pillory. Milton adopts a different approach. While he lobs derisive and disrespectful words at Hall, "hog" being a prime example, he also rejects the criminalization of speech acts and looks instead toward a legal construction that treats injurious language as a merely civil offense.

MILTON, DONNE, AND HERBERT: A MULTIFACETED VIEW

Because Milton's struggle to define what counts as injurious speech has not been the subject of scholarly inquiry, it is worth pausing here to locate his voice within a larger early modern chorus. This section turns to a 1620 sermon John Donne preached at Lincoln's Inn and to the chapter on detraction that George Herbert included in *A Priest to the Temple, or the Country Parson*. Donne's and Herbert's reflections offer a fruitful comparison to Milton's, for all three authors are thinking pragmatically about how to stem the tide of injurious words. Moreover, all three of them look at the problem through a legal lens and offer specifically juridical—as opposed to only moral or religious—solutions. Here, however, the collective alignment ends. Perhaps not surprisingly, Donne the royalist and Milton the antiroyalist take up opposing positions on the rights of the defamed to speak in their own defense. Herbert stands somewhere on Milton's side of the center, for he provides greater latitude than Donne for people to speak derogatory truths about one another while stopping short of Milton's call for a greater "permission of free writing."

In the middle of a sermon delivered on January 20, 1620, to an audience of lawyers and law students at the Inns of Court, Donne unexpectedly digresses into an extended meditation on the contemporary problem of defamation.[45] He had taken as his text John 8:15, in which Christ says, "I judge no man," a verse that allows Donne to reflect on Christ's refusal of judicial

---

45. In context, Donne is using "calumny" as a catchall term for detraction, libel, slander, injurious words, etc., rather than as the technical legal term for the offense cognizable in the ecclesiastical courts.

authority and thereby to castigate the Pope's jurisdictional overreaching. He then turns toward a more insidious form of judgment: impugning others by engaging in slander and detraction. In this way, too, Christ never judged others. Donne then expands on this subject. First, he admits the enormity and intractability of the problem: "when we go about to speak against calumny, and slander, and detraction," we enter "so large a field, as that we may fight out the last drop of our bloud, preach out the last gaspe of our breath, before we overcome it." Precisely because the battlefield is so large and the spiritual enemy so strong, Donne feels obliged to dwell on it, and he asks his listeners' patience as he explores the Christian's duty in the face of injurious words: "but that we may see our danger and our duty, what calumny is, and so how to avoid it actively, and how to beare it passively, I must by your leave to stop a little upon it."[46]

In general, Donne tries to foreclose the very forms of public speech that Milton works so hard to justify. Donne breaks calumnious words into two forms, indirect and direct. Indirect calumny is, in essence, neglecting or refusing to speak well of someone or speaking less warmly than one should have, and since indirect calumny offends only against the law of charity, it occupies less of his attention. Donne spends most of his time on offenses of the immediate, stinging kind: direct calumny, or outright derogatory words about someone else. He then divides direct calumny into three types: (1) bringing a "false and unjust imputation"; (2) aggravating a "just imputation, with unnecessary, but heavy circumstances," a form of verbal piling on; and (3) "to reveale a fault which in it selfe was secret and I by no duty bound to discover it."[47] Milton would have agreed completely with Donne's first type of direct calumny; as we will see in the next section and in chapter 5, he considered it the height of injustice to be the target of "false and unjust imputation." On the other two types, however, he would have responded in more complex and demurring ways. As for the second type, aggravating a "just imputation," Milton would have conceded that under certain circumstances it would be mean-spirited and thus unjust to add to an existing pile of detractions. However, he would have also insisted that those circumstances do not apply when the public welfare is at stake, as in the case of the Smectymnuans' attacks on the bishops. In *Animadversions*, he argues that criticisms of England's prelates need to be supplemented whenever possible, and thus right-thinking men have an obligation to bring all the additional fuel they can.

46. Donne, "Preached at Lincoln's Inne," 4.
47. Donne, "Preached at Lincoln's Inne," 4.

Milton differs most on Donne's third point. Donne claims that those without a direct "duty" to speak out should remain silent. On the surface, this looks a bit like Milton's argument that those who are victims of "private and personal" injuries should suffer them in silence and that only those who know of threats to the commonwealth have a duty to speak out (*CPW* 1:662). However, Donne then clarifies his claim in a way that widens the gap between his view and Milton's: "he is a calumniator directly . . . that discovers any crime extrajudicially."[48] A duty to speak means only a duty to speak in court. When the hidden action in question breaks the law, a man should speak out in a court of law. Otherwise, he should hold his tongue. Donne returns to and elaborates on this point later in his discussion: "Wee are bound where wee have authority to stoppe the mouthes of other calumniators." However, when men "have no authority," their only legitimate response to a "back-biting tongue" is to offer an "angry countenance," for "he that looks pleasantly, and hearkens willingly to one libell, makes another, occasions a second."[49] While Donne does not specify precisely what kind of "authority" separates the man who can act against "calumniators" from the man whose only recourse is a disapproving look, the context of his sermon provides a clue. He delivered his sermon to an audience made up of lawyers and law students, men who had access to judicial positions and who thus already had or hoped to have their hands on the levers of power. He is telling his listeners that as officers of the law, they alone have the authority to "stoppe the mouthes" of those who spread actionable detractions about others. As for those who are not magistrates, judges, or lawyers, their only defensible response to verbal injury is to "avoid it actively" in themselves and to learn to "beare it passively" from others.[50]

Milton and Donne are applying contemporary ideas of law in quite different ways. Donne says that law is the proper way to handle injurious words but that that law belongs only in the courtroom. Milton, however, suggests that law provides a yardstick by which people can regulate their own words and informally prosecute the words of others. Donne argues that men who feel wounded have just two choices: bring a formal action in court or suffer detractions in patient silence. Milton, in contrast, opens up a third option: men may legitimately use books to make known the faults of others, not from a desire to satisfy personal spite but rather to help protect the commonwealth

---

48. Donne, "Preached at Lincoln's Inne," 4–5.
49. Donne, "Preached at Lincoln's Inne," 6–7.
50. Donne, "Preached at Lincoln's Inne," 4.

from bad men. Donne would argue that these authors do not "have authority" and thus have no right to speak. From Milton's point of view, all members of the commonwealth have the authority to offer public criticisms of wrongdoers, provided that they speak the truth. Each of these approaches has its drawbacks. As we will see in the next section, the anonymous Confuter who responded to *Animadversions* argues that Milton's hairsplitting discussion about what counts as libel and what does not simply paves the way for more abusive language. The fact that Milton so repeatedly tries to pin down when and where men can speak against others suggests that he understood the inherent slipperiness of his position. For his part, by suggesting that the courts are the only remedy for injurious words, Donne runs the risk of condoning informants. Like Milton, he too seems uneasily aware of his dilemma. On the one hand, he calls informants "vermine," but on the other, he backhandedly acknowledges their usefulness. While an informant is as lovable as a "Tyger or viper," they all form "one link of Gods chaine," so even if all three life-forms could be exterminated, it would be wrong to do so "for some good use that there is of them." Having both condemned informants and allowed that they have "some good use," Donne offers his listeners the somewhat feeble solution not to stoop to such behavior themselves: "thou shalt not be the man, thou shalt not be the Informer."[51] The differences between Donne's and Milton's positions can be explained by the position of each vis-à-vis the centers of power. Donne was speaking from the very heart of the Caroline judicial apparatus, and he has no doubt that the law will work impartially to protect all with legitimate grievances. Milton, in contrast, was writing from the margins, from the ranks of a nonconforming opposition that knew from firsthand experience that the juridical playing field was not a level one.

Turning now to the writings of George Herbert, we find him standing somewhere in the middle. Herbert includes a chapter titled "Concerning Detraction" in his pastoral handbook, *The Country Parson*, and, as a clergyman tasked with the spiritual health of his parishioners, he struggles with how to define the boundaries between licit and illicit speech. Like both Donne and Milton, Herbert understands the size and severity of the problem. Regrettably, most people, "when they are at leisure, make others faults their entertainments," and "even some good men think, so they speak truth, they may disclose anothers faults." The parson faced with these realities "finds it somewhat difficult how to proceed in this point," for while he naturally cannot

---

51. Donne, "Preached at Lincoln's Inne," 6. On the prominent role that informers play in Donne's legal thinking, see Kneidel, *John Donne*.

encourage detraction, if he forbids men to speak ill of one another, "many an evil may not only be, but also spread in his Parish, without any remedie (which cannot be applied without notice) to the dishonor of God, and the infection of his flock." But having identified the usefulness of detraction as a social diagnostic device, Herbert then checks himself. Regardless of how much gossip and slander can help identify communal problems, the parson cannot condone them if they are inherently wrong, and he quotes Saint Paul: *"we must not do evil, that good may come of it."*[52]

Caught between detraction's wrongness and its potential usefulness, Herbert comes up with a compromise. In a standard line of jurisprudential reasoning, he distinguishes between those faults that are private and those that are "notorious." Although he offers no further discussion of private faults, we can infer his position: when offenses are private matters between individuals (e.g., a man breaks a promise or makes a slur about a neighbor's wife), there is no justification for rehearsing them to others, and both Donne and Milton would likely agree that this kind of speech qualifies as detraction. The trickier issue is whether faults should be aired in the name of one's public duty and whether or not such airing should be confined to a courtroom. Here, Herbert takes a position closer to Milton, for he argues that in the case of notorious faults, the community has a right to know. Herbert subdivides notorious faults into two types. There are those that have been judicially registered through means such as whipping, imprisonment, branding, or stocking. Of these, Herbert writes, "men may talk, and more, they may discover them to those that know them not: because *infamie is a part of the sentence against malefactors."* He continues, "in infamy, all are executioners, and the Law gives a malefactor to all to be defamed," and just as malefactors may be doomed to forfeit life and property, they also lose "their good name."[53] Herbert here echoes the widespread judicial assumption that the point of punishments was to subject the offenders to public opprobrium and thereby to make them literally infamous in the community, a subject that, as we will see in chapter 5, much preoccupies Milton in *Pro Se Defensio*.

But what about known faults that have not risen to the level of judicial conviction and punishment? For example, a man may be widely suspected of cheating his customers but never have been caught. Or a private matter, such as oath-breaking, might have risen to the level of a public concern, as in the case of a man newly moved to the neighborhood who is reputed to have jilted

52. Herbert, *Country Parson*, 163.
53. Herbert, *Country Parson*, 164.

creditors at his former place of residence. Or a woman who has caught a village girl in a lewd act might wish to warn neighbors not to betroth their sons to her. Herbert reflects on situations when evil behavior is known only by "common fame," and he concludes, "those that know them may talk, so they do it not with sport, but commiseration."[54] This position is indebted to the juridical standard of *animus corrigenda*, the virtuous motive that transforms detractive words into corrective ones. However, while many early modern writers stipulated that such corrective words should be offered only in private, Herbert gives them a place in public discourse. Not only may a parishioner speak *to* another, he or she may also speak *about* another. Herbert defends his position on the grounds that "it concerns the Common-Wealth that Rogues should be known," and he then bolsters this sociopolitical justification with a theological one: just as men and women must practice "private Charitie," so too they have an obligation to show "Charitie to the publick."[55] These sentiments are close to Milton's argument that men have a sober duty to the public to make malefactors known, the difference being that while Milton is focused on print as the medium for airing evils, Herbert is thinking more about tavern talk and hedgerow gossip. Neither man, however, agrees with Donne's argument that it is always wrong to talk ill of others "extrajudicially," and neither would restrict the right to act to those in "authority." Instead, Herbert and Milton seem committed to the idea that members of the community have a duty to regulate relations among themselves, and this position requires both authors to define what kinds of speech are collectively allowable in the name of maintaining order.

While the account above stresses the ties that bind Herbert to Milton on the subject of injurious words and the distance that separates both of them from Donne, along another axis Milton stands apart. Donne and Herbert both operate within the conceptual framework of a single legal system, the common law. Although Donne does not specify that the common law is the forum within which men can proceed against detractors, the fact that he is preaching to a Lincoln's Inn audience leads toward that inference. Herbert has a similar juridical orientation. When he argues that communities may speak ill of those who have been whipped or branded as a result of criminal offenses, he imagines public discourse as reinforcing the verdicts of common law judges, who had the authority to impose these penalties. Neither author is interested in putting different legal constructions into the balances to see

---

54. Herbert, *Country Parson*, 164.
55. Herbert, *Country Parson*, 164–65.

how they offer more or less just approaches to defamation. In this respect, Milton is quite different. Faced with a problem such as injurious words, his instinct is to compare different legal systems and to invite his readers to think with him about which one offers the best solution. The gap in this regard between "Preached at Lincoln's Inne" and *The Country Parson*, on the one hand, and *Animadversions*, on the other, illustrates the deeply jurisdictional turn of mind that makes Milton unique.

APOLOGY AGAINST A PAMPHLET AND THE "LIBELOUS" CONFUTER

Milton's last antiprelatical treatise, *An Apology against a Pamphlet*, extends and deepens his reflections on free speech and his understanding of common law jurisprudence as providing the best guardrail against injurious language. Some months after the publication of *Animadversions*, an anonymous treatise titled *A Modest Confutation of a Slanderous and Scurrilous Libell* appeared in which the author (hereafter, the Confuter) defended Hall and attacked Milton. In his biography of Milton, John Toland stresses this work's injurious nature and the legitimacy of Milton's response: the Confuter's pamphlet was full of "Defamation," which, because it was entirely false, needed to be exposed as "Lying and Slander," and having been "unworthily defam'd," Milton has the right to respond.[56] *An Apology* opens on a strongly legal note: he says he has been moved to write out of a concern with "justice and equity"; he models his behavior on a "law of *Solon*" that made neutrality a crime in questions of sedition (*CPW* 1:868); he promises to "defend" that which he regards as "lawfull"; he will act in the name of "justice"; and he trusts to be "acquitted of presumption" by his readers (*CPW* 1:869). This broadly juridical approach quickly narrows to the subject of injurious words. The Confuter called the claims in *Animadversions* "immodest and injurious Libell," "slanderous and reproachfull calumnies," and "the most bitter and Atheisticall libels."[57] Recognizing that the best defense is a good offense, Milton retorts that since *A Modest Confutation* is "full of slanders" and "many libelous endorsements," it is guilty of the very offense that the Confuter protests against (*CPW* 1:878, 870). *Animadversions* had made a case for a wider scope for critical speech, and in response, the Confuter scoffed that Milton hypocritically sought "to maintain and defend libelling" and to "condemn it on the Bishops side" but

---

56. Darbishire, *Early Lives*, 107.
57. *Modest Confutation*, A3, B1, B2v.

to "defend it on [his] own."[58] In reply, Milton asks, "how long is it since [the Confuter] hath dis-relisht libels," alleging that Hall and his supporters have been the chief authors of them against the Puritans (*CPW* 1:905). The Confuter said that Milton's defense of his "rougher accent" (*CPW* 1:662) was just a pretext for a toxic attack. In *An Apology*, Milton responds, "to defend Libels, which is that whereof I am next accuse'd, was farre from my purpose," and "I had not so little share in good name, as to give another that advantage against my selfe" (*CPW* 1:907). As in *Animadversions*, thinking about injurious words leads Milton to think broadly about free speech. He is pleased that "both sides" on the episcopacy debate now "have equall liberty to write" (*CPW* 1:907). Where the Confuter claimed that Milton wants libelous speech to go unpunished, Milton himself claims a different motive: "The summe of what I said, was that a more free permission of writing at some times might be profitable, in such a question especially wherein the Magistrates are not fully resolv'd" (*CPW* 1:907).

As Hall did in *An Humble Remonstrance* and *A Defense of the Humble Remonstrance*, the Confuter attacks Milton using the language and assumptions of seditious libel. And as he did in *Animadversions*, Milton defends himself using the language and assumptions of common law defamation. For example, Milton stresses the different penalties he and his opponent have in mind for one another. Shocked by the fact that *Animadversions* accused England's bishops of having stinky socks, the Confuter accuses Milton of "horrid beastlinesse," and then he entreats his readers to "stone him to death" (*CPW* 1:895). Although stoning was a uniquely biblical form of punishment, the Confuter's call for corporal punishment against an author summons up the criminal penalties attached to seditious libel. Milton, in contrast, wants to live in a world where critical words are not crimes. Whereas the Confuter is as good at "slitting sentences" as his prelatical friends are at "slitting noses" (*CPW* 1:894), Milton never once argued "that any mans skin should be rais'd." Thus the Confuter's work, not his, is the true "scandalous and Butcherly Speech" (*CPW* 1:896). Milton also repeats the common law argument seen in *Animadversions* that truth was a valid defense. He was at first reluctant to answer the Confuter because he feared to be thought "too much a party in mine owne cause," and he hesitated "to molest the publick view with the vindication of a private name," however much that name had been "unworthily defam'd" (*CPW* 1:870). This is the early modern assumption that one's first response to injurious words should be to suffer in silence or to at-

---

58. *Modest Confutation*, B2.

tempt a private correction. But Milton's fight with the Confuter deserves a public audience because the Confuter has sought to "render odious the truth which I had written" (*CPW* 1:871). Because Milton is a "member incorporate into that truth whereof I was perswaded," he must speak out in its defense (*CPW* 1:871). A similar appeal to truth also anchors Milton's claim that he can justifiably use "a sanctifi'd bitternesse" and "tart rhetorick" against "the enemies of truth" and can proceed "vehemently" against an opponent who stands with "the chiefe defenders of old untruths" (*CPW* 1:901). He can even "deride and scoffe" at his adversary (*CPW* 1:903). He writes that if his opponent complains about Milton's libels, "it is because he feels [them] to be right aim'd" (*CPW* 1:905). If the words are "right aim'd," then they must be true, and true words are not defamatory.

Milton's common law reasoning emerges most clearly when he imagines his readers as a jury and asks them to judge the Confuter's tactics. He asks, "what can equally favour of injustice, and plaine arrogance, as to prejudice and forecondemne his adversary" (*CPW* 1:876). That is, the issue to be decided—whether or not *Animadversions* met the bar of seditious libel—was predetermined in the title of the Confuter's work: *A Modest Confutation of a Slanderous and Scurrilous Libell*. The Confuter violated due process with his "preoccupying direction," meaning that the allegation of libel was put in place—literally, it "pre-occupies"—before the evidence was presented (*CPW* 1:876). The Confuter offers "prejudice"—literally, prejudgment—instead of justice, and his work "forecondemne[d]" its opponent. Milton's complaint quickly takes on an added jurisdictional edge. He writes that the Confuter sits "as a Judge and Party" to the litigation and passes a verdict "before the jury of Readers can be impannell'd" (*CPW* 1:876).[59] Milton imagines reading books as analogous to the common law trial. In the common law courtroom, the judge supervised the proceedings but did not pronounce innocence or guilt. But this is exactly what the Confuter has done by handing down a verdict before the "jury of Readers" has had a chance to view the evidence. Moreover, the Confuter is not only a "Judge" but also a "Party" to the litigation. Only in a deeply corrupt set of proceedings could a judge have a personal stake in the outcome. Milton then asks his juror-readers to contrast the Confuter's

---

59. Cynthia Herrup has studied the deeply participatory nature of the common law in her *Common Peace*. See also J. A. Sharpe's claim that "most Englishmen (and possibly women) of moderate property would have been involved in civil litigation at some time, and for some of them litigating was a familiar experience." Sharpe, "Law Enforcement," 224. On the way that popular "law-mindedness" informed even crowd actions, see Walter, "'Law-Mindedness.'"

unjust manner of proceeding with his own: "Nor is my meaning, Readers, to shift off a blame from my selfe, by charging the like upon my accuser, but shall only desire, that sentence may be respited till I can come to some instance, whereto I may give answer" (*CPW* 1:882). The verb "to respite" had overwhelmingly judicial meanings in the period related to granting a stay or reprieve of punishment,[60] so when Milton asks "Readers" to give their "sentence" a "respite" until he can provide "some instance" or evidence, he models a proper form of judicial process.

Even more than *Animadversions*, *An Apology* works to pinpoint the difference between allowable verbal sparring and language that goes too far. If we think of seditious libel as setting a low threshold for injurious words (i.e., many utterances merit legal action) and defamation as setting a higher threshold (i.e., there is more latitude to speak without penalty), then the Confuter has violated even defamation's more permissive standards. First, rather than "confuting" the arguments advanced in *Animadversions*, the Confuter has resorted to "a reasonlesse defaming" of them (*CPW* 1:882). Second, he has gone one impermissible step further: "the method of his madness hurries him to attempt the like against the Author" (*CPW* 1:882). A textual attack has turned into an *ad hominem* attack, and defaming the book has led to defaming the author. Third and worst of all, the Confuter has no "proofes and testimonies" of Milton's bad character so he has relied instead on his own "slanderous inventions," throwing out "falsities" at will to make a case for Milton's personal degeneracy (*CPW* 1:882). Milton quotes the Confuter's frank admission in his preface: "I have no further notice of him, than he hath been pleased, in his immodest and injurious Libell to give of himself."[61] Without any evidence, the Confuter has made a series of outrageously "false accusations" (*CPW* 1:893): that Milton lives in a plague-ridden "*Suburbe sinke*," that he frequents whorehouses and lascivious plays, that he is a foul-mothed devotee of sack, etc.[62] These claims would qualify as common law defamation. As David Ibbetson points out, the common law construction of defamation had expanded in the sixteenth century to include "allegations of incompetence in one's profession,"[63] and the Confuter's allegations would harm Milton's ability to support himself as a teacher, his main occupation in the early 1640s.

60. *OED Online*, s.v. "respite," v.
61. *Modest Confutation*, A3.
62. *Modest Confutation*, A3v.
63. Ibbetson, "Edward Coke, Roman Law," 490.

Milton is all for free speech but not when that speech crosses certain boundaries and becomes wantonly injurious.

As both Achinstein and Sauer have demonstrated, Milton often thinks of his readers as playing an active role analogous to that of jurors, and we can logically extend their arguments further: when he installs his readers in the metaphorical role of the common law jury, Milton also assumes that they can bring basic forms of common law reasoning to bear. His contest with the Confuter presumes that readers can distinguish between the jurisprudence of seditious libel and the jurisprudence of defamation with their associated thresholds for proof. He trusts that readers understand that within a common law framework he, Milton, is innocent of the charge of libel because he has spoken the truth, because his motive for truth-speaking was an honorable desire to protect the commonwealth, and because none of his comments caused material damage to his opponent. In contrast, the Confuter has invented wildly untrue claims against Milton, has done so out of pure spite, and has brought Milton into the danger of the law. Thus Milton argues that the Confuter may "justly be said to have libell'd" him; the Confuter—not he himself—must be termed "this libeler" (*CPW* 1: 906, 883). As we will see in the next chapter, similar ideas about libel and injurious language preoccupied Milton two years later when he sat down to write *Areopagitica*. Like *Animadversions* and *An Apology*, his famous argument for a free press operates inside a jurisprudential framework that is concerned as much with the potentially damaging power of books as with their ability to liberate hearts and minds.

CHAPTER 3

Monstrous Books: *Areopagitica* and the Problem of Libel

Perhaps the most bedeviling feature of Milton's 1644 *Areopagitica* is what critics have called its "logical reversals" and its "shifty and contingent" claims.[1] On the one hand, *Areopagitica* offers an impassioned argument for why books of all kinds should circulate as widely as possible, and Milton writes, "Give me the liberty to know, to utter, and to argue freely according to conscience, above all liberties" (*CPW* 2:560). And yet on the other hand, he coolly recommends that some books should be "justly burnt, or sunk into the Sea" (*CPW* 2:505). In another of the treatise's notorious reversals, Milton argues, "hee who destroyes a good Booke, kills reason it selfe," but then he later says that some books deserve "sharpest justice" and should be delivered to "the fire and the executioner" (*CPW* 2:492, 569). This bafflingly divided stance has understandably led to a divided critical field. Some critics have emphasized Milton's desire to liberate books and have hurried past his less-tolerant comments. For them, Milton is one of the original champions of the individual's right to free speech, in effect an early advocate for the ideas enshrined in the First Amendment of the US Constitution. But others have lingered over the moments when Milton seems to endorse censorship. For them, *Areopagitica* looks repressive and authoritarian. Recognizing the way that *Areopagitica* appears to provide evidence for both positions, others have argued that Milton was attempting to appeal to

---

1. LaBreche, "*Areopagitica* and the Limits," 144. Fulton, *Historical Milton*, 90.

as wide a variety of factional readers as possible and so his treatise is simply contradictory.²

I argue in this chapter that Milton's position on book licensing and censorship is more consistent than critics have recognized. *Areopagitica* explores the same question that we saw in the previous chapter's discussion of *Animadversions* and *An Apology against a Pamphlet*: How does one allow as much freedom of speech as possible while still preventing people from launching unfounded attacks on one another? Milton answers this question in much the same way as in the two antiprelatical tracts. He advocates for free speech as a fundamental political and ethical right, meaning that people should be allowed to speak their minds and merely transgressive or heretical ideas should not be censored. However, he pairs this insistence on freedom from political or ideological censorship with an equal insistence that defamatory words should not be tolerated.³ Over and over again, *Areopagitica*'s contradictory passages seem less so if we think of Milton as arguing for a broad toleration of books up to the point where they begin saying viciously untrue things about other people. Milton's treatise thus illustrates Shuger's claim that the seventeenth century was on balance more preoccupied with the potential damage caused by injurious words than with the danger of heretical ones.⁴

---

2. For the argument that *Areopagitica* supports an emergent liberal ideology, see Belsey, *John Milton*. For a more skeptical readings, see Illo, "*Areopagiticas* Mythic and Real," and Mohamed, *Milton and the Post-secular Present*, 56. Annabel Patterson concludes that Milton's stance was inconsistent: A. Patterson, *Censorship and Interpretation*, 117. On *Areopagitica* as sensitive to parliamentary realities, see Hughes, "Milton, *Areopagitica*." Good overviews of the critical divisions about *Areopagitica* can be found in Kolbrener, *Milton's Warring Angels*, 15–16, and LaBreche, "*Areopagitica* and the Limits," 144–45.

3. Admittedly, an awareness of injurious words does little to resolve statements such as "I mean not tolerated Popery and open superstition," so I am not claiming that an awareness of defamation solves Milton's stance on religion (*CPW* 2:565).

4. While my argument would not have been possible without Shuger's groundbreaking book, she and I disagree about Milton's treatise. She points to *Areopagitica* as the point at which a new and recognizably modern idea of censorship as ideological control—as "Daddy State" looking over one's shoulder—first enters early modern discourse in a significant way (Shuger, *Censorship*, 162). After that point, Shuger touches on Milton now and then as a means to remind readers that Milton stands on our side of a line in the sand dividing older, civility-based controls on transgressive speech from newer, ideologically driven ones, and in her reading, issues like libel and defamation detain Milton "only in passing" (Shuger, *Censorship*, 14). But as my discussion below argues, Milton is quite invested in questions of defamation and civility. Especially when we read *Areopagitica* in concert with the two antiprelatical tracts dis-

In *Animadversions* and *An Apology*, the jurisdiction of Star Chamber was the greatest threat to free speech, but by the writing of *Areopagitica*, the greatest threat Milton saw was licensing. However, the antidote remains the same in both cases. The common law courts' jurisdiction over injurious words meant that these courts provided the ideal forum where damaging books could be weighed in the balances. Common law jurisprudence treated defamation as a civil matter, one that was initiated, disputed, and often settled between private individuals. Thus defamation suits kept the control over books out of the hands of state licensers. For the secretive judgments of the licenser and the hidden workings of state censorship, Milton would substitute the forthright standards of the common law courts and the public processes of that most English of institutions, the common law jury.

THE SPECTER OF LIBEL

A number of threads connect *Areopagitica* to the earlier *Animadversions* and *An Apology against a Pamphlet*. In the opening of *Areopagitica*, Milton contrasts his own sincere praise for Parliament to the "triviall and malignant *Encomium*" that prefaces *A Modest Confutation* (*CPW* 2:486, 488). By nodding toward *A Modest Confutation*, Milton suggests that *Areopagitica* to some degree continues his debate with the Confuter about the proper limits of injurious speech. There are other intertextual links as well. For example, Milton first uses the term "Areopagi" in *Animadversions* (*CPW* 1:666), and his reference in *Areopagitica* to the "Temple of *Janus*" with its "two *controversal* faces" revisits a reference in *Animadversions* to the "subtile *Janus*" who displays sometimes his "bolder face" and sometimes his "cautious, and wary" one (*CPW* 2:561, 1:679). In *An Apology*, he claims that even offensive books can be useful as a "way to lessen tumult . . . as anger freely vented spends it self, ere it break out into action" (*CPW* 1:907–8). *Areopagitica* takes a similar position: even "bad books . . . serve in many respects to discover, to confute, [and] to forewarn" (*CPW* 2:512). *Animadversions* reasons that books allow readers to hear opinions in safety. The ruler or magistrate who wishes to hear the thoughts of "free-spoken and plaine harted" men can read their books instead of eavesdropping in alleys. A related line of argument reappears in *Areopagitica* when Milton asks, "how can we more safely, and with lesse danger scout into the regions of sin and falsity then by reading all manner of tractats,

---

cussed in the previous chapter, we can see Milton's commitment to the very forms of civility that Shuger exempts him from.

and hearing all manner of reason?" (*CPW* 2:516–17). Given these and other similarities, it is hardly surprising that the precis he provides for the earlier pamphlets could serve equally well for *Areopagitica*: "the summe of what I said, was that a more free permission of writing at some times might be profitable" (*An Apology, CPW* 1:907).

As he did in *Animadversions* and *An Apology*, Milton suggests in *Areopagitica* that a broad tolerance for different kinds of speech should end when the speech becomes injurious. He stakes out this position early on in his historical overview of censorship practices. Beginning his survey in ancient Athens, he compliments the Athenians because they had laws "against defaming," and in order to stamp out "the open way of defaming," they decreed "that none should be traduc'd by name." He adds approvingly, "we may guesse how they censur'd libelling." The Athenians refused to surveil books in a general sense, and there were only two kinds of books "which the Magistrate car'd to take notice of": those that were "blasphemous and Atheisticall" and those that were "Libellous" (*CPW* 2:494). Libel and blasphemy were cognate offenses since both were forms of injury. A heretical book might express wrong belief, but a blasphemous one actually insulted God. Thus blasphemy was essentially defamation aimed at heaven, a point I return to at the end of this chapter. Milton next moves to a discussion of the Romans where he finds a similar tolerance of books with the exception of libel and blasphemy: "Except in these two points, how the world went in Books, the Magistrat kept no reckning" (*CPW* 2:498). Displaying his wide reading in Roman jurisprudence, Milton explains that Roman jurists had laws for "what was to be don to libellous books and Authors." He gives as an example the poet and dramatist Naevius, who "was quickly cast into prison for his unbridl'd pen," specifically for his attacks on members of the Metelli family. Similar laws marked the reign of Augustus, when "libels were burnt, and the makers punisht" (*CPW* 2:498). After that point, Rome deteriorated into "tyranny," and so "we may not marvell, if not so often bad, as good Books were silenc't" (*CPW* 2:500). By "bad . . . Books," Milton clearly means defamatory ones. A state becomes tyrannous not only when it destroys honorable books but also when it fails to destroy injurious ones. This same intolerance of defamation appears again when Milton explains why readers should ignore the positive role that censorship plays in *The Republic*: Plato liked Aristophanes even though he was a "malicious libeller" of Plato's friends. Clearly any man undiscriminating enough to approve of defamation is not to be listened to on the subject of censorship. Lest we miss Milton's disdain for this kind of injurious writing, he follows up by calling it "such trash" (*CPW* 2:523).

Milton's focus on defamation in his survey of Athenian and of Roman societies has attracted surprisingly little critical attention, and I will hazard two guesses as to why. First, most critics who study early modern libels regard them as a subgenre of scurrilous verses whose primarily goal is to satirize dominant institutions and authorities. For example, consider the titles of two recent studies of early modern libels: "'The Pooremans Joy and the Gentlemans Plague': A Lincolnshire Libel and the Politics of Sedition in Early Modern England" and *'Railing Rhymes': Politics and Poetry in Early Stuart England*.[5] In both cases, libel is modified by words such as "sedition" and "politics." I do not mean to suggest that these works are flawed. To the contrary, both usefully show how early modern libelous verses were part of an ideological tug of war between popular and official views. My point is simply that if we think of libels only as forms of political critique, we are not in a position to understand *Areopagitica*. In fact, look at what happens if we plug an idea of libel as a biting expression of political dissent back into *Areopagitica*'s discussion of classical societies: Milton appears to give censorship a big thumbs-up by suggesting that the Greeks and Romans were right to stamp out "libellous" works that questioned authority and dared to adopt a satirical stance toward institutional structures. We can see why critics have scratched their heads at the image of Milton the regicide claiming that "libels" cannot be tolerated. As I remarked in the previous chapter, "libel" is one of the most protean of early modern words, so to understand what Milton means, we have to read carefully for context. And in this section of *Areopagitica*, all of his complaints about "libels" refer to personal defamation. When he says that the Athenians wanted to prevent "the open way of defaming" and thus ordered "that none should be traduc'd by name," he expresses an aversion to personal skewering, not to political dissent.

Second, Milton's discussion of libel invites misunderstanding because he refers generally to the actions of the Athenian and Roman state rather than specifically to those of the law courts. We moderns tend to create clear distinctions between different branches of government, but early moderns did not. To give an example, Parliament was both a legislative body and a judicial one, a dual identity Milton highlights in *Areopagitica* when he both asks Parliament to reconsider a law and addresses it as a "High Court" (*CPW* 2:486).[6]

---

5. Walter, "'Pooremans Joy'"; McRae, "*Railing Rhymes*." McRae's collection provides a useful starting point for studying early modern literary libels, as does his *Literature, Satire*.

6. For more on Parliament as both a judicial body and a legislative one, see McIlwain, *High Court of Parliament*.

When Milton talks about those Athenian officials who "censur'd libelling," it is easy for us to assume that he means top-down censorship of the Big Brother variety, one in which some unspecified "they" of officialdom decide which books to allow and which to suppress. But given the context, Milton is more likely using "magistrates" as synecdoches for the judicial system. Milton was comprehensively familiar with the law of *iniuria* in both its common law and Continental manifestations, and so he knew that defamation actions were typically initiated by private individuals. State officials refereed suits as they moved through the legal system and were the ones to enforce sentences, but the judicial process was powered by individual plaintiffs who felt that they had been injured and who sought legal redress in local jurisdictions.[7] Insofar as *iniuria* suits qualify as censorship, it is censorship in the sense of a body of citizens using the courts as a means to enforce collective norms of behavior.

In his other works, Milton underscores this sense that defamation is a private matter and thus not an appropriate concern for state agents. When he calls his opponent "this libeler" in *An Apology against a Pamphlet*, he is decidedly *not* suggesting that state agents should intervene in *deus ex machina* fashion to destroy the book. Rather, he means that the Confuter's allegations meet the legal bar of defamation and that he, Milton, could hypothetically bring a civil suit.[8] In *Pro Se Defensio*, Milton provides an even clearer expression of the individual's control over defamation prosecutions: "shall any private person have done violence upon my reputation in an infamous book . . . and shall I be compelled to swallow that insult, so that I cannot, when the time seems right, vindicate myself with a defense both just and anxiously expected?" (*CPW* 4:731). As I will argue in chapter 5, *Pro Se Defensio* is Milton's textual version of a prosecution for *iniuria*. A blind man living in a common law country, he cannot literally press charges against an opponent who lived under Continental Civil law. Instead he turns his treatise into a metaphorical courtroom where the evidence for *iniuria* can be weighed and a verdict rendered. The assumption on which *Pro Se Defensio* rests is that *iniuria* charges, if proved true, should lead to the destruction of the offending book and some form of penalty for the author. This outcome would not be an instance of state censorship. To the contrary, when Milton refers to his opponent as a "private

---

7. The structure of *iniuria* suits reflects that of Roman law as a whole, which was "fundamentally a body of *private* law": Lee, *Popular Sovereignty*, 18, emphasis in original.

8. I say "hypothetically" because both Milton and the Confuter were writing anonymously and thus boxing at shadows. Common law defamation was a strictly personal jurisprudence, meaning that attacking someone veiled by a pseudonym was not an actionable offense.

person" and to his own right to "vindicate" himself, he insistently moves the issue out of the public realm of state censorship and into the private realm of legal actions between individuals.

By emphasizing the private, civil nature of defamation, Milton rejects the legal category of seditious libel both because it criminalized words and because it allowed political dissent to be punished as libelous, regardless of whether the words were personally injurious.[9] For example, the state surveyor Roger L'Estrange writes that ideas such as those found in *Tenure of Kings and Magistrates* were "Libell."[10] Although *Tenure* was not personally defamatory (it never once mentions Charles Stuart), L'Estrange views it as libelous because its radical ideas send out dangerous political shockwaves. Satirizing this construction of libel in *An Apology*, Milton writes, "I see not how *Wickleffe* and *Luther* . . . could avoid the imputation of libelling" (*CPW* 1:878). He uses the word "libel" in an entirely different way than L'Estrange. When he writes that *A Modest Confutation* is full of "many libelous endorsements" or when he criticizes Aristophanes as a "malicious libeller" in *Areopagitica*, he is not talking about seditious libel, libel of magistrates, scandalous libel—any of the loose cluster of terms that broadly denoted biting words intended to express dissatisfaction with authorities (*An Apology*, *CPW* 1:870; *Areopagitica*, *CPW* 2:523). Instead, he is talking about people who have defamed their peers.

Milton's aversion to defamation appears repeatedly in *Areopagitica*. In another of the treatise's seeming U-turns, he argues that licensing books leads to "the discouragement of all learning, and the stop of Truth." Books should be liberated from such "hindring and cropping" constraints so that further discoveries can be made in "religious and civill Wisdome" (*CPW* 2:491–92). However, in the next sentence he writes, "I deny not, but that it is of greatest concernment in the Church and Commonwealth, to have a vigilant eye how Bookes demeane themselves, as well as men; and thereafter to confine, imprison, and do sharpest justice on them as malefactors" (*CPW* 2:492). In addition to its specific sense of a felon or criminal, the word "malefactor" had the general meaning of "a person who behaves badly or wickedly toward another."[11] Similarly the verb "demeane" indicated behavior toward other

---

9. Historian Leonard W. Levy calls seditious libel an "accordion-like concept, expandable or contractible at the whim of judges": *Emergence of a Free Press*, 8.

10. L'Estrange, *Answer to the Appeal*, 35. For further discussion, see Maltzahn, "Naming the Author," 4.

11. *OED Online*, s.v. "malefactor," n., def. 1 and 2.

people.[12] In both cases, the emphasis falls on interpersonal conduct, on the potential harm books inflict on those around them. Milton is not reversing course in this passage so much as specifying that defamatory language is the one exception to the permissiveness books should enjoy. This passage also suggests that authors who commit defamation should be subject to the judge's gavel rather than to the licenser's pen, a point I take up in more detail in the next section. The word "malefactor" was often applied to those actually facing legal prosecution, as when Milton writes of a "malefactor" who does not have a "sufficient Plea to acquitt him from being . . . judg'd" (*Eikonoklastes, CPW* 3:597). Milton's verbs "confine" and "imprison" similarly point to actual judicial processes, as does his claim that malefactor books should face "sharpest justice."[13] This judicial vocabulary suggests that the punishing of books should be the prerogative of England's court systems, not of its licensers, stationers, and civic administrators.

Two other examples show a concern with injurious words sitting at the heart of *Areopagitica*'s puzzling passages. First, having argued that licensing is an invention of the Inquisition and that books should be "as freely admitted into the World as any other birth," Milton abruptly shifts gears: if a book is "prov'd a Monster," it should be "justly burnt, or sunk into the Sea" (*CPW* 2:505). Since he is clearly not using "monster" in its contemporary sense of a mythical creature or one of extreme size, the most likely definition is something or someone "exhibiting such extreme cruelty or wickedness as to seem inhuman."[14] Again the stress is on hurtful conduct. Six years later, Milton would cut and paste this same wording from *Areopagitica* into *Tenure of Kings and Magistrates*: He imagines a case in which two men make a "covenant" to do good to one another. If one of them "prove afterward a monster" to the other, then the covenant is replaced by a "disobligement," and Milton pictures the injured man lawfully "demanding Justice" on the other (*CPW* 3:232). In both *Areopagitica* and *Tenure of Kings and Magistrates*, people and books "prove . . . a monster" when they turn on their friends and neighbors. Second, Milton makes this same point later in *Areopagitica* when he writes that if books "be found mis-

---

12. *OED Online*, s.v. "demean," v., def. 4a and 4b.

13. The question of who had the right to "confine" and "imprison" had become a flashpoint issue in the seventeenth century, especially in the wake of legal battles such as the Five Knights Case. Increasingly, the common law courts claimed the sole right to detain subjects, and the writ of *habeas corpus* had become a rallying cry for ideas of English liberty. See Halliday, "Birthrights."

14. *OED Online*, s.v. "monster," n., def. 5.

chievous and libelous, the fire and the executioner will be the timeliest and the most effectuall remedy, that mans prevention can use" (*CPW* 2:569). The word "libelous" leaves little doubt that bad books are defamatory ones. The word "mischievous" further underlines his views, since like "demeane," "mischief" often carried the legal sense of that which inflicts damage on other people or "a wrong suffered by a particular individual . . . under a law."[15]

Milton's wariness about a book's potential to inflict interpersonal injury also helps explain his allusion to the myth of Cadmus. He writes that books are "as lively, and as vigorously productive, as those fabulous Dragons teeth; and being sown up and down, may chance to spring up armed men" (*CPW* 2:492). This story comes from Ovid's *Metamorphoses* where Cadmus sows dragon's teeth and then sees them turn into soldiers. One of them warns Cadmus to stand clear: "Keep out of this / Our civil warfare." "As he spoke, he struck / One of his brothers, and himself was murdered" by another. Cadmus watches as "the sudden brothers perished / By wounds they gave each other" until only five are left.[16] This image of interpersonal warfare contrasts with a later passage in *Areopagitica* in which Milton imagines London as "the shop of warre" and the busy scribbling of many pens as "anvils and hammers waking, to fashion out the plates and instruments of armed Justice" (*CPW* 2:554). Whereas the men sprung from dragon's teeth turn and fight one another, those in the "shop of warre" work in concert: collectively "assenting to the force of reason and convincement," they present "their homage and their fealty [to] the approaching Reformation" (*CPW* 2:554). Even what looks like combativeness is really a productive exercise in learning, since "much arguing, much writing, many opinions . . . in good men" are evidence of "knowledge in the making" (*CPW* 2:554). Good books are like swords wielded by allies against the enemies of truth. Monstrous books grown from dragon's teeth—ones that are implicitly defamatory—are like daggers stuck in the backs of comrades.

We can see Milton's intolerance of defamation in yet another of *Areopagitica*'s contradictory passages. He argues forcefully that books should not be micromanaged through licensing since "if we think to regulat Printing, thereby to rectifie manners, we must regulat all recreations and pastimes" (*CPW* 2:523). However, this permissiveness holds only up to a point: "that . . . which is impious or evil absolutely either against faith or maners no law can possibly permit, that intends not to unlaw it self" (*CPW* 2:565). Although in modern usage "manners" usually refers to forms of social refinement, in

---

15. *OED Online*, s.v. "mischief," n., def. 4a.
16. Ovid, *Metamorphoses*, 3.117–23.

the early modern period it had a deeper meaning. Failures of manners were failures of morality.[17] When Wordsworth invokes Milton in "London 1802" and asks him to "return to us again; / And give us manners, virtue, freedom, power," he means that Milton can help cure the English of being "selfish men" and give them his "cheerful godliness." In this passage from *Areopagitica*, Milton emphasizes "maners" rather than ideas; he is more concerned with the way that people treat one another than with their political or religious positions. He argues that even ill-mannered books should be tolerated up to a point since why force books to be virtuous when people have so many other means (dance, music, etc.) to express their baser impulses? However, Milton does not give authors *carte blanche*, and he insists that the law must intervene when books become "evil absolutely" against "faith or maners." His earlier intolerance of blasphemy and libel resurfaces here in slightly modified form. Milton explains that the prohibition on deep affronts to "faith and maners" rests on the fundamental logic of civil society: "no law can possibly permit" these actions that "intends not to unlaw it self." Law exists to uphold civil society, and thus a legal system that does not prevent or punish wounds to other people is useless. The flip side to *Areopagitica*'s aversion to personal injury is its insistence that people should act with a certain level of decency toward one another. Milton turns from reflecting on actions that are "evil absolutely either against faith or maners" to exhorting readers to preserve "*the unity of Spirit*" and "*the bond of peace*" (*CPW* 2:565). Elsewhere he writes that people should display "patience and humility" toward one another and be "full of meeknes and breathing charity" (*CPW* 2:561). They should cultivate a "grain of charity" toward one another, and differing ideas should be "tolerated in peace, and . . . charity" (*CPW* 2:554, 563). He asks authors to give even their adversaries "gentle meetings and gentle dismissions" (*CPW* 2:567). Throughout *Areopagitica*, Milton suggests that the strength and integrity of the social order are threatened far more by failures of charity than by failures of right belief. *Areopagitica*'s permissiveness toward merely heretical or radical books and its intolerance toward attack-dog books echo comments from his other works. For example, in *An Apology against a Pamphlet*, Milton's greatest frustration is that his textual opponent, the Confuter, has crossed over from advancing offensive ideas to making offensive personal allegations. Instead of "confuting" Milton's arguments, the Confuter has resorted to "defaming" Milton himself with "false accusations" (*An Apology, CPW* 1:893). Milton reasons along the same lines in the introduction to *Tetrachordon*, written about

17. For example, see *OED Online, s.v.* "manners," n., def. 4d.

three months after *Areopagitica*. The minister Herbert Palmer had attacked *Doctrine and Discipline of Divorce* in the pulpit and in print. Milton says that if Palmer had "burst out onely against the opinion" of his treatise, he would have "silently born" the attack. However, Palmer's hatred has led him "to inveigh opprobriously against the person," i.e., against Milton himself. Therefore Milton feels bound to come "to the defense of an honest name, or to the reputation of those good men who afford me their society" (*CPW* 2:581). Having been treated in an "illegal manner," Milton claims the right to "defend myself publicly against a printed Calumny" (*CPW* 2:581, 582).

Perhaps the strongest indicator that *Areopagitica* puts injurious words beyond the acceptable pale comes from one of the earliest known references to it. In 1649, the Puritan-leaning writer and scholar John Hall (also Milton's junior colleague in the Commonwealth government) published *An Humble Motion to the Parliament of England Concerning the Advancement of Learning and Reformation of the Universities*. Hall laments the sorry state of education at England's universities, and having complained about matters such as the stale curriculum and the poor "pecuniary endowments," he warms to his subject: "I could lay open abundance of [the universities'] customes, both superstitious, irrational, uncivill, and ridiculous; I could instance how some vices are growne generall in some degrees of them, how many *slugs* there are, how some courses they take will prove merely the choaking of all literature." But he backs away from further vituperation by invoking Milton. Such a cataloging of evils would "degenerate into some *Satyre* or *Pasquill*, rather then an *Areopagitick*," and so Hall resolves to "lay aside all bitternesse" and speak instead with "meeknesse and equanimity."[18] While William Haller, who first drew attention to this allusion, suggests that Hall invokes *Areopagitica* because he wants the same "humanistic type of education" that Milton supported, the quotation's context indicates a different concern.[19] For Hall, "an *Areopagitick*" is the opposite of a "*Pasquill*," which was a variant of "libel." In Hall's view, *Areopagitica* serves to remind readers that while muscular and even fractious debate is a healthy part of civil society, abusive language is not.

COMMON LAW JUSTICE

Having argued to this point that *Areopagitica* is centrally concerned with the problem of defamation, I turn now to Milton's thoughts about definition and

---

18. John Hall, *Humble Motion*, 28–29.
19. Haller, "Two Early Allusions," 208.

enforcement. Assuming that defaming other people is unacceptable, then what exactly counts as defamation? What are the proper mechanisms for prosecution? And what kinds of penalties can be justly applied? As this section argues, Milton apparently wants cases involving injurious words to go to the common law courts, not to Star Chamber. They should be treated as civil actions and heard and decided by a jury of peers.[20]

We see Milton's preference for common law justice when he objects to licensing on the grounds that it requires that a book "stand before a Jury ere it be borne to the World," as if to undergo the judgment of "*Radamanth* and his Collegues," an allusion to the judges Rhadamanthus, Minos, and Aeacus, who judged the souls of the dead in Greek mythology (*CPW* 2:505). Milton's image is built upon two implied oppositions. The first is between being judged before and after the fact. In Greek mythology as in the New Testament ("Doth our law judge any man before it hear him, and know what he doeth?" [John 7:51]), judgment should come after deeds have been done, not before. Thus prepublication licensing contravenes a basic principle of justice. The other opposition is between two types of juries, one illegitimate and the other legitimate. Milton is being ironical in applying the term "Jury"—a word rooted in *jus/jure* or "justice"—to the panel of licensers, since his point is that their verdicts are unjust. In place of this false jury, Milton would have books judged by a better one. At one level, he means the metaphorical jury of readers, and this passage from *Areopagitica* echoes his earlier claim in *An Apology* that the Confuter sits "as a Judge" and passes a verdict "before the jury of Readers can be impannell'd" (*CPW* 1:876). In likening readers to a jury, both *An Apology* and *Areopagitica* also look toward the real jury, the panel of adjudicating laymen that was the signature feature of the common law trial. The analogy of readers to jurors in both treatises works in part because of the highly participatory nature of English common law, which relied upon laymen to serve as jurors, constables, justices of the peace, etc.[21] Because educated readers often served as jurors and because jurors were often readers, it was easy to imagine each form of judging in terms of the other. As we will see in chapter 7, Milton's

---

20. Ironically, the common law courts later stepped into Star Chamber's shoes and took over prosecutions for seditious libel, precisely the outcome that Milton would have wanted least. This change is thoroughly traced in Hamburger, "Development."

21. The central role that juries played in the administration of the common law is a reminder of Hutson's point about the participatory nature of English law. Hutson connects the nation's participatory law to the way that English dramatists invited audiences to apply forensic tools to "solving" problems represented onstage: Hutson, *Invention of Suspicion*.

views of the jury may have darkened over time, but in the 1640s, he still sees a link between juries and the discerning powers of the English people.[22] For example, in *Pro Populo Anglicano Defensio*, he argues that even kings should be subject to the people, "judging all suits by juries of twelve men." This same association of the jury with native English liberty informs this passage in *Areopagitica*. A book should be sent before a jury of readers who will use their own God-given reason to judge its worth. And in the event that a plaintiff thinks that a book has become a "Monster" (i.e., crossed over into actionable defamation), the jury of readers will be replaced by the real jury of twelve good men. The faith Milton expresses in the jury shows the trust he still has in the English people and his hope that the "puissant nation" is stirring itself to erect a more just social order.[23]

Milton's belief that books should be judged by the due processes of law and not by censorship appears clearly in the following passage, one that has been rarely discussed in Milton criticism: "He who is not trusted with his own actions, his drift not being known to be evill, and standing to the hazard of law and penalty, has no great argument to think himself reputed in the Commonwealth wherein he was born, for other then a fool or a foreigner" (*CPW* 2:531–32). The reasoning here is deeply juridical. Milton imagines three kinds of men who might not be "trusted with [their] own actions": the fool, the foreigner, and the man whose "drift" is "known to be evill." The first category refers to those who lacked mental capacity and so did not qualify as adult subjects. The second were foreign nationals. And the third, those "known to be evill," alludes to the legal doctrine of infamy, a common element in Civil law and one whose assumptions had soaked into English common law as well.[24] These three kinds of men did not have the same range of legal rights as ordinary English subjects. Excluding these three groups, Milton says that all others should be trusted to act—and therefore to write—as they please. He defines the liberty of these fully enfranchised men in terms of their legal liability. When he imagines these men "standing to the hazard of law and penalty" in the event that they write actionable words, Milton draws on one

---

22. On juries and readers, see also Chapman, *Legal Epic*, and Achinstein, *Milton and the Revolutionary Reader*, 60–62. For more on Milton's commitment to his readers, see Dobranski, *Readers and Authorship*, 207–9, and Ainsworth, *Milton and the Spiritual Reader*.

23. For more on the English attachment to the jury trial, see the essays collected in Cairns and McLeod, *Dearest Birthright*, and Syme, "(Mis)Representing Justice."

24. Chapter 5 provides a fuller discussion of infamy in Milton's thinking.

early modern meaning of "to stand" as "submit to judicial trial or sentence."[25] In his study of the chaotic variety of early modern censorship practices, Joad Raymond arrives at a similar conclusion about Milton's commitment to the rule of law. He argues that Milton opposed the many informal restrictions placed on authors since these often amounted to *sub rosa* forms of harassment. Instead, Milton favored the clarity and forthrightness of the rule of law: *Areopagitica* "contends that if you wish to punish [an author], then as a free man . . . you need to argue with him in court."[26] For the solitary, secretive, and executive processes of censorship, Milton would substitute the collective, discursive, and highly public processes of English common law trials. And if a jury considers the evidence in a defamation suit and concludes that the plaintiff has proved his case, then the defendant can be justly fined and his book or treatise justly removed from circulation.

Milton's view that the law courts are the best means for controlling injurious words explains his complaint about the anti-Parliament newspaper *Mercurius Aulicus*: "Do we not see, not once or oftener, but weekly that continu'd Court-libell against the Parlament and City, Printed, as the wet sheets can witnes, and dispers't among us, for all that licensing can doe?" (*CPW* 2:528).[27] The term "Court-libell" is anomalous. Milton uses it nowhere else in his writings, and it does not appear in either the *Oxford English Dictionary* or the Early English Books Online database. By creating this compound word, Milton appears to be stressing that he means the kind of libel that can actually be tried in a court of common law. In addition to its generally derisive tone about Parliament (such as its references to the MPs as "the Coxcombs of State," "these precious things," and "their Mightinesses"), *Mercurius Aulicus* sometimes crosses over into defamation. For example, in 1649, Parliament voted

---

25. *OED Online*, s.v. "stand," v., def. 11a. Jurisdictionally speaking, this is an innovative idea since the common law courts usually dealt with spoken injuries and left written ones to Star Chamber. This was not because the early modern period saw any categorical legal difference between written and spoken words but rather because written *iniuria* was almost by definition more premeditated and thus more apt to be seen as a crime. Milton suggests that all forms of defamation should be handled in the common law courtroom, and other, nondefamatory forms of transgressive speech should simply be ignored.

26. Raymond, "Censorship," 527. Raymond and I differ primarily in the legal framework we adopt. In his essay, he studies the laws that specifically related to printing, whereas my own focus is on the jurisprudence of defamation.

27. For further discussion of *Aulicus*, see Raymond, *Invention*, 26–27 and 31–32.

Henry Marten a stipend to compensate him for his losses during the Civil War. The August 14–21, 1649, edition of *Mercurius Aulicus* reports that the money was awarded to Marten "to maintain his *Mol* in Aldersgate street, and his *Mopsa* at Charing-Crosse."[28] In his *Actions for Slaunder* about the ins and outs of actionable defamation, John March reminds readers that "words spoken of a man, which scandal him in his profession or function by which he gains his living, will beare an Action."[29] Since the allegation that Marten keeps not one but two whores would have damaged him in his professional capacities as a lawyer and an MP, it would qualify as a "Court-libell" in Milton's lexicon. Milton's point is that since even the highly developed mechanisms of the nation's main legal system have not succeeded at controlling the defamatory *Aulicus*, then licensing does not stand a chance.

Milton contrasts the due process of common law defamation with two examples of legal processes gone awry. First, he likens the licensed book to the man who needs another to act as his "bayl and surety" (*CPW* 2:532). Second, he relates the condition of licensed books to men and women in prison for debt: "dettors and delinquents may walk abroad without a keeper, but unoffensive books must not stirre forth without a visible jaylor in thir title" (*CPW* 2:536). Both examples show Milton thinking inside the framework of English common law. In his 1661 *Glossographia*, Thomas Blount writes that the term "baile" is "used in our Common Law" to refer to freeing someone imprisoned in return for a fronted security. Similarly, imprisonment for debt was initiated by a writ of *capias ad satisfaciendum*, also a common law action.[30] Both of Milton's images show violations of due process. Men who were attached and imprisoned might have to make bail and find sureties, but authors should not have to. Defaulting debtors might deserve a jailor (there is no indication that Milton the moneylender saw the writ of *capias ad satisfaciendum* as inherently unjust),[31] but books do not. Milton's goal is not for authors and books to be exempt from all legal constraints but rather for the proper ones to be applied under the proper circumstances. Otherwise, "the law must needs be

---

28. *Mercurius Aulicus*, 2, 7 [August 14–21, 1649].
29. March, *Actions for Slaunder*, 77.
30. Blount, *Glossographia*, F3.
31. While the legality of imprisonment for debt was one of the glaring flaws of the early modern common law, we should remember that in a world where loans were made primarily between friends and neighbors, a defaulting debtor could have "a domino effect on each link in chains of credit," thus having an impact on many families and even whole communities: Muldrew, *Economy of Obligation*, 3. See also 181–84. Carl Wennerlind also explores the ubiquity of credit relationships in his *Casualties of Credit*.

frivolous which goes about to restrain things uncertainly yet equally working to good and to evil" (*CPW* 2:528). What Milton opposes is not law but rather "frivolous" law and legal processes that are applied arbitrarily, foolishly, or inconsistently.

These two examples highlight the central role that civil actions play in Milton's thinking. For moderns with positivist assumptions that law exists to further the agenda of the state, Milton's emphasis on law and order can make him sound repressive. But throughout *Areopagitica*, he alludes to the kinds of legal matters that were conducted "horizontally" between equals. For example, sureties were a standard part of early modern loans and contracts, and Milton was personally familiar with them from his experience with defeasible bonds.[32] His image of licensed books as analogous to "dettors and delinquents" has the same inflections. Debt was a civil offense, and "delinquent" is cognate with "delict," which was the Roman law term for a tort (*CPW* 2:536). This civil law orientation appears elsewhere in *Areopagitica*. Contrary to the modern association of monsters with bloodshed, Milton seems to have thought of "monstrous" behavior as merely tortious, for when he reuses *Areopagitica*'s phrase "prov'd a Monster" in *Tenure of Kings and Magistrates*, he does so in the context of contracts: in the event that one man acts like a monster, any "covenant" between him and another is void. Indeed, the covenant is replaced by a "disobligement," another civil term since legal "obligations" usually meant indebtedness instruments such as bonds and mortgages. "The 'disobliged' man stands 'demanding' Justice," and here too we step into the realm of civil jurisprudence since justice pursued by the individual typically involved what Coke called matters of "*Meum* and *Tuum.*"[33] *Areopagitica*'s reference to books as "mischievous" has a similar juridical orientation. Perhaps because it stemmed from a French word meaning destitute or needy, "mischief" often shows up in legal discussions of property.[34] For example, in a 1648 report on various King's Bench cases, the word "mischief" appears repeatedly in the context of damages, legacies, and replevin, all actions involving private disputes between individuals and ones where the penalties were financial rather than corporeal.[35]

---

32. For example, a London goldsmith named William Hearne served as a surety on the loan that Richard Powell took from Milton in 1627. For more details about this transaction, see *MC* 100–102.

33. Coke, *Third Part of the Institutes*, B1.

34. *OED Online*, s.v. "mischief," n., etymology.

35. *Reports, or, New Cases*.

Milton's interest in the civil aspects of the common law appears also in his wariness about monopolies. He writes, "Truth and understanding are not such wares as to be monopoliz'd and traded in by tickets and statutes and standards," and he likens licensers to "some old *patentees* and *monopolizers* in the trade of book-selling" (*CPW* 2:535, 570). As Blair Hoxby and Elizabeth Sauer have shown, Milton here has his eye on landmark cases at common law such as *Davenant v. Hurdis* and *Darcy v. Allen* in which monopolies were ruled to be violations of Magna Carta. By imperiling the livelihoods of England's tradesmen and artisans, monopolies thereby imperiled their liberty.[36] Behind Milton's metaphor of licensers as monopolists lies a jurisdictional argument. In 1624, Parliament passed the Statute of Monopolies, which gave the common law courts jurisdiction over all issues of trade patents and thus the authority to dismantle monopolies. However, this law had almost no impact since Charles I simply rerouted cases involving trade patents through Star Chamber instead.[37] When John Lilburne complained in 1646 about "Prerogative-Monopolizing arbitrary-men," he meant that England's monopolies—which he calls "Illegall"—were being sustained by the prerogative courts. Lilburne argues that the nation should be governed only "by the *Fundamentall Lawes and Constitutions of this* Kingdome . . . and by no other," by which he means the common law.[38] In opposing monopolies, Milton similarly opposes the conciliar court that upheld them, and he suggests that the free trade in both material goods and ideas should be regulated instead by the jurisprudence of the common law.

I stress the presence of civil law references because scholars who find *Areopagitica* repressive often miss the civil/criminal distinction Milton is trying to draw. In a famous argument that *Areopagitica* is tinged with fascism, John Illo describes its "massive intolerance," and he claims that Milton champions a system in which "books, like men, should be subjected to surveillance, and punished or destroyed when bad."[39] But Illo's reasoning cuts misleadingly across legal categories. Like almost all of his contemporaries, Milton accepted the justice of capital punishment assuming that the defendant had been duly

---

36. Hoxby, *Mammon's Music*, 25–56; Sauer, *"Paper-Contestations,"* 20–34. For a wider discussion of the role of monopolies in early modern printing and censorship, see J. F. Loewenstein, *Author's Due*, 132–51.

37. See the discussion of this jurisdictional contest in Walterscheid, "Early Evolution," 771–74.

38. Lilburne, *Londons Liberty*, 40.

39. Illo, "*Areopagiticas* Mythic and Real," 6.

convicted in a court of law of offenses at or above the level of felony. However, by repeatedly alluding to civil legal processes in *Areopagitica*, Milton resolutely separates books—and thus authors—from all criminal processes. His image of "mischievous and libelous" books being sent to "the fire and the executioner" is still not a comfortable one for modern readers, who might ask themselves, "Why destroy the books at all?" But this question applies only if we are thinking inside the framework of censorship. If we adopt instead the framework of defamation, then the question disappears since Milton's views are strikingly in line with those of our modern courts. In the United States, the most recent libel cases have targeted electronic materials, and in the wake of guilty verdicts, defendants have been required to take down websites and delete social media posts. Under the more plaintiff-friendly libel laws in the United Kingdom, judges have even ordered entire print runs of books to be destroyed. While Milton's image of "libelous" books being delivered to the "fire and the executioner" has made many modern readers recoil, it is hardly different from modern court orders that send whole print runs of books to be pulped.[40]

ANONYMITY

The juridical argument that Milton mounts in *Areopagitica* has an Achilles heel: victims of defamation cannot bring suit if they do not know who their opponents are. As he writes in *Defensio Secunda*, the problem with anonymous authorship is that those who conceal their names "do not risk their own property," meaning that they cannot be subject to damages awarded in the wake of litigation (*CPW* 4:560). Thus anonymous authorship presents a significant threat to Milton's claim that thousands of civil defamation suits levied by individuals are a far more efficient means of regulating books than the state could ever muster. In the early modern world of printed books, as in the modern world of social media, anonymity could turbocharge injurious attacks, and so those who wrote anonymously were more likely to descend into defamation than those who acknowledged their own works. Eyeing the threat of anonymous authorship, Milton is careful to argue in *Areopagitica* that books should be printed with names attached. Joseph F. Loewenstein has connected

---

40. For recent examples of books destroyed pursuant to U.K. libel cases, see Pidd, "Rushdie Wins Apology," and A. Johnson, "Music Critic's Book." This example supports Leonard's point that Milton's positions in *Areopagitica* predict modern debates and concerns. See *Value of Milton*.

Milton's concern with identifying authors to the emergence of copyright, as when Milton refers approvingly to the parliamentary statute that "preserves justly every mans Copy to himselfe."[41] But Milton also balances an awareness of authorial rights with an awareness of authorial obligations, specifically the obligation not to use the printed page as a platform for defaming other people. With this issue of obligation in mind, Milton compliments Parliament for a different statute, one requiring that "no book be Printed, unlesse the Printers and the Authors name, or at least the Printers be register'd" (*CPW* 2:569). *Areopagitica* is at heart an antilegislation argument, meaning that Milton wants Parliament to roll back the 1643 Licensing Order, an impulse consistent with the advice that he offers to Cromwell in *Defensio Secunda*: "propose fewer new laws than you repeal old ones" and retain "only those laws that are essential" (*CPW* 4:678–79). However, the statute requiring names on title pages is an exception, for unlike licensing, which is harmful, it qualifies as an "essential" law. If all books bear "the Authors and Printers name," then the prosecution of bad books can be left to private individuals and the civil courts. But if anonymous books continue to scurry from the presses carrying insult and injury, then no amount of common law action will be able to stamp them out.

Milton had ample personal experience with the problem of anonymous authorship.[42] In 1641, he was attacked in the anonymous *A Modest Confutation*. In 1644, a few weeks after he published *Areopagitica*, the same thing happened again, this time in *An Answer to a Book, Intituled, The Doctrine and Discipline of Divorce*, which took aim at his views on divorce. Milton calls this work a "brute Libel" against him (*CPW* 2:753). He was clearly bothered by the anonymous nature of the barrage since he adds the word "nameles" to the title of his follow-up response: *Colasterion: A Reply to a Nameles Answer against The Doctrine and Discipline of Divorce*. He also stresses the facelessness of his opponent in the treatise itself: "Only this I marvel'd . . . when as I, in a Subject so new to this age, and so hazardous to please, conceal'd not my name, why this Author defending that part which is so ceded by the people would conceal his?" (*CPW* 2:724). Even though he has popular opinion at his back, the Answerer hides his name, and Milton detects the tang of cowardice.

---

41. J. F. Loewenstein, *Author's Due*. On the effect of the 1710 Act of Anne on both copyright and authorial liability, see Greene, *Trouble with Ownership*.

42. For a broader study of the role that anonymity played in early modern writing, see M. L. North, *Anonymous Renaissance*. Randy Robertson discusses the problem that anonymity posed for state censors, in contrast to my focus on the problem it posed for those private individuals who wanted legal redress for injurious words: *Censorship and Conflict*, 62–76.

In 1652, Milton had much the same experience again. The anonymous *Regii Sanguinis Clamor* made scalding allegations about Milton for his *Pro Populo Anglicano Defensio*, his first defense. In his response, *Defensio Secunda*, Milton asks himself, "Shall I then always contend with those who are nameless?" (*CPW* 4:560). The editors of the *Complete Prose* assume that Milton is referring to the immediate textual exchange of the first and second defenses, and so in their view Milton's complaint "exaggerates the importance of the matter" (*CPW* 4:560n54). But if we adopt a wider view, the scene changes. Over the course of more than a decade, Milton was harried by three separate anonymous authors for his treatises on episcopacy, divorce, and regicide, and so the note of weary frustration in *Defensio Secunda* is understandable.

The more Milton tangled with anonymous authors, the more committed he became to putting his own name on his title pages. All those involved in the debate over episcopacy, Milton included, wrote anonymously or under pseudonyms such as "Smectymnuus." This debate provided Milton with his first taste of how anonymity could add accelerant to the flames of insult, and perhaps as a result, when he published his last antiprelatical tract in 1642, he added his name to his title page for the very first time: *The Reason of Church-Government Urg'd against Prelaty by Mr. John Milton.* A year later when he published the first edition of *The Doctrine and Discipline of Divorce*, Milton did so anonymously, but by the second edition in 1644, he added "*The Author J. M.*" to the title page. *Tetrachordon* also has "By the Former Author J. M." in the title, a phrasing that puts Milton's stamp on *Tetrachordon* while simultaneously reminding readers that he wrote the "former" *Doctrine and Discipline* as well. In the body of this treatise, Milton draws attention to his decision "to subscribe my name to what I was to own" (*CPW* 2:581). "To own" in this context means "to acknowledge as belonging to oneself, esp. in respect of kinship or authorship."[43] This phrase occurs in a passage where Milton has been discussing Herbert Palmer's decision to "scandalize" him in "the most open and invective manner" (*CPW* 2:579). The context is defamation, and Milton's point is that those who put their names on works have the integrity to "own" them, in the sense of accepting the consequences of their own words.

This determination to "own" his words and not hide behind the veil of anonymity explains the title *Areopagitica; A Speech of Mr. John Milton for the Liberty of Unlicenc'd Printing to the Parlament of England.* In deciding to walk out into the open plain of his title page, Milton displays his growing confidence in himself as an author, and this decision is also a key part of his juridi-

---

43. *OED Online*, s.v. "own," v., def. 3b.

cal argument.⁴⁴ In a treatise that draws the line at defamation, he implicitly proclaims that he himself is innocent of that offense. *Areopagitica* was published without a license, and Milton implicitly says, "if you wish, prosecute me, *Mr. John Milton*, for an unlicensed book, but no man can justly claim that he has been defamed here." Ten years later, Milton would again respond to an anonymous attack by inserting his name into his title. Milton wrote his second defense to respond to the personal insults leveled in the anonymous *Regii Sanguinis Clamor*. While the critical practice is to refer to Milton's work as the *Second Defense* or *Defensio Secunda* or even, to give a longer version, *Pro Populo Anglicano Defensio Secunda*, its real title is as follows: *Johannis Miltoni Angli Pro Populo Anglicano Defensio Secunda*. Milton moves his name to the very front of the title. The author of *Clamor* (whom Milton believed to be the Franco-Scots cleric Alexander More) had hurled mud at Milton, and in *Defensio Secunda*, Milton does not hesitate to hurl mud back. Whether or not one thinks that *Defensio Secunda* engages in the kind of defamation that Milton deprecates in *Areopagitica* (and while he is not kind to More, Milton justifies himself on the grounds that More fired the first shot), at least there is no ambiguity about who its author is.⁴⁵

The juridical argument that Milton mounts in *Areopagitica* struck home with at least one early modern reader. In his seventeenth-century biography of Milton, John Toland writes, "Such was the effect of our Author's *Areopagitica*, that the following year *Mabol*, a Licenser, offer'd Reasons against Licensing; and, at his own request, was discharg'd that Office."⁴⁶ Toland mistakes the name since the licenser in question was Gilbert Mabbott, who appeared before the Council of State in May 1649 to ask to be released from his duties. While Mabbott's petition makes no direct reference to *Areopagitica*, his reasoning is close enough to Milton's treatise that the influence seems unmistakable. Mabbott complains that the "Imployment . . . is unjust and illegall," and echoing Milton's analogy between licensers and monopolists, he adds,

---

44. On Milton's title page as an expression of his autonomy as an author, see Blum, "Author's Authority."

45. The title of Milton's first defense makes a similar point: *Joannis Miltoni Angli Pro Populo Anglicano Defensio contra Claudii Anonymi, Alias Salmasii, Defensionem Regiam*, or, "John Milton Englishman offers a defense of the English people against the anonymous author Claude, also known as Salmasius, in response to his defense of the king." Here too we see Milton both putting his name on a title page and stressing the anonymity of his textual opponent.

46. Darbishire, *Early Lives*, 133.

"Licensing is as great a Monopoly as ever was in this Nation" (*LR* 2:251).[47] Mabbott goes on to suggest that if authors were required to put their names on their title pages, then the common law courts could offer a more efficient and more just means of regulating books than licensing does: "it is lawfull . . . to print any Booke, Sheete, etc. without Licensing, so as the Authors and Printers do subscribe their true Names thereunto," since thereby the authors and printers "may be liable to answer the Contents thereof." And if the books "offend," then the authors and printers should be "punished by such Lawes as are or shall be for those Cases provided" (*LR* 2:252).

In *Areopagitica*, Milton stresses the need to "ordain wisely as in this world of evill, in the midd'st whereof God hath plac't us unavoidably" (*CPW* 2:526), and for both him and for Gilbert Mabbott, this work of proper ordaining means not putting the fetters of licensing upon books and authors. This is not because either man believed that people could be trusted to write only good books. In *Paradise Lost*, Milton shows how sin ushers in "anger, hate / Mistrust, suspicion, [and] discord" (*CPEP* 9.1123-24), and he could look out at his contemporary world and see all these same problems. The English Civil War was raging in the countryside as he sat writing *Areopagitica*, and while this war was notionally fought in the name of varying political and religious doctrines, it was also fought because men hated one another. As Milton writes in *Doctrine and Discipline of Divorce*, "hate is of all things the mightiest divider, nay, is division itself" (*CPW* 2:345). As the divorce tracts respond to the problem of conjugal hatred,[48] *Areopagitica* is Milton's response to the problem of civic hatred. Words could cut right through social bonds and turn friends and neighbors into bitter foes. Milton argues that law is needed because fallen people have lost the ability to self-regulate. The issue that *Areopagitica* takes up is, what kind of law? Should it be the law of licensing? Milton's answer is "no" since licensing books "pulls along with it so many other kinds of licensing, as will make us all both ridiculous and weary, and yet frustrat" (*CPW* 2:526). For both Milton and Mabbott, licensing laws are redundant since England already has another legal framework—the jurisprudence of defamation in the common law courts—that can do the job of regulating books more effectively. And unlike licensing, which in Milton's view treats authors like children, the civil legal system rests on the bedrock assumption that legally enfranchised adults should have the right to choose whether they wish

---

47. Masson, *Life*, 3:431 and 4:87-88.
48. Achinstein, "'Law in This Matter,'" 175.

to bring suit or whether they wish to turn the other cheek. Thus the juridical argument of *Areopagitica* is fundamentally an expression of Milton's overriding interest in liberty.

ACTIONS FOR SLAUNDER

At this point, a reader might reasonably ask why Milton did not make his juridical argument more explicit. That is, the nature of bad books ("defaming," "libelous," and backstabbing ones) is more clearly stated than the solution to them (civil suits rather than licensing). The slightly elliptical nature of Milton's argument makes more sense if we compare it to a book written three years later, in 1647, John March's *Actions for Slaunder*, the first work devoted to the common law jurisprudence of injurious words.[49] *Areopagitica* and *Actions for Slaunder* both point to the deep cultural anxiety about anything that appeared to encourage litigation. In March's case, this anxiety is so profound that forced to choose between letting insults increase or letting lawsuits increase, he chooses insults.

Actions for Slaunder provides a thorough and workmanlike survey of what counts as legal defamation in English common law courts, and its title aptly sums up March's approach: *Actions for Slaunder, or, A Methodicall Collection under Certain Grounds and Heads, of What Words Are Actionable in the Law and What Not*. Basing his work on extensive research in legal manuscripts and printed law books, March has compiled a *"Methodicall Collection,"* meaning that he has organized a wide array of cases about injurious words into broad categories (or *"Grounds and Heads"*), with the goal of showing what words *"Are Actionable . . . and What Not."* In his chapters, March explains why judges ruled the way they did on different issues. For example, a man named Benson sued a man named Morley for saying, *"thou hast rob[b]ed the church . . . and hast stollen the Leads of the Church."* The judge ruled that Morley's words were not actionable because "the Church" implies the universal church, which, as an immaterial entity, cannot actually be robbed. March then gives it as his opinion that had Morley said that Benson robbed "a church," an action could be brought, "because this must of necessity be understood of

---

49. March was a barrister and legal writer known for his defense of the Long Parliament's Militia Act in 1642 and his 1651 *Amicus Republicae, The Commonwealth's Friend, and For Preventing and Determining of Tedious Law-suits*, which includes sensible, moderate suggestions for law reform, such as abolishing imprisonment for debt and the death penalty for petty theft. Orr, "March, John."

some perticular material Church."[50] In a similar vein, someone who has been called a "thievish knave" or "seditious knave" cannot bring a common law suit because these are "adjective words." However, someone who has been called a "perjured knave" can. While "perjured," too, is an adjective, it imputes a real crime (presumably, "thievish" and "seditious" are blurrier in this regard), which fell comfortably within the common law courts' understanding of the scope of defamatory language.[51]

March's reason for writing *Actions for Slaunder* is crystal clear: like many of his contemporaries, he thought that defamation had hit an all-time high in English culture, and he was especially dismayed by the sheer volume of defamation cases clogging the courts. This concern appears first in his subtitle: his book is "*of very great use and consequence to all men, especially in these times, wherein Actions for Slaunder are more common, and do much more abound then in times past.*" March then expands on it in his introduction. Because "the intemperance and malice of men increases," these cases "doe abound more in these dayes then in times past." This malice has spawned "numerous progeny" in the form of lawsuits that appear on almost every page in the law reports.[52] For March, the worst consequence of this increase in suits is the misuse of the law itself. He admits that it is only just that a man should be able to sue when his "life, liveliehood, or reputation is much endangered by scandalous words." However, men too commonly "flee to the Law out of malice and make the Courts of Justice maintainers of every small and vaine brabble," which is "utterly unlawfull and intolerable amongst Christians."[53] "Though the tongues of men be set on fire," there is no reason why "the Law should bee used as Bellowes to blow the Coles."[54]

This overriding aversion to anything that fans the flames of litigation explains the deeply contradictory nature of some of March's arguments. Having explained the jurisprudence of injurious language in copious, painstaking detail, March rejects the possibility that his book might actually be useful to would-be plaintiffs—i.e., that it might teach people when they can profitably sue one another. He first adopts this seemingly disingenuous posture in his lengthy subtitle, where he asserts that his book is a "*Directory*" for the "*tongue*" to help men stay out of hot legal water. Expanding on this line of

---

50. March, *Actions for Slaunder*, 47–48.
51. March, *Actions for Slaunder*, 42.
52. March, *Actions for Slaunder*, 8, 4.
53. March, *Actions for Slaunder*, 4.
54. March, *Actions for Slaunder*, 9.

reasoning later in his treatise, he insists that he has no "intent to incourage men in giving ill and unworthy language, or to teach them a lawless Dylect." That is, his goal is not to instruct men how to insult others with impunity. However, in the next sentence he undercuts that claim. He says that he wants instead to help them manage that "little member," the human tongue, because when the tongue runs amok it can "subject men to dammages and costs . . . which usually trench to the great hinderance and impoverishment of the speakers."[55] Here is the contradiction: a book that teaches men how to avoid the "dammages and costs" of a defamation suit is also, almost of necessity, a book that teaches them how to defame without crossing a crucial line in the legal sand (in effect, to say "the church" instead of "a church"). Thus March cannot convincingly claim that *Actions for Slaunder* deters men from "ill and unworthy language." If anything, it accelerates it. March is between a rock and a hard place. The rock is writing a book that teaches men how to defame strategically without suffering legal consequences. The hard place is teaching them how and when to sue one another. Faced with this unenviable choice, March prefers the rock. That is, he is willing to do almost anything—even to write an apparent guidebook for defamers—that will help reduce the growing volume of lawsuits.

Actions for Slaunder helps us understand why Milton, handling the same incendiary issue of when men can profitably seek legal redress against one another, adopts an oblique approach. He probably takes it for granted that his readers understand the juridical nature of his argument. Lorna Hutson and others have demonstrated the deep saturation of legal knowledge through many levels of English society, and so Milton's references to bail and sureties and his image of authors "standing to the hazard of law and penalty" (*CPW* 2:531–32) would have been clearer in an early modern context than in a modern one, where law has been sequestered in its own professional silo.[56] Second, Milton did not need to spell out that he is thinking about the liberty that men have to bring legal action against bad books or insulting speech because this was already happening all around him. Indeed, if March's claims in *Actions for Slaunder* are a reliable indicator, it was already happening at epidemic levels. Third and finally, we might think of *Areopagitica* and *Actions for Slaunder* as providing a before and after picture. Milton tacitly nudges men to take their grievances against one another to court, and he does so because

---

55. March, *Actions for Slaunder*, 2. March's use of "trench" in this context probably draws on the obsolete sense "to extend in effect to." See *OED Online, s.v.* "trench," def. III.6.a-b.

56. See Hutson, *Invention of Suspicion*.

he is more worried about what he sees as the greater problem of state-based licensing. March, however, shows us what happens when men follow Milton's advice. Lawsuits proliferate, and a book like *Actions for Slaunder* is regrettably needed so that those who want to insult one another can do so without winding up in court.

THE LEGAL AFFRONT OF BLASPHEMY

Having focused to this point on *Areopagitica*, I conclude this chapter by turning to a textual knot in a later work. Once again, Milton's aversion to injurious words can help us make sense of a claim that otherwise looks like stark contradiction. In his 1659 *A Treatise of Civil Power*, Milton offers his clearest and most sustained argument that the civil magistrate has no right to compel any form of religious observance, and *Civil Power* is thus the quintessential expression of his commitment to freedom of conscience: "for beleef or practice in religion according to [his] conscientious perswasion no man ought to be punishd or molested by any outward force on earth whatsoever" (*CPW* 7:242). Milton imagines unpersuaded readers asking whether such toleration should apply even in the face of heresy and blasphemy. His answer is yes, and he defends his position by tracing the etymology of both words. As for "heresy," he argues that the Greeks used the word in a neutral sense to mean "any opinion good or bad in religion" (*CPW* 7:247). Thus those who flinch from the bugbear of "heresy" miss the point that it simply means the individual's choice about what to believe. In this sense, all people are heretics. While critics have often cited this passage as an example of Milton's broad-minded commitment to toleration, they have been less attentive to his accompanying discussion of blasphemy.[57] It is easy to see why. In a treatise that argues passionately that "no man or body of men . . . can be the infallible judges or determiners in matters of religion to any other mens consciences but their own," Milton then matter-of-factly asserts that magistrates have a duty to proceed harshly against blasphemers (*CPW* 7:243). He even pauses to compliment the 1650 Blasphemy Act, which provided criminal penalties for blasphemous utterances: six months' imprisonment for a first offense and banishment for a second.[58]

---

57. On Milton's views of blasphemy in the context of his views of treason, see D. Loewenstein, "Treason."

58. While these penalties will strike modern readers as harsh, they were considerably softer than those in the earlier *An Ordinance for the Punishing of Blasphemies and Heresies*, enacted

Areopagitica can help us understand why in *Civil Power* Milton can balance tolerance of heresy and intolerance of blasphemy. In fact, we have already encountered an incipient version of this position, for in his account of how the Romans treated books, he claimed that "the Magistrate car'd to take notice of" only two related categories of books, those that were "blasphemous and Atheisticall" and those that were "Libellous" (*Areopagitica, CPW* 2:494). For Milton, blasphemy is unacceptable primarily because it is a form of libel. He makes this point explicitly in *Civil Power* by detouring again into etymology. The word "blasphemy," he says, comes from a "usual and common" Greek word that is used "to signifie any slander, any malitious or evil speaking, whether against God or man" (*CPW* 7:246). Blasphemy is thus indistinguishable from "slander," and it is odious not because the words fail to be properly orthodox but because the blasphemers are "malitious" and seek to smear the characters of others. This explains why in a work that repeatedly proclaims the sovereignty of conscience Milton can hold that "Blasphemie or evil speaking against God malitiously is far from conscience in religion." In support, he cites Mark 9:39, in which Jesus says that "no man which shall do a miracle in my name . . . can lightly speak evil of me." Speaking evil of God is by its very essence unconscionable, since the conscience cannot condone malicious insults aimed at a being who is the source of all holiness and goodness. Milton offers a similar definition in *De Doctrina Christiana*: "it is a fact that all Greek writers, sacred as well as prophane, use the word *blasphemy* in a general sense to mean any kind of evil-speaking, directed against any person" (*CPW* 6:699). Those who blaspheme "abuse God openly" (*CPW* 6:700). In this construction, all injurious speech, whether aimed at Heaven or at one's neighbor, falls within the scope of blasphemy since it wantonly injures the good name of another. For Milton, the real problem is that blasphemy has been wrenched from its proper context and used instead to indicate merely wrong belief. Whereas blasphemy was originally "a general term to mean only evil-speaking against God," some "misleading and ill-advised" authors chose to "limit" the term. They did so because this redefinition allowed them to criticize any belief in "religious matters which did not tally with their own" (*CPW* 6:699).

This understanding of blasphemy may explain why he regards the Blasphemy Act of August 9, 1650, as a "prudent and well deliberated" law (*CPW* 7:246). This act opens by explaining that because many men and woman are "most monstrous in their Opinions, and loose in all wicked and abominable

---

by the Long Parliament in May 1648, which prescribed the death penalty for a much wider range of beliefs.

Practices," some legal controls are needed to prevent "the notorious corrupting and disordering, [and] even . . . the dissolution of all Human Society."[59] In its initial catalog of what counts as blasphemy, the act seems to be emphasizing ideological conformity as it discriminates between licit and illicit beliefs. For example, it is blasphemous and thus illegal for a man or woman "to affirm and maintain him or her self, or any other meer Creature, to be very God; or to be Infinite or Almighty, or in Honor, Excellency, Majesty and Power to be Equal and the same with the true God" or to "deny the Holiness and Righteousness of God."[60] However, having enumerated all of the specific actions or assertions that warrant punitive measures, the act steps back and offers a summing up: blasphemy is that which leads to "the Dishonor of God, the Scandal of Christian Religion, and the Professors thereof." Blasphemy is known by its social effects. It offers "scandal," or insult, to those who profess Christianity. Worse, it offers "dishonor" to God, an emphasis echoed in the title of the act itself: *An Act against Several Atheistical, Blasphemous and Execrable Opinions Derogatory to the Honor of God, and Destructive to Human Society*. The problem with holding "Opinions" such as that God approves of unclean acts is not just that they are wrong-headed per se but that they aim to injure God's reputation. This definition may explain why Milton waxes so eloquent in its praise. He writes that the act "defines blasphemie against God, as far as it is a crime belonging to civil judicature . . . in plane English more warily, more judiciously, more orthodoxally then twice thir number of divines have don in many a prolix volume" (*CPW* 7:246–47). Milton's language here is characteristically playful. The parliamentary committee that drew up this definition of blasphemy had in fact eschewed orthodoxy in the sense that they did not define blasphemy in terms of how far it diverges from established, orthodox forms of belief. Thus for Milton, they acted "more orthodoxally" than a swarm of churchmen and theologians. One gets the sense that this committee probably had at least some common lawyers as members, for it instead defined blasphemy in a manner more aligned with common law ideas of defamation. In cases of blasphemy, it was the motive that mattered, and the intent to offer "scandal" and "dishonor" to God counted more than the precise flavor of aberrant belief. Thus Milton calls this definition of blasphemy "judicious," one aligned not only with the tenets of moderation and good sense but also with the more literally judicious nature of contemporary laws against knowingly injuring the reputations of others.

59. Parliament, *Act Against Several*, 979.
60. Parliament, *Act Against Several*, 980.

CHAPTER 4

Civil Law and Equity in the Divorce Tracts

In the previous two chapters, I traced Milton's thinking as he moved deep into the world of common law jurisprudence. This chapter and the next follow him into the world of Roman or Civil law. Together, these pairs of chapters illustrate the way that Milton refused to give his unquestioning allegiance to any one legal system. Instead he regarded different corpuses of law as useful or compelling insofar as they offered unique solutions to different kinds of problems. In a work such as *Areopagitica*, the common law jurisprudence of defamation provides him with a means to control injurious words without infringing on individual liberty. However, at the same time that he was thinking about free speech in *Areopagitica*, Milton also became interested in the subject of divorce, and here the common law was of no use to him. Almost all regulations about marriage came not from the secular traditions of the common law but instead from English canon law, which allowed for separation in the event of abuse, adultery, or abandonment, but which reserved true divorce only for cases in which the marriage had never been valid in the first place, usually owing to consanguinity, frigidity, or lack of consent.[1] When Milton began thinking sometime around 1643 about how to dismantle the canonists' position, he swiveled away from English common law and began probing instead the jurisprudence of the Continental *ius commune*. He did so because the texts of the Civil law helped him to argue for what he saw as a more just understanding of marriage.

   1. For a survey of the work of the church courts, see Ingram, *Church Courts*; Marchant, *Church under the Law*.

While Milton's two major divorce tracts, *Doctrine and Discipline of Divorce* and *Tetrachordon*, have been productively studied for his theological and marital views, they have not been explored as legal arguments.[2] This is a striking omission in view of the sheer density of legal references in these works. The words "statute" and "law" appear more times in these two treatises than anywhere else in Milton's writings, and while many of these references point to Mosaic law, others refer to contemporary legal systems. Moreover, Milton often underlines the juridical nature of his argument, as when he calls it a "moot" (*Tetrachordon, CPW* 2:657), a term for the legal debates conducted at the Inns of Court, or uses a "Lawyers maxim" from Sir Francis Bacon as part of his discussion of God's "legall justice" (*Doctrine and Discipline, CPW* 2:291, 292).[3] At a broad structural level, both *Doctrine and Discipline* and *Tetrachordon* are sophisticated works of comparative jurisprudence. Milton addresses each to a body of English legislators—the Long Parliament, largely made up of men who had trained in English common law at the Inns of Court—and asks them to pass a statute that would strip jurisdiction over divorce from the ecclesiastical courts. In the process, he makes an argument about the true nature of Mosaic law in which he contrasts the failings of canon law to the higher justice of both natural law and Roman law. As much as any of the texts studied in this book, Milton's divorce tracts show his remarkable jurisdictional agility.

This chapter argues that the legal principle of equity is foundational to Milton's jurisprudential strategy in both *Doctrine and Discipline* and *Tetrachordon*. In early modern English contexts, "equity" is often used to refer to those practices specific to courts of equitable jurisdiction. In 1654, when Milton filed a bill in Chancery against the estate of Sir John Cope, he was hoping that the mechanisms of equity would allow him to recover debts owed to him since he had been unable to recover the money through the regular courts of law. However, jurists also used the word "equity" when they were thinking broadly about fairness, impartiality, and consistency, principles that should apply to all systems of legal justice.[4] When Milton

2. Warren offers a partial exception, for he considers the role that the law of nations, or international law, plays in Milton's understanding of divorce as a kind of universal right: Warren, "Milton and the Epochs."

3. Maxims were accepted principles or propositions of law much like axioms in mathematics.

4. The fact that Chancery's applied equity coexisted with the more conceptual understanding of equity as a form of fairness raises the question of their relationship. For example, was the equity practiced in the Chancery the same as the equity that a writer such as Cicero

writes about equity in the divorce tracts, he is thinking at a broad jurisprudential level, not about the operations of a specific English court—although it seems likely that his experiences in English equity courts heightened his sensitivity to equity as a deep principle of legal justice. Milton turns repeatedly to Roman law in his divorce tracts because this body of law offers what he sees as the best model of equitable interpretation, one that allows statutes to be read not in a restrictive way for the letter of the law but rather in a more accommodating way for their perceived intent. While canon law too prided itself on being a supremely equitable system, the canonists' approach to equity was subtly but crucially different from that of Roman and Civilian jurists, a point I explore further below. For centuries, theologians had read the Bible's passages on divorce through the lens of canonical equity, and the upshot was that divorce had been effectively banned. But Milton wants his readers to view these same biblical passages as Roman jurists would and thus to bring a different understanding of equity to bear. Read in this way, he argues, the Bible allows divorce to all. Thus we cannot fully understand Milton's pro-divorce argument without also understanding the way he navigates between different legal systems with their different core assumptions about how law should be applied to the varied field of human action. Milton's ultimate goal is to put divorce outside the cognizance of all courts, as when he claims that marriage should not be subject to "an external and unbefitting judicature" (*Doctrine and Discipline, CPW* 2:344). Ironically, this argument would not have been possible without the approach to statutory interpretation that Milton finds in Roman law and applies to the Christian Bible. Thus his attempt to limit the jurisdiction of real-world judicatures depends upon core principles taken from the same legal systems that he ultimately aims to transcend.

CIVIL LAW V. CANON LAW

While some critics have remarked in passing on the prominence of Roman law in the divorce tracts, Milton's use of Roman law is more surprising and

---

argued should lie behind all law? If, as Christopher St. German argued, English common law contained the principles of equity, then what was the point of Chancery? These questions have been the subject of widespread critical discussion. For a brief sampling of studies, see Macnair, "Equity and Conscience"; Macnair, *Law of Proof*; Cormack, *Power to Do Justice*, 85–132; Brand, "Equity of the Common Law Courts"; Ibbetson, "Earl of Oxford's Case (1615)."

anomalous than these critical glances allow.⁵ This section provides an introduction to the role that Roman law plays in *Doctrine and Discipline* and *Tetrachordon*. It situates his use of Roman law in the context of contemporary juridical arguments, and then it turns to his treatment of canon law. Most nonconformists were hostile to the jurisdiction of the ecclesiastical courts, and Milton's rejection of what he calls the "canonicall infection" is a typical Puritan response (*Tetrachordon, CPW* 2:600). What is atypical is that even as he pours disdain onto canon law, he assiduously tries to keep any of that disdain from splashing onto Roman law. Legal historians today often use the consolidated term "Romano-canon law" because by the early modern period, Roman law and canon law were affiliated legal systems that together formed the conglomerated jurisprudence of the Continent. But unlike virtually all of his contemporaries, who looked at Roman law and canon law and saw juridical similarity, Milton looked at them and saw juridical difference. His divorce tracts are unique from a juridical standpoint in that he tries to split these two legal systems apart. As later portions of this chapter demonstrate, he does so because Roman law instantiates a form of equitable reasoning that crucially supports his argument for divorce, while canonical equity threatens it.

While Milton relies heavily on Roman law throughout *Doctrine and Discipline* and *Tetrachordon*, in each treatise he adopts a somewhat different stance toward this legal source material. In *Doctrine and Discipline*, he most often touches on Roman law in connection with discussions of the great seventeenth-century jurist Hugo Grotius.⁶ For instance, he cites the "statutes and edicts" of the "Christian Emperors" as a way to compliment Grotius's adherence to "those imperiall decrees" about marriage (*CPW* 2:238). Later, he writes that Grotius uses the "maxims of civil Law" to build out overarching ideas of legality that should be binding on all peoples (*CPW* 2:330). Grotius used Roman law as the framework for his theories of natural law, so in *Doctrine and Discipline* Milton is largely content to see Roman law as mediated

---

5. For more on Milton's interest in Roman law, see Dzelzainis, "Liberty and the Law"; Skinner, "Milton and the Politics of Slavery." Achinstein notes the role of Roman law in the divorce tracts in "'Law in This Matter.'" Because Rome was an empire, Roman law was inherently multinational, and so it served as the ideal armature for those early modern jurists, such as Alberico Gentili and Hugo Grotius, who were working to create the system that we call international law. For Milton's awareness of the emerging field of international law, see Warren, *Literature and the Law of Nations*, 160–228.

6. On Grotius's use of Roman law as the foundation of his natural law theory, see Straumann, *Roman Law in the State of Nature*.

through Grotius's natural law theories, especially as exemplified in his 1625 *De jure belli ac pacis*. However, in *Tetrachordon*, Milton alters his approach. Grotius drifts into the background, and Milton engages more directly with Roman and Civil law sources. For example, the very first nonbiblical source Milton cites is Cicero's *De inventione*: "*No man observes law for laws sake, but for the good of them for whom it was made*" (*CPW* 2:588). From this opening interest in classical Roman law, Milton widens his field of vision to take in Justinian's magisterial *Corpus Juris Civilis*, as when he cites the "*Pandects* out of *Modestinus*" (*CPW* 2:600) and the opinions of Ulpian and Hermogenian, a reference to the early Roman jurists whose writings formed important parts of the *Digest*—also called the *Pandects*—one of the three main parts of the *Corpus Juris Civilis*. Justinian's work was augmented over the centuries, and Milton also cites later jurist-commentators such as "*Tuningus* a famous Lawyer" and the collected learning of "the Civil lawyers" (*CPW* 2:611).

Because common law was case law and because it said almost nothing about marriage, Milton needed to look outside his native borders to find relevant statutory support. In this respect, his use of Roman law makes sense. However, given the larger rhetorical argument, his decision to wield Roman law in defense of his argument is an odd one. *Doctrine and Discipline of Divorce* is addressed "*TO THE* PARLIAMENT OF ENGLAND" (*CPW* 2:222), and in his opening address, Milton urges these English legislators to take action. Not merely a scholarly disquisition, *Doctrine and Discipline* is meant to spur real change. *Tetrachordon* is similarly addressed "To the PARLAMENT" and aims at a similar legislative result: he asks Parliament to pass a "*just Law*" (*CPW* 2:585). While J. G. A. Pocock's thesis about the insularity of the "common law mind" has been convincingly challenged, it remains true that Roman jurisprudence played little overt role in common law arguments.[7] When Coke cites Justinian in the 1602 *Case of the Monopolies*, he does so in a perfunctory way, using Roman law as mere window-dressing to his own legal innovations.[8] The seventeenth-century judge Roger North encourages an even more minimalist approach to Romanist learning. In his *Discourse on the Study of the Laws*, North remarks that "a man of the law would not be willing to stand mute to the question, what is the difference between the Civil and the Common Law." However, "it is not at all needful to study" the Civil law since common lawyers can get all the knowledge they need "by mere inspection of

---

7. Pocock, *Ancient Constitution*. For sample counterarguments, see Burgess, *Politics*; Tubbs, *Common Law Mind*.

8. Thorne, "Sir Edward Coke," 9–10.

some books and perusing their introductions."[9] This wariness about Roman law was echoed in parliamentary proceedings. In his study of Stuart Parliaments, Conrad Russell observes that debates in the Commons were characterized by a "resistance to foreign parallels, and to foreign law, particularly to the civil law."[10] For example, in 1640 Sir Simonds D'Ewes argued against the imposition of martial law—which was essentially Romanist in nature—on the grounds that it was antithetical to "our own laws."[11] Coke similarly rejected a legislative change that would have protected the two university courts on the grounds that these Civilian courts had no standing at common law.[12] These examples do not mean that Civilian learning had no influence on common lawyers, some of whom—including Coke himself—had read widely in Civilian sources. Rather, as Michael McNair suggests, it was probably more acceptable "to borrow civilians' arguments than actually to cite them directly."[13]

McNair's point only highlights the anomaly of *Doctrine and Discipline* and *Tetrachordon*. Milton is not just silently borrowing Romanist reasoning. He takes the next step and cites Roman jurists directly and repeatedly, and he does so in highly laudatory terms, as when he calls the Civil law "a generous and elegant law" and writes that Civilians have "the honour ... to stand for" this law (*Tetrachordon*, CPW 2:700). A comparison with late-sixteenth-century usury debates suggests how unusual Milton's enthusiastic reliance on Civil law really is. Those MPs who wanted to legalize usury were in much the same situation as Milton: both usury and divorce rested on conflicting biblical evidence; both were forbidden by canon law; both were allowed by the secular Civil law. However, during the heated Commons debates about usury in April 1571, the members offered only glancing references to Civil law and instead rooted their arguments in English custom and the Bible.[14] By the time Milton was writing in the 1640s, most Englishmen had grown even more strongly attached to the idea that the common law protected the Englishman's liberty and property, and most were wary of the Civil law's association with absolutism. Thus Milton's overtly Romanist arguments hardly seem like the best way to sway his target audience.

Jurisprudentially speaking, Milton's treatises are equally surprising for the

9. R. North, *Discourse on The Study of the Laws*, 8–9.
10. Russell, *Parliaments*, 357.
11. Jansson, *Proceedings in the Opening Session*, 78.
12. Russell, *Parliaments*, 159.
13. Macnair, *Law of Proof*, 293.
14. D'Ewes, "Journal."

way they put Roman law and canon law at odds with one another. For instance, in *Doctrine and Discipline*, he writes that the "statutes and edicts" of Roman law are "easie and relenting" whereas "the Canon is inflexible" (*CPW* 2:238), and he contrasts the broad-mindedness of "the Christian Emperours, *Theodosius* . . . and *Justinian*, men of high wisdom and reputed piety" with the "letter-bound servility of the Canon Doctors" (*CPW* 2:334, 342). In *Tetrachordon*, he compliments the Civilians' ability not to "count that for law, which the *pontificall* Canon hath enthrall'd them to" (*CPW* 2:700). Similarly, he praises the "Civilians" who have not been "blinded by the Canon [law's]" prohibition on divorce (*CPW* 2:714).[15] These claims run counter to prevailing juridical realities. In the twelfth-century Bolognese Renaissance, canonists discovered Justinian's *Corpus Juris Civilis* and used it as the foundation for their own highly sophisticated body of canon law. Elaborated and refined over several centuries, this canon law was eventually handed back to the secular states, which adapted it—and the Roman law on which it was based—into the system of Civil law.[16] Together, both kinds of law formed the *ius commune*, the "common law" of the Continental tradition. The sixteenth-century French Civilian Petrus Rebuffus sums up the fusion of the two legal systems: "canon law and civil law are connected to such a degree that understanding one without the other is scarcely possible."[17]

In England, Civil law and canon law were both juridical minorities, and perhaps even more than on the Continent, the boundaries between them often blurred to the point of near-invisibility. Men trained as Civilians regularly practiced in the ecclesiastical courts, as in the case of Sir Julius Caesar, who sat on the bench of the Admiralty (a Civilian court) and also argued cases in the canon courts and who left an extensive set of reflections about pragmatic questions of law in both venues.[18] In his *View of the Civile and Ecclesiastical Law*, the prominent Civilian Thomas Ridley shuttles back and forth between

---

15. Milton may have been modeling himself on Martin Luther, who had burned canon law texts and who stated that the Romans had an "excellent legal and judicial system" that Germany should imitate. Quoted and discussed in Shuger, *Renaissance Bible*, 61.

16. For a fuller discussion of the genealogical relationship between Roman law, canon law, and Civil law, see Berman, *Law and Revolution*; Vinogradoff, *Roman Law*; Stein, *Roman Law*. For an argument that Milton knew this braided history of Roman law and canon law, see Dzelzainis, "'In These Western Parts.'"

17. *Ius canonicum et civile sunt adeo connexa, ut unum sine altero vix intelligi possit.* Quoted and discussed in Helmholz, *Oxford History*, 247.

18. Caesar's notebook appears in Helmholz, *Three Civilian Notebooks*. On the general situation of Civilians in England, see Levack, *Civil Lawyers*.

Roman law and canon law with disorienting speed. In a single page, he moves from discussing the "commerce of Princes with Princes" (i.e., the mercantile questions that the Roman law addressed) to the proper order of worship service (i.e., the purview of the ecclesiastical courts) to last wills and testaments, a subject on which "the Civile and Ecclesiastical Law" collaborate.[19] Richard H. Helmholz reflects on how unconcerned English Civilians and canonists were with the comparative value of the two kinds of law. This issue—which is "seemingly an obvious one today"—simply "did not trouble" them. In fact, "there is little sign that it occurred to them as a relevant question." Faced with two different kinds of Romanist law, Civil and canon, "they used both."[20] From the common lawyers' point of view, the linkage between Roman law and canon law provided a good reason for keeping both at arms' length. In his *History of the Common Law* (probably written and circulated in the 1660s although not published until long after his death), Sir Matthew Hale congratulates the common law for standing apart from the laws of "Rome, as well Ancient as Modern."[21] One of Milton's favorite writers, John Selden, offered a similar linkage in a 1628 speech to the House of Commons: "the canon law and civil law we have from Rome and out of the Empire." While both kinds of law are "*lex terrae* . . . that is such as by the law of the land [i.e., England] are in force," they are both subordinate to and different from "the common law."[22] In their different ways and for different reasons, English Civilians, canonists, and common lawyers all stressed the connective tissue binding Roman law to canon law. Arguing against this consolidated juridical common sense, Milton tried his hardest to pry the two legal systems apart.

THE EQUITY OF THE LAW

The sheer strangeness of Milton's enthusiastic reliance on Civil law in treatises about divorce raises the question of "Why?" Why is he so intent on shielding the Roman law from the "canonicall infection" (*Tetrachordon, CPW* 2:600)? What is so vital about the Civil law such that it must be present in his treatises, even at the expense of making unproductively Romanist arguments to common law legislators? One possible answer has to do with subject matter: Milton needs Roman law because it includes statutes allowing for divorce.

19. Ridley, *View*, 226.
20. Helmholz, *Three Civilian Notebooks*, xlvi.
21. Hale, *History of the Common Law*, 47–48.
22. Johnson and Cole, *Commons Debates 1628*, 463–64.

However, while Milton does indeed address matters such as the Roman law regarding "*Nuptials*" (*Tetrachordon*, *CPW* 2:635) and the way that "*Justinian* or *Tribonian* defines Matrimony" (*Tetrachordon*, *CPW* 2:611), a surprising number of his Roman law references are not about divorce or marriage at all.[23] To give some examples, sometimes he uses Civil law to make broad jurisprudential points as when he cites Ulpian and Hermogenian to argue that customs can be considered legally binding in the absence of statutes (*Tetrachordon*, *CPW* 2:618). Sometimes he refers to the "civil Law" principle that similar offenses should receive similar treatment: "from like causes to like the Law interprets rightly" (*Doctrine and Discipline*, *CPW* 2:330). Consistent judgment was a goal of all judicial systems, and in Milton's day common law jurists were increasingly researching precedents in order to regularize judicial decisions and thus make the common law more equitable. However, instead of citing domestic legal sources, Milton looks abroad, and this impulse suggests the degree to which he wants to associate broad jurisprudential reasoning with the Civil law. Elsewhere he appeals to the "three general doctrines of *Justinians* law": "*To live honestly, To hurt no man, To give every one his due*" (*Tetrachordon*, *CPW* 2:653). Sometimes Milton leaves this more theoretical jurisprudential plane and drills into specific legal issues. For example, he argues by analogy from "the *Roman* law" regarding "contracts and dowries" (*Tetrachordon*, *CPW* 2:620). He uses the laws of "that Civilian Emperor" about "donations" and the "rescript of *Antoninus* in the Civil Law" that governed the treatment of slaves (*Tetrachordon*, *CPW* 2:626). He even detours through the Roman law's provision for "Tutelage" and the "defense of Orfanes" (i.e., the Roman law of guardianship) (*Tetrachordon*, *CPW* 2:660). In all of these instances, Milton is not simply mining Roman law for its precepts about marriage. Instead he relies on it for another, larger reason: it gives him a productive way to think about law in general.[24] Faced with contradictory biblical laws about marriage, Milton turns to Roman law because it offers a sophisticated tool for interpreting written evidence and for understanding how statutes should be applied to the infinitely varied field of human actions. This tool is the judicial principle known as equity.

23. Tribonian was the jurist and advisor whom Justinian commissioned to lead the compilation of the *Corpus Juris Civilis*.

24. Milton's use of Roman law to argue for divorce supports Quentin Skinner's point that Roman law was turned to a wide variety of ideological purposes. See his *Foundations of Modern Political Thought* and "Milton and the Politics of Slavery." Stein argues that Roman law provided a "legal supermarket" of ideas: Stein, *Roman Law*, 2.

Milton's interest in equity is unmistakable. Here is a representative sampling from *Doctrine and Discipline of Divorce*: Milton refers to the "precious equity" of the Mosaic law (*CPW* 2:231); he finds a comparable "equitie" in Roman law (*CPW* 2:238); "all sense and equity" supports his argument (*CPW* 2:245); a good lawgiver takes heed of "equity" (*CPW* 2:289); all people must obey "the law of nature and of equity imprinted" in them (*CPW* 2:297); and "plain sense and equity" can be found in the Bible (*CPW* 2:309). Using the adjectival version, Milton finds an "equall plea of divorce" (*CPW* 2:240); justice proceeds in "ever-equall proportion" (*CPW* 2:263); and the law is "equal" as well as "just" (*CPW* 2:281). *Tetrachordon* shows this same pattern. In just his discussion of Deuteronomy 24:1–2, Milton refers to the "equity" of "Roman law" (*CPW* 2:620), the "true equity" of "*Moses*" (*CPW* 2:621), the "equal" nature of divorce (*CPW* 2:622), the "equity" implicit in "equal" contracts (*CPW* 2:624), and the "equity" of the Civil law regarding gifts (*CPW* 2:626). Given the relative absence of critical commentary on Milton's use of equity, scholars have presumably assumed that Milton is appealing to a basic sense of fairness.[25] However, if we think of equity as merely a synonym for fairness, we flatten out its complexities and particularly its status as a long-standing point of jurisprudential debate.

Virtually everyone in the early modern period agreed that equity was an important part of justice. In his *Treatise of Christian Equity and Moderation*, William Perkins writes that two kinds of men should not be judges: those who have too little zeal for the law and those who have too much. On the second count, Perkins explains, "he is but halfe a Judge, who can doe nothing but urge the law, and the plaine words of the lawe, and is not able also, to mittigate the rigour of the law, when neede so requireth."[26] Perkins is reframing the standard maxim *summum ius, summa iniuria*, the greater the strict adherence to the letter of the law, the greater the potential for injustice. The solution to the problem of *summum ius, summa iniuria* was equity. In one of the earliest and most influential accounts, Aristotle writes that equity (which he calls *epikeia*) is necessary because while temporal laws must necessarily be framed in terms of general, abstract pronouncements, "about some things it is not possible to make a universal statement which will be correct."[27] The role

---

25. The one exception is Mark Fortier, who registers the presence of equity in Milton's thinking in the divorce tracts: Fortier, *Culture of Equity*. For arguments about equity in Milton's other works, see Visconsi, *Lines of Equity*, and Silver, "'Taken Scandal.'"

26. Perkins, *Hepieikeia*, 10.

27. Aristotle, *Nicomachean Ethics* 1137b12–13. See also Chroust, "Aristotle's Conception of Equity," 125.

of equity is to bridge the gap between the generality of laws and the particularity of circumstances.

Although there was broad agreement about the need for equity, there was less consensus about the exact relationship between equity and law. Generally speaking, there were two approaches to equity in the *ius commune*. Milton embraces one and repudiates the other, and this push/pull dynamic, in turn, powers his arguments about God's. Proponents of what we might call "internal equity" regarded it as a principle found inside the law itself. When a judge recognized that following the strict letter of the law in a particular case would result in injustice and when he provided instead a softened outcome, he was obeying the equitableness implicit in the law. Others favored "external equity," meaning that they regarded equity as a principle outside the law that was manifested through extralegal principles such as mercy, humanity, commiseration, etc. Historian Dennis R. Klinck sums up this opposition as follows:

> Thus "equity" could refer to the justice or reason which was regarded as essential to the law, or to a mode of interpretation whereby the true spirit of the law was discerned. Both these meanings emphasize that equity is already *in* the law. Or equity could mean the adjusting of the ordinary law—already "just" in its general application—in response to particular circumstances, or even the merciful application of the law. The latter meanings tend to make equity something that is added to the law.[28]

The legal outcome might be the same in either case (i.e., internal and external equity did not necessarily differ in their effects), but each approach was based on different assumptions about the ontology and authority of law itself.

Each of these philosophies of equity was associated with a different—albeit cognate—group of jurists. Internal equity or *aequitas* had been developed in classical Roman law by writers such as Cicero and Quintilian, who elaborated on the theories of Aristotle.[29] For Cicero, doing equity meant appealing to "an element intrinsic to the positive law and imbedded in any system of law."[30] Milton approvingly cites Cicero's theory of equitable interpretation in *Tetrachordon*: "*All law*, saith he, *we ought referr to the common good, and*

---

28. Klinck, *Conscience, Equity*, 47.
29. Meyjes, *Jean Gerson*, 242.
30. Lefebvre, "Natural Equity and Canonical Equity," 124. However, as Lefebvre notes, equity is also a remarkably slippery concept. At times Civilians speak of equity as supplementing the *ius civile* from without, while at times canonists refer to equity as a principle internal to

interpret by that, not by the scrowl of letters" (*Tetrachordon, CPW* 2:588). The "common good" here is not an external principle that can reach in and adjust the law. Instead it is the actual *telos* and substance of the law itself. Judges are to push past the "*scrowl of letters*" (i.e., the words of a law) to find the equity at the law's heart (*CPW* 2:588). To give another example, we see a characteristically Roman expression of *aequitas* in *Doctrine and Discipline* when Milton writes, "exceptions [to laws] that arise from natural equity are included silently under general terms" (*CPW* 2:330). The magistrate who makes these "exceptions" is authorized to do so by the "silent" logic of the law itself.

In contrast, external equity was associated more with the canonical tradition. Given its core assumption that a transcendent justice should at times override the mandates of merely human law, external equity was particularly consonant with the theological concerns of canon law. Canonists were fond of quoting Saint Cyprian's maxim *aequitas est iustitia dulcore misericordiae temperate*, "equity is justice tempered by sweet mercy."[31] This maxim separates justice (*iustitia*) from sweet mercy (*misericordia temperata*), and equity results when these two distinct principles are properly combined and especially when mercy adjusts the rigors of law. Similarly, the medieval canonist Hostiensis saw equity as an expression in the juridical realm of the compassion that all Christians should display.[32] Over the centuries, this idea of equity had been reified and formalized into the canon law's system of dispensations, exceptions, and indulgences. These practices allowed the rigors of the canon law to be relaxed or suspended in certain instances, and as forms of external equity, they were "understood to function apart from law (*praeter legem*) or against law (*contra legem*)."[33]

These two kinds of equity, and especially the Roman law's internal equity or *aequitas*, are important to understanding Milton's divorce tracts because of the conflicting biblical evidence he faced. One of his foundational texts is Deuteronomy 24:1, which allows for divorce: "When a man hath taken a wife, and married her, and it comes to pass that she find no favour in his eyes, because he hath found some uncleanness in her: then let him write her a bill of divorcement, and give it in her hand, and send her out of his house." However, Jesus says the opposite in Matthew 19:9: "Whosoever shall put away his wife,

---

the law. As a result, the difference traced here between internal and external equity should be viewed as a broad jurisprudential pattern rather than a categorical division.

31. Lefebvre, "Natural Equity and Canonical Equity," 122. On the canon law's association of equity with the extralegal principle of *misericordia*, see also P. Landau, "*Aequitas*," 102–3.

32. Coughlin, *Law, Person, and Community*, 113.

33. Coughlin, *Canon Law*, 46.

except it be for fornication, and shall marry another, committeth adultery: and whoso marrieth her which is put away doth commit adultery." Encountering this tension between the Old Testament and the New, most exegetes reasoned away the former on the grounds that Moses's law had to give way before Christ's. But while they needed to explain away the Mosaic law's allowance of divorce, theologians and canonists did not want to say that that law itself was bankrupt. External equity allowed them both to save the moral integrity of Moses's proclamation and to subordinate it to Jesus's words. According to canonist thinking from Gratian onward, Adam's claim that Eve was "bone of my bone and flesh of my flesh" (Genesis 2:23) showed that God had established marriage as a sacramental bond. Subsequently, the Israelites fell into the lustful practice of divorcing one wife and taking another. Moses wanted to bring them into a closer relationship with God, but faced with a people used to sexual profligacy, he saw the wisdom of permitting divorce as a concession to their hard-heartedness. This view of Moses as giving a concession shows the logic of external equity at work. Although Protestant theologians rejected the sacramental nature of marriage, many of them followed the canonists' interpretation of this passage. For example, Thomas Fuller's *Sermon of Reformation*, published the same year as Milton's *Doctrine and Discipline*, argues that the "Bill of Divorce," which has been "cancelled by Christianity," was "permitted to the Jewes," not because divorce can be regarded as good but "because [the Jews] were bad, and by this Tolleration were kept from being worse."[34] When he uses words such as "permitted" and "Tolleration," Fuller applies external equity to the law. Faced with the tension between an Edenic law that makes marriage unbreakable and a Deuteronomic law that allows for divorce, Fuller follows Protestant orthodoxy in regarding Deuteronomy as an instance when charity intervenes to soften the law's unproductive rigor.

Throughout *Doctrine and Discipline of Divorce* and *Tetrachordon*, Milton is implacably hostile to this reading of Deuteronomy 24:1-2. The problem is that the dispensation or external equity argument makes divorce a failing to be excused under particular circumstances when he wants to make it a liberty allowed to all. It also diminishes the importance of Deuteronomy 24:1-2, which as the most salient section authorizing divorce, forms the cornerstone of his argument. The external equity approach shrinks Deuteronomy down to something of a footnote in the story of sacramental marriage. Instead of a generally valid set of precepts, the Deuteronomic verses about divorce become merely an instance when an exception was made to accommodate a people's weak-

---

34. Fuller, *Sermon of Reformation*, 7.

ness. Moreover, most people thought that this exception effectively proved the Edenic rule that marriage is forever. When he talks about external equity, Milton uses terms such as "permissions," "indulgences," and "dispensations" (he reserves "equity" for the Roman *aequitas*), and he is always being derisive. For example, in *Doctrine and Discipline*'s opening address to Parliament, he scorns the "ungirt permissions" and "venial . . . dispenses" proposed by the canonists (*CPW* 2:233).[35]

Milton attacks the external equity reading of Deuteronomy along two main lines. First, he argues that it is an affront to the law's consistency. If Moses is regarded as having granted divorce as a dispensation, then he must also be regarded as having more or less permanently created an exception to the law. For Milton, this outcome is inconsistent with the nature of God as a just lawgiver. While a "human law-giver may slacken somthing of that which is exactly good, to the disposition of the people and the times" (*Doctrine and Discipline, CPW* 2:284), God cannot be said to have enacted "a dispensation as long liv'd as a law," since such an arrangement effectively highlights the defectiveness of the law (*Doctrine and Discipline, CPW* 2:300). Milton's second, related argument is that the dispensation reading implicates the Mosaic law itself in sin. If one regards marriage as a sacramental bond, then the man or woman who divorces and remarries commits the mortal sin of adultery. Milton is outraged at the logical conclusion: it is a "most absurd and rash imputation fixt upon God and his holy Laws" to think that the Mosaic law has been "conniving and dispensing with open and common adultery among [God's] chosen people" (*Doctrine and Discipline, CPW* 2:250). This reasoning attributes to God an "impure and treacherous dispense," one that betrays believers "under the vizard of Law to a legitimate practice of uncleanness" (*Doctrine and Discipline, CPW* 2:297). Since "*the Law is ordained unto life*" (Romans 7:10), how can God "publish dispenses against that Law, which must needs be unto death?" Milton likens this kind of dispensation to a secular "Judge or Law" indulgently allowing a man to "cut his owne

---

35. This attack on external equity is clearest in the three chapters Milton devotes to a proper understanding of dispensations. He agrees that in some occasions a dispensation should be allowed, as in the face of "some particular accident rarely happ'ning and therfore not specify'd in the Law, but left to the decision of charity" (*Doctrine and Discipline, CPW* 2:299). As an example of an allowable dispensation, Milton points to King David and his hungry followers entering the temple and unlawfully eating the show bread (1 Samuel 21:6). For Milton, this Davidian dispensation differs crucially from the dispensation that the canonists saw in Deuteronomy 24:1 since it was a violation of only the ceremonial law and did not involve intrinsically immoral actions.

throat"—an "absurd and monstrous" conclusion (*CPW* 2:297). He even sardonically compares the dispensation idea of divorce to "such a dispense as that ... which the serpent gave to our first parents" (*Doctrine and Discipline, CPW* 2:300). The permission to divorce, like the metaphorical permission to eat that Satan gave to Adam and Eve, does not remove the sin from the action in question; instead it simply tempts humans to push deeper into sin. Milton concludes that no one, not even God, can issue a dispensation that absolves a sinful action: "God is no covnant breaker, he cannot do this" (*Doctrine and Discipline, CPW* 2:297).

While *Doctrine and Discipline of Divorce* and *Tetrachordon* are distinguished by Milton's adamant rejection of one kind of equity, they are equally characterized by his enthusiastic embrace of another. Milton consistently argues that the Bible verses that underpin and structure his argument should be read through the principle of internal equity. For example, in *Doctrine and Discipline* he writes that Christ refused to abolish even the "smallest jot and tittle of precious equity contained in that Law" (*CPW* 2:231). Equity is inside the law, not waiting in the wings to be added to it. Similarly, he writes that if we regard the Mosaic law "in the best and equalest sense," we will see that God's law itself makes room for divorce (*Doctrine and Discipline, CPW* 2:244). The law itself is both "wise and equal" (*Doctrine and Discipline, CPW* 2:303), "full of moral equity" (*Doctrine and Discipline, CPW* 2:306), and "a most equall and requisite law" (*Doctrine and Discipline, CPW* 2:325). God has provided "just and equal inferences" in "his pure and chast Law" (*Doctrine and Discipline, CPW* 2:312). When Milton looks at God's law, he sees equity already resident within it, and so there is no need to bring in *misericordia* or *humanitas* to arrive at justice. Thus Moses allowed for divorce not despite the Edenic law of marriage but in fulfillment of it.

Milton explicitly connects this internal equity reading of the Bible to Roman jurisprudence. For example, in *Doctrine and Discipline*, he argues against the "stony rigor" of a literal reading of the Bible by looking to the "equitie of those imperiall [i.e., Roman] decrees" about divorce (*CPW* 2:238). In *Tetrachordon*, he reflects on the fact that the "*Roman* law" of contracts and dowries declined to provide exhaustive conditions and offered instead the general stipulation that matters should be conducted honorably and in good faith. As he puts it, Roman law sensibly "left many things to equity" (*CPW* 2:620). He then reasons by analogy that Moses's law of divorce, which consists of "true equity, high wisdom, and God-like pitty," has the same silent elasticity even though provisions and exceptions are not spelled out in detail (*CPW* 2:621). In another passage, Milton considers sections from the *Corpus Juris Civilis* that permit a donor to recall his gifts if the recipient "proves unthankful toward him" (*CPW* 2:626). The Civil law here makes an equitable exception to the principle that gifts are not revocable. Reasoning from this example, Milton argues that Moses acts "with much more equity" when he permits "the giver to recall no petty guift, but the guift of himself" (*CPW* 2:626). On the same page, he points out that a "rescript of *Antoninus* in the Civill Law" provided that in the event of a master's cruelty, the Roman law of slave ownership could be relaxed to allow the abused slave to change masters. Again, he uses the equity he finds in Roman law to understand God's ways: "should God who in his Law also is good to injur'd servants, by granting them thir freedom in divers cases, not consider the wrongs and miseries of a wife which is no servant" (*CPW* 2:626–27). Milton combs through the *Corpus Juris Civilis* not just for its provisions about marriage but for places in which *aequitas* can be shown to be part of the law's basic genetic code. This Roman *aequitas* in turn allows him to argue that God's laws similarly contain and allow for exceptions, and so divorce is simply a fulfillment of those laws' equitable core.

GOD'S INTENTION

As critics have long recognized, Milton approaches the Bible in a new way in the divorce tracts. In Dayton Haskin's words, before he wrote *Doctrine and Discipline*, Milton "was accustomed to accept the familiar doctrine that the plain words of the Bible provide the ultimate criterion for judgment in spiritual matters." In the process of wrestling with the contradictory nature of God's edicts on marriage, he changed his mind. Understanding the Bible, he decided, took great exegetical labor, for its meaning on many subjects was not, in fact, readily apparent. Haskin argues that Milton relied on an interpretive technique he learned from Cicero and Aristotle: "the diligent 'conferring place with place,' whereby difficult texts were to be restored to their meanings and harmonized according to the overall drift and scope of the whole Bible."[36] When faced with a difficult or contradictory text, the interpreter was to compare different sections, since thorny passages often made more sense when read in light of other more accessible ones. The only element missing from Haskin's convincing account is that writers such as Aristotle and Cicero developed this interpretive approach as one means of doing equity, and in context, they were primarily focused on making sense of legal documents such as statutes, wills, and contracts. As Kathy Eden shows, this equitable

36. Haskin, *Milton's Burden*, 55. See also Barker, *Milton and the Puritan Dilemma*, 63–79.

manner of reading was later picked up and absorbed by Christian exegetes ranging from Augustine to Melanchthon, becoming a central component of their hermeneutics.[37]

What Milton calls "comparing other texts" (*Doctrine and Discipline, CPW* 2:282) was just one of the techniques Roman jurists developed for equitable reading. These techniques were intended to solve a real-world judicial problem: merely declaring that a judge should find the equity inside the law did not necessarily help those faced with a gap between the wording of a statute and the circumstances of the case at hand. What was needed was a consistent and adaptable set of interpretive techniques so that judges did not have to fall back on a vague sense of what was fair. While one solution was a comparison of statutes on similar subjects, two other approaches were to consider the intention of the lawgiver and the reason for which the law was established (*ratio legis*). Confronted with a case in which a statute did not clearly address the circumstances, the judge should ask himself: What would the lawgiver himself do on this occasion? What was his intention in establishing this law? What was the reason for this law, or what problem was it meant to correct? While thus far my focus has been on the *Corpus Juris Civilis* and its associated tradition of Continental texts, the forms of equitable interpretation laid out in these works had also migrated into English jurisprudence. For example, the common lawyer Edmund Plowden considers a statute of Westminster requiring that, in the event of shipwreck, salvaged goods should be stored intact for a year and a day so that the owner could claim them. Any failure to follow these provisions was punishable by fines and imprisonment. But, Plowden asks, what about perishable cargo such as fruit and nuts? If the sheriff sells them and holds the money for a year and a day, has he broken the law? Plowden argues that this hypothetical sheriff has rightly used equity to discern the "sense" and "intent" (*le sence* and *lentent*) of the act. Plowden provides a set of disarmingly self-referential instructions to his reader: "it is a good method each time you peruse the words of a statute, to imagine that the institutor of that law is present and to ask him the question you want to know about the statute's equity. And when you have asked him this question, then you must give yourself the answer that you think he would have done if he had been present." While Plowden emphasizes that this manner of equitable reading is an important part of "our law" (*nostre ley*) and can be seen in English writers such as Bracton, he is also aware of its origins in the

---

37. Eden, *Hermeneutics*.

classical tradition since he calls it "Equitas" and associates it with the theories of Aristotle.[38]

In his divorce tracts, Milton turns repeatedly to these juristic principles of *ratio legis* and the intention of the lawgiver, ones that formed a living part of jurisprudence on both sides of the English Channel. For example, he gives the chapters of *Doctrine and Discipline* titles such as "*The first reason of this Law*" (*CPW* 2:245) and "*The Second Reason of this Law*" (*CPW* 2:250). He also pervasively stresses the intention of the lawgiver. Arguing in *Doctrine and Discipline* that the "strictnes of a literall interpreting" (*CPW* 2:242), or *summum ius*, leads to *summa iniuria*, Milton says that the law should be understood instead in relation to "the end of the Lawgiver" (*CPW* 2:243). He identifies "that [which] was chiefly meant" in the Mosaic law (*CPW* 2:254). He considers "the expresse end of Gods institution" of marriage (*CPW* 2:269). He discerns "the intent of [the] Law" (*CPW* 2:306) and what "*Moses* did in the true intent of the Law" (*CPW* 2:307). In one of the most famous phrases from the treatise, Milton says that in "Gods intention," a "meet and happy conversation" is the "noblest end" of marriage (*CPW* 2:246). It is as if Milton has followed Plowden's instructions about imaginatively bringing the lawmaker into his study for questioning: having asked God about his real "intention" for marriage, Milton then confidently supplies the answer. This same interpretive approach is equally prevalent in *Tetrachordon*, as when he writes, "All Ordinances are establisht in thir end; the end of Law is the virtu, is the righteousnes of Law. And therfore him wee count an ill Expounder who urges Law against the intention therof" (*CPW* 2:623). The lawgiver's "intention" was to pass a statute that helped the law fulfill its own end, and since the "end" of the law is virtue and righteousness, the law of divorce must be interpreted in a way that leads to more virtuous lives among its subjects.

Especially in *Tetrachordon*, Milton suggests that charity is the ultimate form of statutory interpretation, in effect an expression of internal equity. For example, he explains that apparent discrepancies in the Bible can be reconciled to one another if we apply the "general rule of charity" (*CPW* 2:596).

---

38. Plowden, *La Second Part*, 466–67. Plowden is writing in Law French, the official language of the early modern common law courts. An English translation can be found in Plowden, *The Second Part*, 466–67. In his popular work about law and equity, Christopher St. German also stresses the need to consider the intention of the lawmaker. Together, Plowden's and St. German's thinking indicate how this aspect of classical jurisprudence had become a standard part of judicial interpretation in England. See St. German, *Dialoges in English*.

It is clear in context that he means that charity operates from inside the law rather than being a salve applied from the outside. He then reflects on Deuteronomy 22:13–19, which provides that a man who unjustly accuses his new wife of unchastity will be fined and forbidden to divorce her. Milton reasons that while the husband cannot use defamation to get rid of an unwanted wife, the wife herself now has the right to leave the husband. "Otherwise this cours had not so much righted her, as deliverd her up to more spight and cruel usage." Following the "common Expositors," Milton argues that the law in this case operates "graciously," for though the wife's ability to divorce her husband is "beyond the letter of his law," it is "not beyond the spirit of charity" (*Tetrachordon*, *CPW* 2:629–30). Similarly, he argues that we should interpret not according to the "stubborn letter" of the law but rather according to the "divine and softening breath of charity which turns and windes the dictat of every positive command and shapes it to the good of mankind" (*CPW* 2:604–5). While the law's body is made up of rigid letters, that body is animated by the "breath of charity," which makes it pliant and able to be "shaped" around the varying needs of true human happiness. This metaphor underscores the fact that charity/equity resides inside the law, much as breath resides inside the body.

By applying the interpretive traditions of *aequitas* to Mosaic law, Milton makes a basic assumption about the potential of human reason.[39] When writers such as Cicero or Quintilian instructed readers that the way to find the equity of a contract, will, or statute was to consider its intention, they took for granted that the mind reading the document was capable of fathoming the mind that created the document. While in practice, the words of the intervening text might thwart this meeting of minds (e.g., if the statute was so poorly worded as to obscure its intention), in theory there was no intrinsic reason why the lawgiver's intentions should be opaque to the judge. When Milton talks about reading the Bible in an equitable way, he makes the same assumption about the mind of God. He even states this fact explicitly. As he explains in *Doctrine and Discipline of Divorce*, "God indeed in some wayes of his providence, is high and secret past finding out: but in the delivery and execution of his Law . . . [he] hath plain enough reveal'd himself." While God's nature might be inscrutable, his laws are not, and men and women should understand laws in accordance with "the law of nature and of equity imprinted" in them (*CPW* 2:297). In *Tetrachordon*, Milton further ratchets up this sense

---

39. On the way Milton echoes Christian rationalist contemporaries such as William Chillingworth and Lord Falkland, see Barker, *Milton and the Puritan Dilemma*, 80–85.

that God's laws are like human laws: their meaning can be decoded by the proper application of juristic thinking and specifically by applying *aequitas*. In the Bible, "God presents himself like to a man deliberating" in order to show that he "intended" to establish the law "according to naturall reason," and this human reason allows us to understand the "reason" behind the law itself (*CPW* 2:595). Thus the fit reader of the Bible uses "all equity" to arrive at proper "construction" and to "comprehend . . . what God spake," meaning to discern the intention behind God's law (*CPW* 2:603). Similarly when Milton contrasts the "perfet scales of [God's] justice" with the "fals and abominable" "ballances" of the canonists, he assumes that he can tell which balances are poised properly and which ones are not (*CPW* 2:658).

Because critics have not recognized that Milton's references to the "intention" of the lawmaker or the "end" of the law spring from his deep reading in Roman jurisprudence, they have often overstated his resistance to law as a whole. For example, John Halkett argues that in the divorce tracts Milton has "taken marriage out of the realm of law and placed it in the realm of affective psychology."[40] W. Scott Howard says that Milton celebrates the way that the "inward ordinance of individual acts of nearly prophetic interpretation—-i.e., the spirit of the law" can be used to correct "institutional practices, or custom—i.e., the letter of the law."[41] In her account of the logical structures of Milton's treatise, Lana Cable cites a passage from *Doctrine and Discipline of Divorce* where Milton refers to what "God intended" to be the "whole reason of the Law," as classic an expression of *aequitas* as one finds in Milton's works (*CPW* 2:310). Cable argues that this passage proves that "the appropriateness of a given point of law to a given individual is determined not by any outside judge . . . but by the individual's makeup and capacity." Similarly citing Milton's reference to "what *Moses* and the Law intended" (*Doctrine and Discipline*, *CPW* 2:308), she reasons that "just law operates from within, realizing its meaning not as a stricture imposed from the outside but as a function of the understanding."[42] At one level, these arguments are true in that Milton indeed refuses to have the meaning of the law imposed from the outside, and he insists that the power to judge rests with the individual. However, what needs to be added is that the interpretive practice he adopts himself and urges on his readers is itself a crucial part of Western jurisprudence. When Milton rejects a literalist reading and thinks instead about the reason for the law and the inten-

---

40. Halkett, *Milton and the Idea of Matrimony*, 8.
41. Howard, "Milton's 'Divorcive' Liberties," paragraph 4.
42. Cable, "Coupling Logic," 154, 155.

tion of the lawgiver, he is not moving from the realm of law into the realm of not-law. Instead, he is applying fundamental juristic techniques that had for centuries been at the center of jurisprudential thinking and that had figured in decisions handed down in countless courtrooms. Thus the great irony of the divorce tracts and perhaps their greatest rhetorical achievement is that Milton's argument—that when it comes to divorce, each man should be "a Law in this matter to himself" (*Doctrine and Discipline, CPW* 2:347)—would not have been possible without the very judicial systems and traditions that he hopes to transcend.

CHAPTER 5

Defending *Pro Se Defensio*

This chapter focuses on Milton's third and most neglected Latin defense, *Pro Se Defensio*, and I argue that in it, Milton uses the assumptions and procedures of the Civil law to arraign his opponent for libel. But before diving into Milton's tract, I want to detour briefly through the work that might well have inspired its jurisprudential strategy: Ben Jonson's 1601 play *Poetaster*. Like Milton, Jonson felt himself to have been the victim of injurious speech, in his case from the playwright John Marston, who had ridiculed him in *Histrio-Mastix* and *Jack Drum's Entertainment*, part of the extended verbal quarrel known as the Wars of the Poets. Like Milton, Jonson imagines his adversary being arraigned for injurious words, and *Poetaster* concludes with the trial and conviction of Crispinus and Demetrius (thinly veiled versions of Marston and his collaborator Thomas Dekker). While this trial occupies only one scene, Jonson clearly thought of it as the play's defining moment, as evidenced by his work's full title: *Poetaster, or The Arraignment*. And like Milton, Jonson judges his opponent using the Continental jurisprudence of *iniuria*, which encompassed a wide range of offenses. Understanding Jonson's use of the jurisprudence of Roman law and the way he adapts his scene for English audiences provides us with a useful starting point for understanding Milton's own use of Roman law under comparable circumstances.

The climactic scene of *Poetaster* shows Jonson's nuanced handling of jurisdictional realities.[1] Crispinus and Demetrius have been arrested for their

---

1. For law's importance to *Poetaster*, see Greenfield, "Trial by Theater." On Jonson's familiarity with various aspects of early modern law, see Wilson, "Ben Jonson and the Law of

slanderous attacks on Horace (the character who represents Jonson himself), and the formal indictment, read by the tribune Tibullus, charges them with violating the "statute of calumny": they have "mutually conspired and plotted at sundry times, as by several means, and in sundry places, for the better accomplishing [their] base and envious purpose, taxing [Horace] falsely of self-love, arrogancy, impudence, railing, filching by translation, etcetera."[2] Jonson's contemporary English audience—many of whom would have served as jurors, bailiffs, sheriffs, coroners, clerks, JPs, etc.—would likely have known that these charges would not hold up in a domestic court of law. Within a common law framework, Crispinus has not imputed a crime to Horace, nor has he damaged him in his profession. Indeed, earlier in the play, Horace says he will not press charges because "I heartily wish a fool should hate me"[3]—i.e., Crispinus's clueless, bombastic insults actually provide him, Horace, with a professional boost. Nor would Crispinus and Demetrius's actions qualify as seditious libel, which, as we saw in chapter 2, targeted private words that endangered the public peace. Nowhere in the play does Horace suggest that Crispinus's attacks stir up social unrest. To the contrary, he characterizes them as merely personal betrayals, as when he describes Crispinus as one of those who "gnaw their absent friends" and "reveal / Each secret that's committed to their trust."[4] Given that neither of the two major English secular jurisdictions—common law or the prerogative court of Star Chamber—would take cognizance of Crispinus and Demetrius's actions, Roman law offers Jonson the perfect solution. As I will explore in more detail during the course of this chapter, Roman law had a broader construction of libel, and dishonoring someone's good name was actionable regardless of whether the perpetrator thereby imputed a crime to his victim, damaged his professional standing, or stirred up civil unrest. Thus Jonson conjures up a Roman law trial on his early modern English stage because Marston/Crispinus and Dekker/Demetrius are clearly guilty of *iniuria* as it was defined and applied in Civilian courts.

This dramatic strategy of using Roman law to convict libelous opponents comes with attendant risks. As we saw in chapter 4, the English were apt to regard their native common law with some patriotic fervor as the guarantor of life, liberty, and property and to be suspicious on principle of Continental

---

Contract"; Klotz, "Ben Jonson's Legal Imagination." On the political functions of detraction in *Poetaster*, see Smuts, "Jonson's *Poetaster*."

2. Jonson, *Poetaster*, 5.3.220–25.
3. Jonson, *Poetaster*, 5.3.174.
4. Jonson, *Poetaster*, 5.3.324, 331–32.

law. This means that Jonson must thread a jurisdictional needle. He needs to show the plaintiffs of *Poetaster* being convicted under Roman law while also ensuring that his English audience feels they are witnessing true justice. His solution is to make this Roman trial feel like an ordinary English one. Whereas later in the Roman empire, evidence was presented in writing to a judge, Jonson situates his trial in the early days of the Roman empire when charges and evidence were presented orally and decided by a jury.[5] As a result, he gets to have it both ways. He can boast of his scene's historical verisimilitude (his jurors even deposit their verdict tokens into an urn) and his own classical erudition, while at the same time he gets to show seventeenth-century English audiences a trial format that looked exceedingly familiar. For example, his depiction of the pleading procedures seems cribbed straight from standard English judicial practice. Common law trials featured the following, highly ritualized exchange of words:

CLERK: How to do you plead?
ACCUSED: Not guilty.
CLERK: How will you be tried?
ACCUSED: By God and my country.

In asking to be tried "By God and my country," the accused man or woman was asking for a jury trial, as opposed to trial by ordeal or by combat. Here is Jonson's version in *Poetaster* of the exchange between Crispinus and Demetrius, the accused, and Tibullus, the tribune:

TIBULLUS: what answer you? Are you guilty or not guilty?
. . .
CRISPINUS, DEMETRIUS: Not guilty.
TIBULLUS: How will you be tried?
. . .
CRISPINUS, DEMETRIUS: By the Roman gods, and the noblest Romans.[6]

Jonson is dressing this Roman trial in English common law garb. He wants his audience to see Marston in the familiar role of the common law defendant being presented with overwhelming evidence of his guilt and in the process to forget the fact that the actions in question—such as verses accusing Horace

---

5. Chroust and Murphy, "Lex Acilia."
6. Jonson, *Poetaster*, 5.3.227–34.

of "*satirical humours*" and "*much self-love and more arrogance*"—were not, in English contexts, actually illegal.[7]

I offer this digression into *Poetaster* to indicate that when he uses the jurisprudence of Roman law to convict an opponent for injurious words, Milton is not inventing a rhetorical wheel. Instead, he adapts a strategy that Jonson, similarly smarting under the sting of libelous words, used to powerful effect. Insofar as Milton's approach differs from Jonson's, it is because he is addressing a different audience and combating a different enemy. Because Jonson was speaking to English audiences, he made Roman legal proceedings look like English ones. But in *Pro Se Defensio*, Milton is writing to a Continental readership whose own contemporary jurisprudence was modeled on Roman law. Because he does not need to accommodate his juridical approach to his readers' understandings, Milton can spend time building a much more thoroughgoing and even technical case against his opponent. Ironically, because Milton simply takes it for granted that readers will understand his jurisprudential strategy, large swathes of *Pro Se Defensio* have been inscrutable to modern English readers, most of whom inhabit a juridical world that is descended from early modern English common law. Milton also has a different kind of adversary in view. For all of Jonson's ire at Marston's abuse, he seems to have regarded Marston mainly as a pompous fool who brought stagecraft into disrepute. Thus Jonson's trial has a lighthearted quality, and the sober mechanisms of trial and conviction blur into the hilarious exchange in which Crispinus, having swallowed pills given him by Horace, begins to vomit up all of the pompous, fustian words that have blotted his verses. There is little levity in Milton's approach, not because Milton was less capable of humor. Rather, as this chapter demonstrates, Milton saw his adversary, Alexander More, as a serious threat to the integrity of the Protestant church. Thus he brings a formidable legal arsenal to bear on exposing his wrongdoings.

MILTON'S USE OF ROMAN LAW

Critics have not been kind to *Pro Se Defensio*. In the very first sentence of his preface in the Yale edition of Milton's prose, Kester Svendsen offers a typical critical assessment: it was "the worst mistake of his public career" (*CPW* 4:687). The "mistake" is the fact that *Pro Se Defensio* apparently takes aim at the wrong man. In the wake of his *Pro Populo Anglicano Defensio*, Milton was

---

7. Jonson, *Poetaster*, 5.3.299, 302.

attacked by the anonymous treatise *Regii Sanguinis Clamor ad Coelum adversus Parricidas Anglicanos* (*The Cry of the Royal Blood to Heaven against the English Parricides*; henceforth *Clamor*), which most of Europe—Milton included—attributed to the Franco-Scots cleric Alexander More who lived in the Low Countries. Milton retaliated by lampooning More in his *Defensio Secunda*. In response, More hastily published *Alexandri Mori Fides Publica* (*The Public Faith of Alexander More*; henceforth *Fides Publica*) to protest his innocence of *Clamor*.[8] Milton then further pressed his case against More in *Pro Se Defensio*.[9] Reflecting on Milton's intransigence on the subject of More's authorship of *Clamor*, Svendsen calls *Pro Se Defensio* a "masterpiece of argumentation in the face of flat denial" (*CPW* 4:687). Milton seems so determined to get revenge for the insulting language of *Clamor* that he ignores what looks like reasonable evidence and relies instead on unfounded or exaggerated claims and vituperative rhetoric. Other critics have found *Pro Se Defensio* similarly distasteful. William Riley Parker regrets that "having accused [More] of the authorship of *Clamor*, Milton was unable to drop the argument." *Pro Se Defensio* is "sadly lacking in the important argument of the first *Defensio* and the varied themes of the second," and it is "single-minded, monotonous, and dull."[10] Douglas Stewart concludes his study of *Pro Se Defensio* by stating that Milton's "obsession" with attacking More is "pathetic."[11]

In this chapter, I argue that critics have profoundly misunderstood *Pro Se Defensio* by reading it in a generally rhetorical instead of a specifically legal context. In his first two defenses, Milton combats his textual opponents by using basic principles of logical argumentation. However, he changes his strategy in *Pro Se Defensio*. Here he argues using the terms and premises of Civil law, casting himself as a defendant and presenting evidence to rebut the claims of Alexander More, the metaphorical plaintiff. This chapter develops the arguments of previous chapters in two main ways. First, when he uses Roman law in the divorce tracts (the subject of chapter 4), Milton applies

---

8. *Fides Publica* is in fact a two-part work: More's original *Fides Publica* published in October 1654 followed by a *Supplementum* he published around April 1655. These two are combined and reprinted in *CPW* 4.1082–1128.

9. For more details about Milton's encounter with More, see W. R. Parker, *Milton*, 1:447–60.

10. W. R. Parker, *Milton*, 1:457, 459.

11. Stewart, "Speaking to the World," 57.

broad jurisprudential principles rather than procedural technicalities, meaning that he writes more like a jurist examining theories of law than like a lawyer confronted with an actual case. But *Pro Se Defensio* is more caselike in that Milton (the defendant) wields the practical aspects of Civilian procedure in order to counter the charges made by More (the plaintiff). Second, because both *Clamor* and *Fides Publica* accused Milton of libel, *Pro Se Defensio* offers an extended reflection on the subject of injurious words. As I argued in chapters 2 and 3, Milton's earlier prose works look at the problem of libel through the lens of English common law. But because common law applied only to domestic offenses and native litigants, Milton had to turn elsewhere when confronted with a foreign opponent. In *Pro Se Defensio*, he imaginatively climbs out of the common law's framework and into that of the *ius commune*, meaning that he wields the same corpus of statutes, assumptions, and procedures that judges in Continental Civil courts brought to bear in cases where the issue was written or verbal attacks. Milton invites his Latinate readers to view *Pro Se Defensio* as a kind of textual courtroom where they can see the evidence and judge the relative claims of both parties.

Milton's deeply juridical approach has led to a widespread misunderstanding of his work because the legal doctrines he relies upon are not familiar ones today. For example, modern English editions of *Pro Se Defensio* consistently fail to capture the legal meaning of key Latin words. Throughout the treatise Milton makes arguments about More's and his own *fama*. *Fama* was both a technical term in Roman law and a foundational concept in the Continental *ius commune*, but it has no real equivalent in modern Anglo-American jurisprudence. When *fama* is translated literally as "fame," it is easy for modern readers to conclude that Milton is indulging his wounded ego rather than making a specific kind of juridical argument. Similarly, Milton's arguments about what counts as authorship have struck modern readers as highly tendentious. However, they were standard in early modern legal argumentation, both in Civilian and in common law contexts. Excavating the judicial strategies of *Pro Se Defensio* not only shows us Milton's remarkable facility with a legal system other than his native common law; it also shows him using that legal system to pursue what he considered to be true justice. Alexander More showed himself to be a bad minister and something of a sexual predator, and Milton brings to bear an impressive array of legal arguments to try to have him defrocked. In *Defensio Secunda*, Milton claimed to be speaking "not on behalf of one people nor yet one defendant" but rather for "civil life and religion" in various countries (*CPW* 4:557–58). In *Pro Se Defensio* he delivers on this claim, for he looks resolutely outside the borders of his own country and wields the Civil law on behalf of Protestant believers in places like Geneva, Leiden, and Amsterdam.

INIURIA: UNDERSTANDING THE CIVIL LAW OF LIBEL

From his title page all the way through to the conclusion of *Pro Se Defensio*, Milton stresses the essentially legal nature of his treatise. For example, by using the phrase *pro se defensio* in his title, Milton positions himself as one of the litigants in a lawsuit: attorneys today still talk about the delicate difficulties of facing *pro se* defendants, those who are acting as their own counsel.[12] The image of a legal face-off is not merely a convenient analogy for his textual contest with More. To the contrary, Milton emphasizes that he is charging More with actual offenses under contemporary Civil law. The author of *Clamor* accused Milton of erecting a "tribunal of no authority," by which he meant Milton's *Pro Populo Anglicano Defensio* and *Defensio Secunda*. According to More, these works violated the law of nations, which held that disputes that crossed national lines should be resolved according to broadly accepted juridical standards. Answering this charge in *Pro Se Defensio*, Milton clearly stakes out his legal ground: "I use your own law; your own tribunal; your own seat of judgment . . . against you" (*CPW* 4:736). When he says that he will use More's "own law," Milton means that rather than judging More according to the standards of English common law or even those of reason and/or conscience, he will instead use Civil law. We see similar references throughout the work, as when Milton likens himself pressing charges against More to the Roman leader Crassus coming into "the court of the Senate and the Roman people" to present the offenses of a "reprobate citizen" (*CPW* 4:767). Milton calls attention to the essentially just nature of using Civil law against a man who lived in a country with a generally Civilian legal system.[13] The legal/textual proceedings in *Pro Se Defensio* lead to "full justice," and Milton says

---

12. While Milton was writing *Pro Se Defensio*, his brother Christopher was busy handling family lawsuits with both the Cope family and Mrs. Elizabeth Ashworth (W. R. Parker, *Milton*, 1:450–51). As a result, Milton's claim that he is acting as his own legal counsel may contain a nod to the fact that he was writing without his lawyer-brother at his side.

13. To be precise, while he resided in the United Provinces, More lived under Roman-Dutch law, which was an amalgam of Roman statutory law with Dutch customary law. However, since the Roman-Dutch law and Civil law aligned in many respects and especially in those aspects that concern Milton in *Pro Se Defensio*, I will use the broader term "Civil law" here.

that by bringing legally valid testimony against a man who is "openly and patently criminal," he will have "prosecuted" More in a "most just" fashion (*CPW* 4:736, 796).

Two critics have noticed the pervasive legal vein in *Pro Se Defensio*, although neither one fully identifies how the law functions in the work. Barbara K. Lewalski follows critical tradition in deprecating the treatise as "Milton's least attractive work," "a tissue of vituperation," and "a strained defense of a serious error." However, Lewalski also admits (albeit somewhat vaguely) that Milton's "struggle with the issues posed by his mistake—proper standards of evidence, the uses of defamation, the meaning of authorship—hold considerable biographical interest."[14] All three of the elements in her appositive phrase are legal ones: evidence, defamation, and the legal implications of authorship. Lewalski is correct that Milton has his eye on all three in this work, but her phrasing suggests that to make his case (i.e., to persist in his "serious error" about More's authorship and to sustain his "vituperation") Milton has to push his way through a spiny hedge of law and that matters like the "proper standards of evidence" are antithetical to his case. However, Milton is working to make a legally valid argument; the law is his ally, not something against which he has to "struggle." For Lewalski, the legal language of *Pro Se Defensio* offers primarily "biographical interest," by which she presumably means that it shows us Milton's familiarity with law. This is true although it underplays the significance of the legal scholarship on display in the work. The strongly juridical tilt of *Pro Se Defensio* demonstrates not only Milton's knowledge of jurists such as Justinian, Coke, and Grotius but also his determination to use this knowledge in pursuit of what he saw as a just cause.

Joad Raymond has come the closest to recognizing how contemporary ideas of law inform Milton's defense. Outlining the differences among the three defenses, Raymond observes somewhat in passing that *Pro Se Defensio* introduces a "new strain of legal terminology" that "suggests that [Milton] had been concerned with the law, especially Roman law, over preceding months."[15] Milton was indeed thinking about Roman law in *Pro Se Defensio*, but Raymond's phrasing conveys two potentially misleading impressions. First, the reference to the "new strain" of legal terms suggests that law was only a recent interest for Milton, one that had emerged "over preceding months." However, the evidence of Milton's other works, including his commonplace book, shows a far more sustained interest in early modern jurispru-

---

14. Lewalski, *Life*, 324.
15. Raymond, "Rhetoric," 287–88.

dence.[16] Second, Raymond implies that by curving into Roman law, Milton was following a primarily academic or even antiquarian interest. What needs to be clarified is that Roman law was hardly a relic of the past for his European readers. As the previous chapter reminds us, Roman law had been absorbed into the church by canonical scholars of the twelfth century, becoming *the* foundation for all ecclesiastical law. This law had later migrated back into the secular states as the Civil law, a transferal that illustrates what Shuger calls the "crisscross exchanges binding canon law, civil law, and theology."[17] When Milton quotes from Justinian's *Institutes*, he is citing a text whose precepts and assumptions still actively animated the jurisprudence of early modern Europe and that had also exerted a profound impact upon English common law.

Milton's ability to wield the Civil law precisely and effectively in *Pro Se Defensio* was the product of both his wide reading in Civilian texts and his personal experience in non-common law courts. Between 1639 and 1645, he made a number of entries from the *Institutes* in his commonplace book,[18] and the range and variety of Roman law references in the divorce tracts indicate that he had read deeply in the *Corpus Juris Civilis* and its surrounding constellation of jural texts.[19] Outside the realm of books, Milton had either personally encountered or was generally aware of the way that Roman law worked in some of England's non-common law courts.[20] In addition to being the foundation of the ecclesiastical courts, Civil law was directly administered in the High Court of the Admiralty and the two university courts, and since Milton's state letters contain multiple references to the Admiralty, we can assume that he had some familiarity with Civil proceedings there.[21] His most direct exposure to something resembling Civil law almost certainly came through his various lawsuits in the Court of Chancery.[22] An equity court, Chancery did not administer the Civil law in any substantive way. However,

16. For example, Fletcher argues that Milton started reading and thinking about law even before his Cambridge years: Fletcher, *Intellectual Development*, 2:530–31.

17. Shuger, *Censorship*, 104.

18. Mohl, *John Milton and His Commonplace Book*, 223, 229.

19. Dzelzainis, "In These Western Parts." For more on Milton and Roman law, see also Dzelzainis, "Liberty and the Law," and Skinner, "Milton and the Politics of Slavery."

20. On the uneasy relations of common law and Civil law, see Ibbetson, "Common Law and *Ius Commune*."

21. On Roman law at the Court of the Admiralty, see Wijffels, "*Ius Gentium*." For the role that the Civil law played in England's common law culture, see Levack, *Civil Lawyers*.

22. *MC* remains the standard source on Milton's experiences in Chancery.

procedurally speaking it operated along Civilian lines. For instance, Chancery proceedings involved written documents such as interrogatories and depositions (as opposed to oral arguments in common law cases), and equity judges, like Civil law judges, could issue both subpoenas and injunctions. As a result, Milton's considerable experience filing Chancery bills and writing interrogatories was to some degree a training in the procedural aspects of Civil law.

Whatever its precise source, Milton's Civil law learning is on full display as early as the title page of *Pro Se Defensio*, where he advances two legal claims that crucially underpin his argument as a whole. First, the phrase "*pro se defensio*" strategically casts Milton as the defendant and More as the plaintiff. Given the sequential volley of attacks and counterattacks launched in *Clamor*, Milton's *Defensio Secunda*, More's *Fides Publica*, and finally Milton's *Pro Se Defensio*, it can be hard to keep straight who is the accused and who the accuser. In context, however, Milton is the defendant, for *Clamor* was a textual ambush attack that made what Milton calls in *Pro Se Defensio* "false accusations [*accusationes . . . falsas*]" (*CPW* 4:700; *PSD* 4).[23] Milton's vocabulary is pointedly judicial. Civil law proceedings were initiated when a plaintiff filed a document called a bill of accusations, and the *ius commune* was particularly concerned with punishing false accusations and vexatious litigants. Near the beginning of his treatise, Milton calls attention to the fact that More has done precisely these things. Writing anonymously, More has brought false changes against Milton, and so Milton has no choice but to act *pro se*. He is writing a defense "of myself, who am wounded by every kind of abuse." He must "defend myself against those slanders, as is fitting and just" (*CPW* 4:724, 726). He trusts that Christian readers "will not . . . snatch from me the right and the power of defending myself." He has "defended" himself "against . . . contemptuous adversaries" (*CPW* 4:729, 735). And he chides More, "Remember that it is you who began this sport" (*CPW* 4:747). In terms of Civil procedure, Milton's treatise is effectively a set of peremptory exceptions: after the plaintiff filed his bill of accusations, the defendant could submit exceptions, and peremptory exceptions were those in which the defendant argued that the plaintiff's case had legal/factual errors (as opposed to dilatory exceptions, which alleged procedural errors such as that the case was filed in the wrong

---

23. When discussing Milton's general rhetorical claims, I use the English translation from *CPW*. When examining Milton's use of specific legal terms, I use instead the original Latin version from *PSD*.

jurisdiction).²⁴ By adopting the position of the defendant, Milton gains an important advantage because in Civil law cases the burden of proof was higher for the plaintiff. The plaintiff had to provide clear, credible evidence to support his allegations, while the defendant had only to demonstrate that the plaintiff's proofs were not legally adequate.²⁵ Thus *Pro Se Defensio* repeatedly calls attention to the fact that the evidence More presented in *Fides Publica* does not hold up to legal scrutiny, as when Milton surveys the testimony More offered and concludes that all of it is either "evilly procured" or "out of date" (*CPW* 4:811).

Second, Milton's title accuses More of libel. His full title is as follows: *Joannis Miltoni Angli Pro Se Defensio Contra Alexandrum Morum Ecclesiasten, Libelli Famosi, Cui Titulus Regii Sanguinis Clamor Ad Coelum Adversus Parricidas Anglicanos, Authorem Recte Dictum*. Milton names the litigants—*Joannis Miltoni Angli* and *Alexandrum Morum Ecclesiasten*—and then the offense, *Libelli Famosi*, which was the Roman law term for libel. And More is *Authorem Recte Dictum*, rightly called the author, of this libel. In effect, the primary basis of Milton's peremptory exception is that the plaintiff's allegations are legally worthless because they are libelous. Modern editions of *Pro Se Defensio* obscure the central legal issue by shortening the title. The Yale Prose gives the title as *John Milton Englishman His Defense of Himself against Alexander More, etc.*, and the Columbia edition renders it as *John Milton an Englishman His Defense of Himself in Answer to Alexander More, etc.*²⁶ Both editions bury the legal offense—*libelli famosi*—in the "etc.," and so they make *Pro Se Defensio* look more like a private quarrel regrettably dragged into print and less like Milton's version of a formal judicial argument. However, Milton is explicit throughout the work that More is guilty of libel. For example, More is "the author of that libel [*illius libelli*]" and "the author of that infamous libel [*illius libelli famosissimi*]" (*CPW* 4:207, 702; *PSD* 6, 7). Milton has had many conversations "concerning this libel [*libello*]," and he is confident that More is "a party in composing this libel [*libelli*]" (*CPW* 4:704, 710; *PSD* 10, 17).

To understand how *Pro Se Defensio* proceeds against More, we have to understand the Roman law of libel. The scope of this law can seem strange to

---

24. For more on the procedural details of Civil law, see Brundage, *Medieval Origins*, 407–63.

25. Brundage, *Medieval Origins*, 131; Helmholz, *Select Cases*, xxiii.

26. *CPW* 4:698; F. A. Patterson et al., *Works of John Milton*, 9:3.

modern readers since it included both physical harms and verbal harms in the same category of injurious actions. Under modern American and British law, to strike a man is legally actionable while to call him a scoundrel is not. But under Roman law, both equally exposed the perpetrator to an *iniuria* action, since *iniuria* included any "outrageous insult" whether "from something done or from words."[27] Throughout *Pro Se Defensio*, Milton stresses that More has committed the offense of *iniuria*. For example, More has done him an "injury" (*injuriâ*), so he, Milton, must write in response to show More's perfidy (*CPW* 4:805; *PSD* 169). More has committed two "crimes" (Milton uses the specifically legal word *res* here), *flagitiorum* and *iniuriarum*, which the translator of the Yale Prose edition, Paul Blackford, renders as "debauchery" and "insult and outrage" (*CPW* 4:701; *PSD* 6). While "debauchery" accurately captures the meaning of *flagitiorum*, the translation "insult and outrage" bleaches out the legal implications of *iniuriarum*. Milton is not simply saying that *Clamor* is insulting and outrageous in a generic sense; he means that it falls comfortably within the definition of *iniuria* in the *ius commune*. Why, Milton asks, did he reply to *Clamor* at all? Because he was "expressly injured [*laesus*]" (*CPW* 4:767; *PSD* 112). Again answering the question of why he responded to *Clamor* and not to other royalist works, Milton says simply that in those other works, "I was not injured [*non laesus*]" (*CPW* 4:767; *PSD* 112). The term *laesus* was common in *iniuria* proceedings (e.g., *laese maiestas* for the offense of "injured majesty"), and so Milton says that he takes up his pen not because More's claims are personally hurtful or ideologically objectionable but because More crossed into the realm of offenses that are actionable at law.

One further example will serve to typify Milton's pervasive reliance on the jurisprudential language of *iniuria*. Here is Milton again specifying that More has committed *iniuria* and asserting his own right to offer a defense:

> Shall any private person have done violence upon my reputation in an infamous book . . . and shall I be compelled to swallow that insult, so that I cannot, when the time seems right, vindicate myself with a defense both just and anxiously expected? (*CPW* 4:731)

As so often happens, this English translation suppresses some of the legal implications of the Latin original. First, "infamous book" is actually *famoso libro*—libel—in the Latin, so Milton is once again saying that *Clamor* is a le-

---

27. Justinian, *Digest*, 47.10.1.

gally actionable civil offense. Second, Milton's concern for "my reputation" also looks to the world of Civil jurisprudence since he uses the phrase *existimationem meam* (*PSD* 50). The term *existimatio* appeared often in *iniuria* suits where one litigant claimed that his good name had been wounded. Writing in the *Digest*, the Roman jurist Callistratus defines *existimatio* as "a position of unimpaired standing, which is established by law and custom." This status may be reduced if "we are assigned a penalty which affects our standing, although liberty remains," as in the case of infamy or public obloquy.[28] Thus this libelous wounding of Milton's *existimatio* has resulted in what Blackford translates as "insult" but what Milton himself calls *iniuria*. And finally, Milton has the law in mind when he calls More a "private person" (*privatus*). (Similarly, on the previous page Milton writes that as a "private individual" [*privatim*] himself, he has a right to punish More [*CPW* 4:731; *PSD* 49]). Milton is relying on the *ius privatum / ius publicum* distinction so fundamental to Roman law in order to argue that whether or not the English Commonwealth government regards More's attack on the English people as an actionable offense, he retains the right to bring a civil suit on his own behalf. Naturally, as a resident of England, Milton cannot actually press charges against More, but by wielding the Civil law so pervasively and to such devastating effect, *Pro Se Defensio* makes it clear that were Milton living under the same legal system as More, he would easily win his case.

Under Civil law, *iniuria* had two components, both of which Milton lays at More's feet. The first was contumely—*contumelia*—or derogatory speech, that which hurt a man's reputation and brought shame upon him in the community. The second was calumny—*calumnia*—or the act of making legally false accusations, that which brought a man into the peril of the law. Milton explicitly says that More has done both: he has acted *ex contumeliis* and *ex perpetuâ calumniâ* (*PSD* 5). On the one hand, the author of *Clamor* is guilty of "the foulest contumelies" (*foedissimis contumeliis*), and Milton deplores what he calls "your contumelies" (*contumelias vestras*) (*CPW* 4:724, 729; *PSD* 38, 47). On the other, Milton writes that he has been assaulted with "abuses and calumnies" (*convitiis omnibus atque calumniis*), and he charges More with "calumny" (*calumniam*) (*CPW* 4:735, 724; *PSD* 58, 39). Milton applies the term *calumnia* with precision since the author of *Clamor* accused the English people generally and Milton specifically "of robbery, of murder, of treason, . . . of parricide" (*CPW* 4:708). In fact in one chapter titled "Against

---

28. Justinian, *Digest*, 50.13.5. For more on the importance of reputation in Roman law, see E. Peters, "Wounded Names"; Bowman, "Infamy and Proof."

that foul rascal John Milton the advocate of Parricide and Parricides," the author of *Clamor* indulges in a violent fantasy of Milton being bound, tortured, and then hanged for an array of "crimes" including "murder" (*CPW* 4:1079). To accuse someone of these things was unquestionably actionable under the Roman law of *iniuria*. These accusations even fell within the more restrictive scope of defamation under English common law, since as we saw in chapter 2, accusing another of a secular crime exposed one to an action on the case for defamation.[29] At one level, Milton's Latin treatise is aimed at those who know the Civil law, specifically Civilians in England and all those who lived in Civil law countries on the Continent. But he can also count on an English readership that would recognize and fundamentally assent to the juridical standards being applied.[30]

Milton's use of the Roman law of libel in *Pro Se Defensio* extends and deepens his awareness of libel in the previous defense, *Defensio Secunda*. In a letter to Milton, Richard Watson discusses the work that triggered Milton's sequence of three Latin defenses, Salmasius's *Defensio Regia pro Carolo I*. Watson calls it a "Pasquil against the Republick of England" (*LR* 2:275). Previous chapters have touched on the fact that a "pasquil" was a term for a libel, so by Watson's logic, when Milton wrote to exonerate the English people in *Pro Populo*, he did so in response to a libelous attack. His *Defensio Secunda* is also a response to libel.[31] Milton uses the second half of his title to pinpoint the offense at issue: *Joannis Miltoni Angli Pro Populo Anglicano Defensio Secunda. Contra Infamem Libellum Anonymum*, "against an infamous and anonymous libel."[32] In *Defensio Secunda*, Milton refers to the "insults and slanders" and "calumny" that Salmasius and More have heaped on him and his fellow countrymen (*CPW* 4:558). Answering those who would say that these attacks "might better have been ignored," Milton asks, "how in the

---

29. On the relationship between ecclesiastical and common law defamation in England, see Helmholz, *Select Cases*, xi–cxi; Helmholz, *Roman Canon Law*, 56–68.

30. Having liberally accused More of *iniuria*, Milton also specifies that *Clamor* is a "defamation of me" (*altero in me diffamatorio*) (*CPW* 4:712; *PSD* 20). As Ingram observes, "defamation causes emerge as peculiarly characteristic of English society": *Church Courts*, 319. See also McRae's discussion of the early modern English preoccupation with libel and slander in *Literature, Satire*.

31. D. Loewenstein, "Milton and the Poetics of Defense," 174–75, emphasizes the importance of reading these defenses as actual defenses, although he regards a defense primarily in rhetorical and military contexts. I would add a jurisprudential layer here.

32. As Brown notes, Salmasius himself was trained in law and in legal forms of argument: Brown, "Revealed Law."

world will everyone else be convinced that the lies our enemy has told are not the truth?" (*CPW* 4:558). This was precisely the danger of libelous words. As David Cressy writes, "people were inclined to believe them."[33] While Milton begins experimenting in *Defensio Secunda* with how to respond to a libel, he does not arrive at the specifically legal approach that characterizes *Pro Se Defensio*. The stumbling block might be that in *Defensio Secunda*, he writes "not on behalf of one people nor yet one defendant, but rather for the entire human race against the foes of liberty" (*CPW* 4:557–58). This collective defense does not lend itself to using the terms and procedures of Roman law, since libel suits were launched by private individuals who felt personally wounded. Milton solved this problem with *Pro Se Defensio* when he meets More on his own legal terms. In *Pro Se Defensio*, he metaphorically crosses the Channel and meets an attack written on Continental soil also using the legal system of the *ius commune*.

LEGAL AUTHORSHIP

One of the greatest stumbling blocks that *Pro Se Defensio* presents to modern sensibilities is Milton's insistence that More can be "justly regarded" as the author of *Clamor* (*CPW* 4:704). What Milton did not know—indeed, what almost no one knew until after the Restoration—was that *Clamor* was actually written by the Huguenot cleric Peter du Moulin, who lived in London. Du Moulin secretly sent the manuscript to Claude Salmasius, Milton's opponent in his *Defensio Pro Populo Anglicano*. Busy with other work, Salmasius gave the manuscript to his protégé More, who was living with him at the time. More in turn supervised the printing of *Clamor*, corrected the presswork, and wrote the fulsome dedication to Charles II, although the preface appeared under the printer Adrian Vlacq's name. In his *Defensio Secunda*, Milton attacked More for his authorship of *Clamor*, and More responded with *Fides Publica*, in which he insists that *Clamor* was not his, quoting from multiple letters in support of this claim. Refusing to back down in the face of what looked like credible contrary evidence, Milton instead pressed his case. As a result, *Pro Se Defensio* is full of claims about authorship that defy our modern common sense. For example, Milton says that "he who published" a scandalous work "must be considered its author." He asserts that even if More is "not the author," he is still guilty, since "either by your labor or by your counsel this book was published" (*CPW* 4:701, 710). And he writes, "If I find that you

---

33. Cressy, *Dangerous Talk*, 34.

wrote or contributed one page of this book, or even one versicle, if I find that you published it, or procured or persuaded anyone to publish it or that you were in charge of its publication, or even lent yourself to the smallest part of the work," then "for me you alone will be the author of the whole work, the culprit and the crier" (*CPW* 4:712–13). These claims have struck modern readers as highly dubious. Commenting on Milton's insistence that the one who published a work is as guilty as the one who wrote it, Svendsen writes, "on this technicality Milton must rest his whole case for More's authorship" (*CPW* 4:701n8). For Svendsen, Milton is committing a form of rhetorical legerdemain by incrementally broadening his definition of authorship to include anyone remotely involved with the production of a book. This strategy enables Milton to have his rhetorical cake and eat it too: he can adopt a stance of wounded outrage at More's perfidy and yet also allow a "gradual admission of More's innocence of the text" (*CPW* 4:718n43).

However, More is innocent of *Clamor* only if we apply modern ideas of authorship. When Milton tells More, "what you say is another man's is now lawfully yours no less than his who you say it is," he is simply reiterating a fact of early modern jurisprudence on both sides of the English Channel (*CPW* 4:750). As Stephen B. Dobranski and others have shown, the modern idea of single, autonomous authorship did not apply in the early modern world of textual production.[34] One consequence of the pervasively blurred lines between authorship, publishing, and printing was that the liability for a printed work could be assigned to any one of several figures. The person whose name could be definitively linked with a work, regardless of seditious intention, could be held liable for the work's contents and thus prosecuted. A survey of Roger L'Estrange's vigorous use of the late-seventeenth-century courts to control the press reveals little of our modern concern to differentiate between the culpability of authors as opposed to that of printers and booksellers.[35] Printers were especially apt to be held accountable since "it was the printer who affixed his/her name to frequently anonymous works." As a result, "it was printers who were frequently tarred with the brush of originative agency" and punished in the place of the authors.[36] The trial of the printer and bookseller Edmund Curll provides a good example. When Curll was brought to trial for publishing the erotic *Venus in the Cloister*, he argued, first,

---

34. Dobranski, *Milton, Authorship*.

35. Hinds, "Roger L'Estrange," 26. On the Stuart tendency to prosecute everyone involved in a transgressive book, see also Dzelzainis, "Managing."

36. Nevitt, "Women in the Business," 104n12.

that he was only the printer, not the author, and second, that the work was simply a translation "not bearing my Name." Although Curll reasoned that he should not be "doomed to suffer for the Sins of other Men," he was convicted and sent to the King's Bench prison.[37] While it is easy for modern readers to interpret such outcomes as symptoms of the period's oppressive judicial system, Curll's imprisonment resulted just as much from a different legal definition of what counted as authorial liability. As Jody Greene argues, the idea that liability for a work should primarily follow the person who actually wrote it began to emerge only after the passage of the 1710 Act of Anne, which established copyright protections. Before that point, booksellers, printers, and authors could all be collectively or severally punished depending on a variety of legal and political factors, and there was no prevailing sense that convicting a printer was less just than convicting the "real" author.[38] Milton's *Areopagitica* shows this societal assumption that either authors or printers could be legitimately pulled up, if necessary, in the law's dragnet, for he refers approvingly to a parliamentary statute requiring that "no book be Printed, unlesse the Printers and the Authors name, or at least the Printers be register'd" (*CPW* 2:569).

The identity of the true author was particularly irrelevant in the case of libel. In his commentary on Star Chamber's examination of John Lamb under suspicion of libel, Sir Edward Coke writes that a conviction for libel can lawfully apply to the man who is "either a contriver of the Libell, or a procurer of the contriver, [or] a malicious publisher thereof, knowing it to be a Libell."[39] The modern idea of authorship—what Coke calls the "contriver"—is only one of three culpable categories, since guilt can be just as readily assigned to the "procurer" or the "publisher." Even just being found holding a libel could expose someone to the penalty of law. This precept was part of Roman law regarding the false accusations characteristic of *famosi libelli*, and it had been absorbed by early modern English common law. As Coke explains elsewhere in his *Reports*, if any man finds a libel "and would preserve himselfe out of danger," he must either "burne it, or presently deliver it to a Magistrate."[40] In England as on the Continent, this definition of liability in the case of libel remained in force through at least the end of the eighteenth century, for the emi-

---

37. Rogers and Baines, "Prosecutions," quoted at 183. For a similar point that liability for printed materials could extend to anyone involved in producing it, see also Johns, *Nature of the Book*, 159–60.
38. Greene, *Trouble with Ownership*.
39. Coke, *Exact Abridgment*, 343.
40. Coke, *Exact Abridgment*, 236.

nent jurist William Blackstone writes that people can be punished "for either making, repeating, printing, or publishing the libel."[41] As in Coke's definition, "making" a libel is one of several ways to expose oneself to the penalties of law, with "repeating," "printing," and "publishing" being equally culpable. Thus when Milton says that More is guilty because he is "a party either in composing this libel" or "in procuring its composition," or when he claims that the one who publishes a work is as guilty as the one who writes it, he speaks the language of both English and Continental jurisprudence (*CPW* 4:701).[42] Procurers, printers, and publishers were particularly imperiled when the libel in question was anonymous. In his *Considerations and Proposals in Order to the Regulation of the Press*, L'Estrange writes that "*the* Person *in whose Possession*" a libelous book is found should "*be Reputed, and Punish'd as the* Author *of the said Book, unless he* Produce *the Person, or Persons from whom he received it.*"[43] Milton had a personal brush with precisely this capacious construction of authorship when he was questioned before the House of Lords on December 28, 1644. The Lords were searching for information about an anonymous libel, and Milton was asked if he knew "the author, printer [or] contriver" of the work.[44] Based on his comments in *Pro Se Defensio*, Milton agreed with the Lords' assumptions about who could be held responsible for injurious words. He writes that he has assigned authorship to More, "seeing that no one else comes forth" and because "no one but yourself has yet appeared" to claim the work (*CPW* 4:713, 701).

Milton repeatedly pauses to remind his readers that his construction of

41. Blackstone, *Commentaries*, 4:151.

42. As an experienced and learned man of his time, More almost certainly knew that his role in *Clamor* had exposed him to legal liability. This knowledge perhaps explains why he omitted his name from the dedication and asked Vlacq, the printer, to sign his name instead. More's position of aggrieved innocence in *Fides Publica* is more or less what Milton deems it: after-the-fact scrambling intended to avoid the unintended consequences of his actions. Milton quotes from three of the recently ratified Articles of Peace between the English Commonwealth and the Dutch United Provinces, all of which provide that neither country shall receive the enemies of the other and that any known enemies must be expelled under pain of death (*CPW* 4:706–7). As Milton points out, More translated these articles, and so he understood the stakes for concealing his role in a work that attacked the English people. Milton writes, "to confess is so very perilous to you" and "to forswear that book is a matter of so much importance to your safety, your comforts, and almost your life" (*CPW* 4:708).

43. L'Estrange, *Considerations and Proposals*, 2. L'Estrange considers "*Authors* or *Compilers*" as a single category of "*Grand Delinquints*," and they are only one shade guiltier than the "*Printers* and *Stationers*" (32).

44. Masson, *Life*, 3:295.

authorship follows early modern legal norms. He pronounces More's guilt and then says, "by right and by the most just laws the same judgment has been agreed upon by almost all nations." He writes, "I adduce that which is admitted by everyone, the civil imperial law," and then he backs up this claim with two excerpts from Justinian's *Institutes* on the law of *iniuria* (*CPW* 4:713). The first holds that "if any, to the infamy of another, shall write, compose, or publish any libel or poem or history, or with evil intent shall cause any such to be done, etc.," then that person is liable to prosecution. The second excerpt specifies that blame can be attached to the one who writes, composes, publishes, or causes to be published, "even though he publish under the name of another or without a name." Given that these standards were more or less universally shared across the *ius commune*, Milton reasons that European nations would "all decree" that the man who procures, publishes, or edits a work "shall be considered and punished as the author" (*CPW* 4:713). Two pages later he tells More, "I am not concerned over whether [*Clamor*] is yours or not," because since More is "its publisher, or supervised its publication," he is guilty "by the general agreement and intent of all laws." The "laws and justice of all nations declare" More to be "the Overseer as the Author" of *Clamor* (*CPW* 4:715). As "the proven overseer and editor of that book," More can be "considered the author by the justice and laws of all nations" (*CPW* 4:746, 736). Milton is relentlessly grounding his argument in the broad assumptions of the *ius commune*.[45]

Here is Svendsen's response to these arguments and particularly to the except Milton quotes from the *Institutes*: "Luckily . . . [Milton] found a passage in Justinian which declared the editor or publisher of an anonymous writing legally responsible for it and in the eyes of the law its author. This is Milton's neck verse, so to speak, for he was right in asserting that More edited the *Clamor* and composed the dedication." So skillfully does Milton build his flawed case that by the end "the reader is prepared to believe More the author in fact as well as in law."[46] Svendsen is mistaken on three fronts. First, his comment about Milton's "lucky" find of Justinian hardly gives credit to

---

45. The anonymous biographer (probably Cyriack Skinner) underscores the justness of Milton's approach: More had represented Milton as an "injurious Defamer" by labeling him as the author of *Clamor*. However, Milton had "very good testimonies" and "circumstantial proofs" that "justify'd" his belief, and More's protests to the contrary were ultimately "shallow Evasions." Like Milton, Skinner is drawing on early modern legal assumptions about the nature of reliable evidence in cases of anonymous authorship. See Darbishire, *Early Lives*, 28.

46. Svendsen, "Milton's *Pro Se Defensio*," 18.

the titanic stature of the *Institutes*. Second, Justinian's precept had migrated outward over the centuries and become the animating principle behind most legal pronouncements regarding liability for printed materials, so in citing Justinian's view of libel, Milton is effectively citing the entire corpus of Civil law. Moreover, as Helmholz shows, the Roman law of *iniuria* had shaped defamation as construed by English canon law, which then transmitted its underlying assumptions about transgressive speech to the common law courts.[47] As a result, Justinian's ideas about libelous speech were as foundational to native English common law practices as to Continental jurisprudence. Third, Svendsen creates a tendentious opposition between authorship "in fact" and "in law," suggesting that the former is real and compelling while the latter is just a matter of niggling technicalities. We see here evidence of the modern impulse categorically to separate law and morality, an impulse that the seventeenth century did not share. Svendsen sees Milton as being both specious and logically slippery. To the contrary, Milton is building a perfectly coherent juridical argument, and it seems strange to us only because its premises are ones that the modern world does not share.

FAMA: THE IMPORTANCE OF REPUTATION AND HEARSAY

Just as Milton's definition of authorship does not match modern common sense, so too his pervasive reliance on hearsay evidence seems an affront to fair and evidence-based argumentation. For example, Milton claims that he can convict More because the "common report" ascribes *Clamor* to More, and in support of his claim for More's authorship, Milton quotes a letter from a correspondent in Leiden who refers offhandedly to "that book of More's entitled *The Cry of the Royal Blood*" (*CPW* 4:704, 710). These hardly seem like just legal grounds. Similarly, justifying his claim that he is proceeding "lawfully" against More, Milton cites the fact that he has relied only upon "that report which, arising from informants both honest and well known, jurists teach us to approve as testimony" (*CPW* 4:704). In a modern court governed by strict rules of evidence about what is and is not admissible, Milton's reliance on the "report" about More or on a secondhand comment in a letter would be immediately disallowed. As a result, when Milton claims that this hearsay evidence moves his argument out of the realm of "rumor" and into the realm of "just proof and . . . witnesses," he seems to be indulging in outrageously thin argumentation (*CPW* 4:710).

47. Helmholz, *Select Cases*.

However, the world of early modern Civil jurisprudence did not share the modern restrictions on hearsay evidence. Judges were allowed to listen to hearsay evidence, and the courts had even developed elaborate rules for how and when hearsay about a person or event could be used. The different outlook of Civilian jurisprudence on derivative proof hinges on the crucial role played by *fama*. The *fama* about a person was her general reputation or the common report about her actions and character. In contrast with our modern world, *fama* in the *ius commune* "was one basis of proof and status." For example, the statutes of Renaissance Florence, like those of many other cities, "liberally allowed public fama as both a sufficient basis for initiating judicial proceedings on a number of matters and as evidence in them."[48] Commenting on the degree to which judges could act on the common report about an individual or an event, Richard M. Fraher writes that "an entire subcategory of jurisprudence" had developed concerning *fama* and its subsets of *notorium* and *manifestum*.[49] Echoes of the rules of *fama* also informed legal proceedings under English common law. As Coke writes about *Hext v. Yeoman*, a man "for suspicion of felony" could be imprisoned "and his life [brought] in question" by means of a trial.[50]

Throughout *Pro Se Defensio*, Milton explicitly appeals to the Civil law understanding of *fama*. When he cites "the common report, unanimous, invariable," he uses the Latin phrase *famam communem* (*CPW* 4:704; *PSD* 9). He refers to "the report [*fama*]" that has "obtained universally" and "the common opinion [*fama*]" (*CPW* 4:704, 705; *PSD* 10, 11). He points to the "rumor" (*fama*) against More, to the "invariable report" (*famam constantem*) of More's authorship (*CPW* 4:710, 711; *PSD* 18, 19), and to "ubiquitous report" (*passim fama*) (*CPW* 4:732; *PSD* 52). As is evident from these excerpts, Milton is hammering relentlessly on the word *fama*. Moreover, he is at pains to show that the *fama* about More would hold up in a Continental court of law since it comes from what the courts called *bones et graves*, good and wise men. For example, Milton says that the *fama* about More's authorship comes from "many men of passable discernment" and from "no vulgar men" (*CPW* 4:708, 705). He bases his argument for More's guilt on the standard of what the "good and sensible man" would credit and on the report of "a very intelligent and honorable man" (*CPW* 4:717, 711).

48. Kuehn, "*Fama* as a Legal Status," 29, 35.

49. Fraher, "Preventing Crime," 225. As Fraher points out elsewhere, *fama* had something of the same standing that probable cause does in the modern legal world since it provided enough reason to initiate an investigation: Fraher, "Conviction," 33.

50. Coke, *Exact Abridgment*, 105.

Early modern assumptions about *fama* also underpin Milton's account of how More seduced Pontia, a lady-in-waiting in the house of Salmasius. Responding to More's claim in *Fides Publica* that Milton has no evidence and no witnesses to this fact, Milton writes, "call into judgment, if you wish, common and constant Fame [*Famam ipsam communem, constantem*], and those hundred or rather thousand mouths. There are many witnesses. If credit is often publicly given them, why should I not credit them about a public adversary" (*CPW* 4:758; *PSD* 94). To modern eyes, this looks like evasiveness: unable to produce a witness, Milton invokes the general rumor mill. But Milton is again standing on solid legal ground since the story of More's conduct in the house of Salmasius was so widely bruited as to have passed beyond the purview of any single witness and into the realm of what everyone simply knew. Critics who do not appreciate the jurisprudential functions of *fama* can arrive at a mistaken understanding of Milton's work. For example, Stewart scoffs, "'the common report, unanimous, invariable' . . . is [Milton's] exalted characterization of the anonymous witnesses vouching for More's authorship of Clamor." Stewart sees this reliance on *fama* as evidence of how far Milton has strayed from the paths of reasonable argumentation: "the blind Milton's dependence on the hydra-headed 'Fama' is perhaps the most telling sign of the extent to which this controversy has . . . [become] a contest for personal credibility."[51] But while Stewart views *fama* as mere rumor and thus as inadequate grounds for any serious allegation, Milton's Latinate, European readers would have thought of it quite differently, steeped as they were in Civil law assumptions and procedures.[52]

However, *fama* is not the sole basis for Milton's argument, and having established the *fama* about More, he then moves beyond it. The direct testimony of eyewitnesses was an even stronger form of proof, and so Milton is careful to base his attribution of authorship not on "report alone" (*non famâ solum*) but also on "that testimony than which nothing can be more certain," including "eye-witnesses" (*CPW* 4:714; *PSD* 22). Elsewhere, he says that his charges against More come "not from rumor alone" (*non famâ, inquam, solâ*) but also from "very scrupulous witnesses" (*CPW* 4:715; *PSD* 25). When he refers to the "very clarity of the testimony" offered by these witnesses, Milton

---

51. Stewart, "Speaking to the World," 56.

52. Milton was not the only person who was interested in the *fama* about More's conduct. Sometime in late 1652, More was reported to have started a lawsuit against Salmasius. Then by early 1653, More and Salmasius's wife were fighting openly in court, and Salmasius was collecting evidence about More as a "fornicator" (*scortatorem*) (*LR* 3:319–20).

echoes the Civil law benchmark that proofs had to be "as clear as the light of day" in order to be credible (*CPW* 4:718).[53] In the *ius commune*, the testimony of two reliable eyewitnesses was required in order to convict someone, and *Pro Se Defensio* conspicuously adheres to this standard. Milton reproduces an anonymous letter from the Hague indicating that More had delivered *Clamor* to the printer, and then on the grounds that Civil law "rejects a single witness," he also provides an excerpt from a letter from Amsterdam: "It is very certain that almost everyone throughout these parts considers More as the author of that book ... for he himself corrected the sheets as they were taken from the press, and some copies display More's name subscribed to the dedication, of which he was likewise the author" (*CPW* 4:717). Having met the legal bar of two credible eyewitnesses, Milton then pushes beyond it, introducing into evidence another letter that he calls a "a third witness." As he says to More, "you shall not say that any part of the law due to you was abridged by me" (*CPW* 4:717).

The only greater form of proof was a confession, and Milton says that he has this too. Focusing on More's authorship of the preface of *Clamor*, Milton writes that "there are many who have heard from your own lips that the preface is yours" and that More has "confessed [himself] to be the writer" (*CPW* 4:715). Milton is also thinking about what counted legally as a confession when he describes the trial of More that almost happened in Geneva. As Milton narrated in *Defensio Secunda*, More had had sexual relations in Geneva with a woman named Claudia Pelletta. He had seduced her by making promises of marriage and then later rejected her, and when she complained against him, he accused her publicly of slander. Although Pelletta then filed civil charges, the case was never brought to trial, not because More was innocent but because the Genevan Council wanted to avoid scandal.[54] In *Fides Publica*, More argued that Milton had neither proof nor witnesses to support his claims. In *Pro Se Defensio*, Milton answers this charge:

> Why do you require witnesses of me ... when you fled those places where there were? Return to Geneva where you were long ago found guilty of

---

53. Milton's witnesses in *Pro Se Defensio* are excerpts from letters that he has obtained, and it is worth remembering that unlike the modern common law world where a trial is fundamentally a personal encounter based on oral testimony, Civil legal proceedings centered on the steady compilation of a dossier of written evidence. Moreover, any explicit restrictions on the use of hearsay did not extend to written documents. Damaska, "Of Hearsay," 436.

54. Svendsen, "Milton's *Pro Se Defensio*."

those crimes. Say only that you wish a legal judgment to be made concerning these matters for the sake of suppressing these calumnies; you will find those who, with the greatest good will, would share your wish to try these crimes by law. . . . Witnesses will not be lacking. (*CPW* 4:756)

Since More "fled the trial offered," he is "condemned by [his] own judgment" and thus has no right to require that Milton produce witnesses and proofs. Milton here argues with the full force of law at his back. Conspicuously avoiding a trial was tantamount to a confession. By agreeing to leave his position in Geneva in return for a quashing of Pelletta's lawsuit, More tacitly confessed to wrongdoing, and therefore the Civil law threshold for conviction has been met.

INFAMIA: WHY MORE CAN'T TESTIFY

Much of what scholars have read as Milton's rehashing of salacious stories and an unsportsmanlike heaping of abuse on More is instead Milton's attempt to show that More has met the legal bar of *infamia*. As its name implies, *infamia* meant that one's *fama* was bad. An infamous person was someone of poor character, one about whom the whole community had nothing good to say. Milton's reliance on the standard of *infamia* is unambiguous. For example, More is "sunk in every kind of infamy [*omni infamiâ*]" (*CPW* 4:711; *PSD* 20); he is "infamous" (*infami*) (*CPW* 4:793; *PSD* 148); his turpitude brands him with "infamy" (*infamiam*) (*CPW* 4:802; *PSD* 164); and he has been unable to conceal his "private and domestic infamy" (*privatae atque domesticae . . . infamiae*) (*CPW* 4:817; *PSD* 188). Importantly, *infamia* was not simply an indicator of one's low reputation. It also brought with it a whole set of specifically legal disabilities. When Milton sets out to show that More is "sunk in infamy," he is not just undertaking what Svendsen calls a "character assassination unworthy of him."[55] He is trying, through the careful presentation and management of evidence, to demonstrate that More meets the legal bar of *infamia* and thereby to win the legal challenge that he mounts in *Pro Se Defensio*.

Legal and social infamy could be acquired in many ways. For example, infamy could be assigned to those who had committed a crime and been formally sentenced, to certain kinds of professions (e.g., pimps, prostitutes, gladiators, actors, etc.), and to those who had committed "insult, fraud, [or]

---

55. Svendsen, "Milton's *Pro Se Defensio*," 18.

trickery."[56] *Pro Se Defensio* turns crucially on the fact that infamy was also applied to those who could be shown to have committed adultery or to have engaged in loose sexual behavior. More's sexual predations are thus at the heart of Milton's jurisprudential argument. As he says, his title page should have addressed *"Alexander More, Adulterer and Lecher"* instead of *"Alexander More, Priest"* (*CPW* 4:723). As a subset of *fama*, a verdict of *infamia* could be applied when the evidence against someone was "public knowledge that is . . . so widespread as to constitute in effect the testimony of an eyewitness," and so merely the presence of general notoriety became "a sufficient if merely presumptive proof."[57] In order to establish a presumptive proof of More's rapacious libido, Milton emphasizes the unanimous outcry against him. For example, he quotes a letter from Ezekiel Spanheim that More's sexual predations were "commonly repeated in the mouths of all . . . charges which can be clearly corroborated by the authority and assent of the whole assembly, nay by the accession of still more charges" (*CPW* 4:781). More's loose behavior with women is "the common talk," and a letter from John Dury shows that "the opinion of almost all men" is against him (*CPW* 4:779, 781). Milton aims at the legal bar of infamy in other ways. When he accuses More not only of "lecheries" but also of "perjuries [*perjuria*] by the help of which you escaped from judgment," Milton seems mindful of the fact that known perjurers were considered *infames* (*CPW* 4:758; *PSD* 94). Those with criminal reputations were also infamous, and toward the end of *Pro Se Defensio* Milton increasingly argues that More's "depravity" (*scelera*) has pushed him over the criminal threshold (*CPW* 4:781; *PSD* 132). He alludes to More's "previous crimes [*facinora*]" (*CPW* 4:778; *PSD* 129) and to men ready to "offer in testimony your crimes [*tua crimina*]" (*CPW* 4:780; *PSD* 131). Describing the charges brought against More in Geneva, Milton calls him a "criminal" (*reum*) (*CPW* 4:789; *PSD* 142). While words like *scelus* and *facinus* had the broadly generic meaning of a wicked deed whether illegal or not, *crimen* and especially *reus* carried more specifically legal inflections. Milton is not just saying that More is a bad man; he is also saying that More is a bad man who has broken the law.

As a set of peremptory exceptions, *Pro Se Defensio* hinges on the fact that as a legally infamous man, More has no right to press a case against Milton or generally to be believed about any issue. Under the provisions of Civil law, *infames* were subject to a wide range of legal disabilities (for example, they

---

56. Justinian, *Digest*, 3.2.1.
57. E. Peters, "Wounded Names," 69; Fraher, "Preventing Crime," 225.

could not make a will or hold public office). For Milton's purposes, one of the most important of these was that infamous persons could not be witnesses or be parties to lawsuits. The *Digest* makes this point emphatically. For the Roman jurist Paul, "A person found guilty of corruption cannot witness a will or give evidence." For Arcadices Charisius, "A person held liable for a defamatory verse is an incapable witness." And for Callistratus, some people cannot give evidence because of "marks of bad repute in their way of life."[58] In effect, the testimony of the *infamis* was legally worthless. This logic explains why Milton so repeatedly emphasizes the evidentiary flaws in More's case. For example, in asserting More's responsibility for *Clamor*, Milton can cite the widespread public *fama* about More's role in writing or procuring it. In contrast, Milton draws attention to the fact that most of More's evidence boils down to More's own assertion about himself. He writes, "you mean to reduce the whole affair to a few words: 'I am not,' you say, 'the author'" (*CPW* 4:745). When More claims, "My friends are not silent," Milton replies, "Out of your [own] mouth." When More says that preachers support him, Milton replies, "On your credit." More says that "Ambassadors confirm" his innocence, and Milton answers, "Out of your letters." Milton steps back and summarizes More's case: "what is all of this save that singular denial of yours made in the beginning, 'I am not the author'" (*CPW* 4:745). In modern jurisprudential terms, Milton is displaying a mulish and unreasonable determination not to believe More's testimony about himself, for in our contemporary court system, unsavory people are not automatically barred from testifying in court. However, a whole branch of Civil jurisprudence rested on the assumption that those shown to be infamous would simply not be listened to. For example, the jurist Papinian asks, "can someone found guilty of adultery witness a will?" The answer is no, "he is barred from testimony," and thus a will "witnessed by such a person is invalid at civil law."[59]

These contemporary ideas about *infamia* and valid testimony explain Milton's anecdote about the visit paid to him by "two noble gentlemen, friends of mine." Worried about his precarious professional position and aware that Milton was preparing another work (*Pro Se Defensio*) against him, More sent a letter to the Dutch ambassador, who then approached John Thurloe, the English secretary of state. As a concession to English/Dutch relations, Thurloe asked two men (whose names we do not know) to visit Milton and ask

---

58. Justinian, *Digest*, 22.5.15, 22.5.21.1, 22.5.3.5. For an extended discussion of infamy in Roman law, see Tatarczuk, *Infamy of Law*.

59. Justinian, *Digest*, 22.5.14.

him to "give credit to [More's] letter" and thus to refrain from writing *Pro Se Defensio*. Milton describes his response to this attempted intercession:

> I replied that what they demanded was not honest; that More did not deserve such faith and that it was not customary, against the common report and a fact otherwise sufficiently proved, to credit a mere letter of an adversary and an accused party making a denial concerning himself. (*CPW* 4:740)

When he says that a man of More's character does not "deserve such faith," Milton is not necessarily being vengeful. He speaks instead the juridical logic of infamy. More supervised the printing of *Clamor* and wrote the preface, and so for him to disavow all relationship to the treatise amounts to perjury. Imagining the scales of justice with, on the one hand, "the common report" (again, Milton uses the term *fama commune*) and "a fact otherwise sufficiently proved" (here he uses the legal term *res*) and, on the other, the "letter of an adversary" who is also the "accused party," Milton reasons quite correctly that "it is not customary" to credit the latter. According to the translation above, Milton told the two visitors that their request "was not honest." But the Latin original, *non esse aequum*, also carries another set of inflections (*PSD* 67). *Aequum* could indeed mean "honest," but in context it more properly carries the sense of "equitable" or "just." The translation "honest" keeps us in the realm of Christian morality, but *aequum* is as much about early modern jurisprudence. Milton says that the visitors are making a legally invalid—literally, inequitable or unjust—request. Even the two gentlemen seem to have agreed. Milton writes that recognizing "that they had nothing which they could say in answer to this," they ceased to plead More's case.

The logic of legal infamy also explains why, having first traced all of More's so-called witnesses to his innocence of *Clamor* back to More himself, Milton then moves in the second half of his treatise into a consideration of More's sexual reputation:

> But since I have duly proved, contrary to your hope and opinion, that you are the author of [*Clamor*], though a lying and protesting one, I do not doubt that I shall be able to produce an impartial belief among all fair judges of affairs concerning your debaucheries also. (*CPW* 4:755)

Milton closely examines all the evidence for More's sexual transgressions, adding to some of the stories he first told in *Defensio Secunda* about More's inability to control himself around women. He writes, "it seems that, wherever you go, the maids can never escape you" (*CPW* 4:777). First, there was the woman in Geneva, Pelletta, whom More debauched with promises of marriage and who tried to bring a civil suit against him. Then there was Elisabeth Guerret, the lady-in-waiting to Mme. Salmasius (Milton refers to her as "Pontia," evidently unaware of her real name). When he seduced Guerret at the home of Salmasius in Leiden, More was not only committing adultery with a married woman but also betraying his host. Again, there were signs that More would be the target of a civil suit, and again, the Leiden synod decided not to arraign More owing to his legal and political maneuvering, although it did ban him from all Leiden pulpits.[60] Milton also mentions a widow whom More was said to have sexually assaulted and a woman in Amsterdam whom More reputedly seduced. As Svendsen shows, these were not empty allegations. Having narrowly escaped prosecution in both Geneva and Leiden for his sexual predations, More was charged by the Synod of Tergou in 1659, and Svendsen calls the indictment "a lurid document, accusing More of the most spectacular venery," including soliciting a girl in Middelburgh, visiting a prostitute in Amsterdam, and being a regular at brothels.[61]

Milton critics have generally misunderstood the role that More's sexual offenses play in *Pro Se Defensio*. Svendsen shows that More was clearly guilty of various sexual crimes, but then he adds, "his guilt of course had no bearing whatever upon his authorship of the *Clamor* . . . but few patriots in the seventeenth century could be expected to admit that, least of all Milton."[62] Svendsen is here making modern juridical assumptions that simply did not apply in the early modern world. Since we have no legal equivalent to infamy, Milton's attacks on More's sexual proclivities in a work about his authorship of *Clamor* look like gratuitous character assassination. But in the early modern *ius commune*, as in early modern English common law, a broad-spectrum weighing of character had everything to do with how legal guilt was apportioned. Milton welds More's two offenses together: More has both denied any responsibility for *Clamor* and also denied the "reproaches" (i.e., the sexual reproaches) against him. Thus in response Milton proceeds along both axes: "If I show our calumniator to be lying, dishonorable, perfidious throughout his life, I do thereby make it more easily believed" that he is lying about the authorship issue (*CPW* 4:737). Similarly, when he accuses More of both *flagitiorum*

---

60. Sellin, "Alexander More," 244, 246.
61. Svendsen, "Milton's *Pro Se Defensio*," 2.
62. Svendsen, "Milton's *Pro Se Defensio*," 22.

and *iniuriarum*, "debauchery" and "injury," Milton is not gratuitously hooking together unrelated offenses, for establishing the first is a crucial part of his argument for the second (*CPW* 4:701; *PSD* 6). More complained in *Fides Publica* about precisely this linkage of his sexual conduct with the authorship question, writing that Milton's many jabs at his character are not "honorable" because they "have nothing to do with the case" (Milton quoting More at *CPW* 4:736). More's claim seems credible to modern eyes because it has become our modern jurisprudential norm: while a man accused of, say, embezzling might reasonably expect to be cross-examined about whether or not he paid his taxes, most judges would disallow inquiries into his sexual misconduct as being irrelevant to the case at hand. But when Milton and More were writing, an assessment of character—including sexual misconduct—was central to the process of weighing guilt or innocence. According to the *Digest*, "the value of testimony depends on the dignity, faith, morals, and gravity" of the witnesses, the plaintiff, and the defendant.[63] Thus Milton articulates a basic jurisprudential assumption of his day when he answers that men of "proper judgment" will agree that "nothing is of greater moment in the judgment of a cause [*causam*] than the quality and manners" of those involved (*CPW* 4:736–37). A *causa* was the term for a case in Civil law court, and so Milton is saying that those who pronounce legal as well as moral judgments in the *ius commune* understand the importance of knowing the character of both the plaintiff and the defendant.

In order to clinch his claim that More meets the legal bar of infamy, Milton must also demonstrate that he himself does not. This is not simply because he wants to feel righteous by comparison. Rather, as with so much about *Pro Se Defensio*, Milton's stress on his own good *fama* serves a jurisprudential end. If a bad man besmirched the name of a good man, he was infamous. If he besmirched the name of another bad man, he was not, because the *infamis* had no reputation to lose. Thus an important component in Milton's claim for More's infamy is a corresponding stress on his own clear reputation. For example, he says that he has "credit among good men," and he carefully refutes each one of the "crimes" that More laid to his account, such as the fact that he had had the temerity to praise Christina of Sweden and that he had traveled abroad with only one servant (*CPW* 4:767). He challenges More to swear with him the following words: "I call God as my witness that I have always lived upright and undefiled" (*CPW* 4:773). The implication is that More could not do so without committing perjury. Svendsen reads Milton's emphasis on his

---

63. Justinian, *Digest*, 22.5.2.

own good character as evidence of his neurotic "preoccupation with integrity" (*CPW* 4:791n230), but Milton is not displaying a narcissistic absorption with his own virtues. Rather, he is simply making a legally sound argument.

SHAMING OPPONENTS, PROTECTING THE CHURCH

By failing to see the essentially legal nature of *Pro Se Defensio*, many critics have arrived at a misunderstanding of Milton himself, for this treatise has often been read as showing us an unpleasant side of Milton's character. In Michael Lieb's words, *Pro Se Defensio* regrettably "says at least as much about the victor as the victim."[64] The most common lament is that Milton stoops to personal attack. Svendsen, for instance, calls it Milton's "most sanguinary *argumentum ad hominem*; nothing in its treatment of Salmasius or Hall equals its violence" (*CPW* 4:687). Similarly, Stewart writes that Milton's determination to use More's sexual misdeeds against him "underscores his commitment to an extreme form of the *argumentum ad hominem*."[65] But Milton is not committing the logical fallacy that Svendsen and Stewart accuse him of. He makes personal attacks not because he has no other ground on which to proceed but because personal reputation was the very foundation of *iniuria* and *infamia* claims.[66] *Pro Se Defensio* can also offend modern sensibilities because of the degree to which Milton tries to shame his opponent, and it is hard for us not to feel some sympathy for the poor underdog More bearing the brunt of Milton's attacks. Admittedly, the author of *Clamor* first shamed Milton, but we want our favorite author to be above returning tit for tat, to refrain from retaliatory mudslinging. But once again, these are sensibilities that fail to appreciate the role that honor and character played in the early modern juridical world. As Samuel Edgerton shows, Renaissance Florence often punished criminals and delinquents by ordering their pictures—literally, *pittura infamandi*—to be painted on city walls. The whole point of these pictures was to bring public shame and humiliation on the offender and thereby to exert communal pressure for him or her either to leave the community or to repent and reform.[67] Florentine officials were just following precepts they found

---

64. Lieb, *Milton and the Culture of Violence*, 220.
65. Stewart, "Speaking to the World," 52.
66. Moreover, as McRae points out, in the early modern period "the spheres of the personal and the political were intricately intermeshed" and so this kind of language was more central to public discourse than modern readers have typically appreciated: *Literature, Satire*, 52.
67. Edgerton, *Pictures and Punishment*, 91–125.

in the *Digest*. Libelers should be named publicly so that "public good [can] emerge from the exposure," and "the sins of those who do wrong should be noted and noised abroad."[68] As we saw in chapter 2, this idea of collective policing was not confined to the Continent. Herbert speaks the language of infamy on both sides of the English Channel when he reasons that people can sometimes speak ill of one another "because infamy is a part of the sentence against malefactors, which the Law intends, . . . that they may be known."[69] The crucial role that shame played in policing public norms also explains why Milton says that "to defame the villainous and to praise the good . . . are at the same time both equally just and constitute almost the sum of justice" (*CPW* 4:794). Lieb reads statements such as this as indicators of Milton's psychic frailty: having been wounded in print by More's *Clamor*, Milton needs to "repristinate" himself by piling up odium on his opponent's head, and so the many *ad hominem* attacks in the treatise and especially the descriptions of More's sexual activity reveal Milton's intense anxiety about his own sexual purity.[70] However, when we situate the treatise within its contemporary legal context, we can see that what Lieb sees as evidence of an unstable psyche is actually sound jurisprudential reasoning.

Ultimately Milton frames his attacks on More as an attempt to protect the international Protestant church. Toward the end of the treatise, Milton dwells at length on the fact that More the sexual predator is also More the Protestant minister. In his archival investigations of the charges brought against More by the synod of Tergou, Paul R. Sellin observes that despite More's undisputable sexual misconduct, he still managed to leapfrog from one clerical position to the next. Svendsen comments on the same phenomenon: More would get into hot water for his promiscuous actions and then "would obtain some kind of clearance, even testimonials"—usually issued to avoid scandal—and "move on to another post, where he repeated himself."[71] Milton is outraged at the fact that More has so abused his clerical position. He can hardly believe "that there is a man so unregenerate in the church—in the Reformed Church, indeed" (*CPW* 4:763). More's actions are a "disgrace . . . insufferable in the church," and he has "afflicted God's church with . . . great ignominy" (*CPW* 4:718, 760). Given that the laws of Solon prevented anyone known to be *infamis* from orating to the people, "how much more shameful is it that

---

68. Justinian, *Digest*, 47.10.5.11 and 47.10.18.
69. Herbert, *Country Parson*, 166–67.
70. Lieb, *Milton and the Culture of Violence*, 207–25.
71. Sellin, "Alexander More," 17.

a fornicator and adulterer . . . should possess the most pernicious right to preach in a church" (*CPW* 4:761–62).

Because men shown to be *infames* were barred from public service and especially from clerical office, by making a case for More's infamy Milton is effectually trying to prevent him from finding a ministerial position. More has "deserved reviling and infamy," and so Milton encourages European readers to "drive far off from the walls of the church this prowling wolf" (*CPW* 4:761). Milton takes particular aim at the officials in Geneva who allowed More to escape trial because they wanted to avoid scandal. Milton imagines them as "partly worn down, partly persuaded, partly afraid that some of the man's ignominy might overflow upon the public, partly thinking it the obligation of their own virtue to pardon offenses" (*CPW* 4:792). But this stance just allowed More's "contagion" to creep "from the pastor into the flock, from the doctor into the school," a reference to the fact that More subsequently obtained a university position. Milton worries that More might harm "those same good men's children who are entrusted [to him] for their learning." He fears that the fact that no one has punished More may inspire others to think that they can "cast off a like villainous character upon the schools and churches, with no danger to themselves" (*CPW* 4:793). This is the problem that Milton aims to correct, for he uses *Pro Se Defensio* to exert what leverage he can to keep More out of pulpits and out of schoolrooms.[72] He writes that "sometimes from private enmities public transgressions are wont to be censured," meaning that a private lawsuit intended to redress a personal wrong may at times result in a more widespread benefit to society (*CPW* 4:796). Milton says that *Pro Se Defensio* is impelled by precisely this motive: he has "stooped to this contention with More," a task he calls "not at all pleasing, but still necessary," precisely because "there is no place for pests of this kind . . . in the reformed church" (*CPW* 4:793, 792).

---

72. On Milton's horror at the news that More had been given a church in Charenton, see Masson, *Life*, 5:366–69.

CHAPTER 6

The Tithes of War: Paying God Back in *Paradise Lost*

In his divorce tracts, Milton criticizes the canon law for what he calls its "obstinate *literality*." The canonist is the "extrem literalist" who is "literally superstitious" (*Doctrine and Discipline, CPW* 2:279, 340, 343). An overly literal reading of God's words is not simply spiritually injurious; it can lead to material damage, even annihilation: "the strictest observance" of biblical precepts "may oftime prove the destruction not only of many innocent persons and families, but of whole Nations" (*Tetrachordon, CPW* 2:588). As I argued in chapter 4, *Doctrine and Discipline* and *Tetrachordon* juxtapose the canonists' literality with the more equitable approach Milton finds in Roman law, and this equity allows him to argue that "Christ meant not to be tak'n word for word" (*Doctrine and Discipline, CPW* 2:282). This same opposition between literality and equity is equally central to his 1659 pamphlet *Considerations Touching the Likeliest Means to Remove Hirelings Out of the Church* (henceforth *Likeliest Means*). In this work, Milton shifts his gaze away from the canon law of marriage, and he looks instead at the canon law of tithes. During most of the early modern period, tithes were required by canon law, and Milton and his like-minded contemporaries were dismayed that while the Interregnum government had abolished many elements of the canon law courts, tithes had not changed. In June 1659, tithes became even more compulsory since instead of being enforced by the canon courts, they were mandated by an act of Parliament, and common law judges on their provincial circuits were required to read the statute.[1] Milton

---

1. Woolrych discusses the circumstances leading up to this act and subsequent developments in *CPW* 7:73–82. Hutton points out that tithes were an important pressure point in 1659

argues in *Likeliest Means* that the tithing mandate destroys "Christian libertie" (*CPW* 7:292). As in the divorce tracts, he associates the canon law of tithing with a rigidly literal reading of the Bible, as when he argues that pro-tithers fail to see that tithes in the Bible "were fitted to the *Jewes* only, a national church of many incomplete synagogues" (*CPW* 7:292). He says that the Bible verses about tithing should be read not as stipulating a "legal right" but as open to "the rule of common equitie" and the "very light of reason and of equity" (*CPW* 7:290, 280). Similarly, Milton argues that the canon law's literal approach leads to violence, and he describes the "violent and irreligious exactions" that result from forced tithes: men blinded by "covetousnes and rapine" will "fetch by force that which is not thir own." Ultimately the canon law of tithing makes "the name of Christ accessory to violence" (*CPW* 7:296-97).

About the same time that he wrote *Likeliest Means*, Milton began composing *Paradise Lost*, and the same aversion to the canon law of tithes seen in the prose treatise also plays a key role in his epic poem. Scholars have traditionally identified only one brief moment when the issue of tithing impinges on the epic: right after Satan leaps the border hedge around the Garden, Milton writes, "So since into his [God's] Church lewd hirelings climb," a simile that likens Satan to those men drawn to the ministry by the scent of money (*CPEP* 4.193). However, as I argue in this chapter, the contemporary problem of tithing has left a wider footprint in Milton's epic than critics appreciate. Indeed, it profoundly shapes his depiction of Satan. A whole series of legal and financial allusions weave through Satan's puns during the second day of the war in heaven as he exults in the power of his newly forged cannons. These allusions summon up both general ideas about financial indebtedness (the subject of this chapter's first section) and also the specific question of tithes (the subject of the second section).[2] By putting the language of indebtedness in Satan's mouth in book 6, Milton connects the war in heaven to the sense of oppressive debt that Satan expresses in his soliloquy in book 4. Because

---

and that debates over them contributed to the collapse of the Protectorate: *Restoration*, 47. Although *Likeliest Means* includes Milton's most sustained discussion of tithes, other, equally unfavorable comments can be found in *Of Reformation* (*CPW* 1:613); *Animadversions* (*CPW* 1:717-22); *Tenure of Kings and Magistrates* (*CPW* 3:196, 241); and *Defensio Secunda* (*CPW* 4:65-51).

2. My discussion of the legal/financial allusions in these puns differs from previous discussions that emphasize their scatological and sexual elements. See J. N. King, *Milton and Religious Controversy*, 122-24, and Fish, *How Milton Works*, 95-97. On the puns as Milton's attempt to "expose the nature of rhetorical bad faith," see Gregerson, *Reformation of the Subject*, 227.

he feels burdened by the "debt immense of endless gratitude," Satan seeks symbolically to "quit" that debt on the battlefield through the most violent means he can devise (*CPEP* 4.50, 49), and Milton glances at the fact that "to quit" could mean both to repay someone and to revenge a wrong.[3] Satan's engines of war are his way of paying God back for what he experiences as the humiliation of indebtedness. Instead of paying tithes to God with the proper currency of gratitude, Satan converts his debt into cannonballs, and as we will see below, this act of paying a tithe through an alternative currency was itself the subject of intense legal debates during the seventeenth century. When Satan alludes to forced tithing on the battlefield, Milton delivers on his claim in *Likeliest Means* that the canon law of tithes creates hostility and violence.[4] Echoing Satan's own puns but at a larger conceptual level, Milton shows how easily the ecclesiastical law's ordinances can be turned into ordnance and its canons into cannons.

SATAN'S "DEBT OF GRATITUDE" AND "TERMS OF COMPOSITION"

People who supported tithes in seventeenth-century England often characterized them using the early modern language of debt. For example, the pro-tither John Carter writes of the "*eternall* debt of tithes" that all people owe to Christ, and the antiquarian Henry Spelman says that "Tithes are required as a debt."[5] Thus in order to understand what Milton thought about the canon law of tithes, we have to understand prevailing early modern ideas about debt itself. In *Paradise Lost*, Satan chooses war as a means of debt relief because he understands his debt in a particular way. In his book 4 soliloquy, he accurately sees the true nature of this debt but then almost immediately distorts it. Satan is correct that he owes God a "debt . . . of gratitude" (*CPEP* 4.50). As scholars

---

3. *OED Online*, s.v. "quit," v., def. 1a and 3b. For general discussions of the war in heaven, see Revard, *War in Heaven*; Lieb, *Milton and the Culture of Violence*; Freeman, *Milton and the Martial Muse*.

4. Satan's struggle against God has most commonly been connected to the emerging seventeenth-century discourse of international law: J. S. Peters, "'Bridge over Chaos'"; Warren, "Milton and the Epochs." I am interested instead in how Milton invokes domestic laws of tithing and debt. By doing so, he ironically emphasizes that Satan remains under God's jurisdiction.

5. J. Carter, *Vindiciae Decimarum*, 4; Spelman, *Larger Treatise*, 91. Spelman's work was regarded by many in the period as the definitive treatise supporting tithes. Its anti-tithing counterpart was John Selden's 1618 *History of Tithes*.

such as Peter Medine and Seth Lobis have shown, Satan's book 4 soliloquy reprises the thinking of Aquinas, Cicero, and Seneca on the subjects of gratitude and obligations.[6] All three writers distinguish between legal and moral debts. Legal debts can be paid off through material means in a manner agreed upon by the parties involved. In Aquinas's words, "proportionate repayment" is a fitting response to "the legal [debt] due," as when "it is contracted that so much be paid for so much." If one has enough time and/or resources, the legal debt can be discharged. Aquinas contrasts the legal debt with the moral one: "the repayment that belongs to the virtue of thankfulness or gratitude answers to the moral debt and is paid spontaneously."[7] It is impossible to pay a moral debt through purely material means since the moral debt springs from within the individual. Aquinas gives as an example the fact of having been brought into the world by one's parents. Strictly speaking, this moral debt can never be repaid since the child can never return to the parents the same gift of life that she received. In this sense, moral debts are endless. However, regarded from another angle, moral debts are more easily acquitted than legal ones. As Lobis points out, for Seneca as well as for Aquinas, "willingness, not wealth, is all one needs to repay the debt of gratitude."[8] Thus a beggar can repay a king simply through the act of saying "thank you." At one level, Satan understands that his moral debt to God could have been easily repaid. He says, "a grateful mind / By owing owes not, but still pays, at once / Indebted and discharged; what burden then?" (*CPEP* 4.55–57). This is a classic expression of the Thomistic/Stoic/Ciceronian idea that the moral debt of gratitude is "discharged" in the very act of sincerely attempting to pay it.

Although Satan momentarily recognizes that his debt to God is a moral one, Milton also shows him working to convert it into a legal debt. For example, Satan asks himself, "What could be less than to afford him praise, / The easiest recompense, and pay him thanks, / How due!" (*CPEP* 4.46–48). Words like "afford," "recompense," "pay," and "due" suggest that Satan is thinking of his debt in quasi-financial terms. Similarly, his sense that his debt is "burdensome" and "a burden" tells readers that he understands his debt in the wrong way. As Aquinas explains, the moral debt that created beings experience is not burdensome because its currency is love. Paying that debt is no more onerous than loving someone because the more we receive, the more we

---

6. Medine, "Gratitude"; Lobis, "Satan and the Problem of Gratitude." I am grateful to Prof. Lobis for the chance to read his conference paper.

7. Aquinas, *Summa Theologica*, 2a2ae 106, 2.

8. Lobis, "Satan and the Problem of Gratitude," 8.

have to give back, a reciprocal dynamic that epitomizes Milton's ideal of true conversation. In fact, as Medine argues, the Thomistic idea of moral debts paradoxically opens up the possibility of a radical freedom. God pours down tremendous gifts, and in the process, he gives human beings and angels the choice to repay these gifts through voluntary acts of reverence. Repaying the debt of gratitude is thus an "exertion of ultimate freedom" in that it "makes one godly—godlike—and reveals the state of grace."[9] The fact that Satan experiences this debt of gratitude as a burden suggests that he thinks of it in a legal rather than a moral register.[10]

Although Satan feels unjustly oppressed by his legal debt, he actually has strategic reasons to want to reconceive it in legal rather than moral terms. First, legal debts were contracted between relative equals. To give an example from Milton's own experience, in 1627 Richard Powell gave Milton a defeasible bond in which he confessed his indebtedness in the amount of £300 (*LR* 1:137). This was a freely contracted exchange between two men who were social equals. If Satan can think of himself as owing God a legal debt, then God is not infinitely above him in the cosmic hierarchy. Second, the person with a legal debt does not have to pay from the heart. When considering legal debts, one asks "did the debtor pay?" and not "did he pay in a spirit of love or hatred?" Thus thinking of his debt in legal terms allows Satan to imagine rendering a payment other than reverence. Third, legal debts are more easily evaded than moral ones, in the sense that they do not endlessly renew themselves. Although it took some legal effort on his part, Milton was eventually able to distrain the rents from Powell's estate for long enough to repay the debt owed to him and cancel the bond. Satan is in a different situation. His debt to God results from his status as a created being and not from a signature on a defeasible bond or statute staple. As a result, he carries that debt around inside him in much the same way that he eternally bears a "Hell within him" (*CPEP* 4.20). By converting his moral debt into a legal one, Satan thereby externalizes it, as when he fantasizes that by moving "one step higher" in the heavenly hierarchy, he could "quit / The debt immense of endless gratitude" (*CPEP* 4.50–52). His hope recalls the modern financial phrases "to climb out of debt" or "to be in the hole" of debt. Satan thus construes his debt as the result of circumstances, not as an intrinsic fact of his existence. This impulse

---

9. Medine, "Gratitude," 122.

10. For discussion of how the language of debt in this passage reflects early modern financial concerns, see Hawkes, *Culture of Usury*, 71–88; Hawkes, *John Milton*, 312–13; Haydon, "*Paradise Lost* and the Politics of the Corporation," 147–48; Im, "Between Habbakuk and Locke."

to externalize his debt echoes his approach to most problems. As Steve Fallon shows in his study of Milton's materialist monism, Satan is the voice of Cartesian dualism who most intransigently "attempts to separate the material from the spiritual."[11] In effect, Satan treats his sense of indebtedness much like the rich man in *Areopagitica* treats his religion. Too busy to cultivate his religion himself, he commits its care to another, and so his religion "is now no more within himself" but has become instead a "dividuall movable" (*CPW* 3:544). For Satan, the advantage of turning his debt into a "dividuall movable" is that he can then weaponize it.

The legal/financial language Satan uses in his book 4 soliloquy recurs two books later in the middle of the war in heaven. Sardonically anticipating the results of firing his newly invented artillery into the puzzled ranks of good angels, Satan says that he and his followers have come to "discharge / Freely our part," an echo of his desire in book 4 to be "discharged" of his obligation to God (*CPEP* 6.564–65; 4.57). Satan's battlefield pun depends on the fact that "discharge" looked in two directions. On the one hand, it could mean the act of firing a gun. On the other, it had a number of early modern meanings relating to shedding or paying off obligations. For example, to "discharge" could mean "to relieve of a duty, debt, or other obligation," often used in relationship to those who were bankrupt; "to pay (a debt)"; "to pay (a creditor)"; and "to pay for (goods, services, etc.)."[12] The word "part" in Satan's claim functions similarly since in addition to its relevant usage as one side in a battle, a "part" could also mean a duty or obligation.[13] Satan wants to "discharge" his weapons into his enemies and in the process to "discharge" any legal debt to God. This attempt to discharge his cannons/debt reveals the anxiety running underneath his earlier claim to Abdiel that the angels were "self-begot, self-raised / By our own quick'ning power" (*CPEP* 5.860–61). As Lobis argues, Satan refuses to see that God ceaselessly gives the gift of love throughout eternity. Instead he "held in his mind only one of God's manifold gifts, the first one, creation, and became fixated on and paralyzed by its unrequitability." Thus the fantasy of self-creation he expresses to Abdiel is "the fantasy of a debt-free existence."[14] When he characterizes his cannons as engines of debt repayment, Satan reveals how persistent his sense of indebtedness really is.

---

11. Fallon, *Milton among the Philosophers*, 224.
12. *OED Online*, s.v. "discharge," v., def. 3a, 3b, 3d, 3e.
13. *OED Online*, s.v. . "part," n., def. 17a, 11.
14. Lobis, "Satan and the Problem of Gratitude," 5.

Because he could not simply cancel it out with a boast of being self-begot in book 5, Satan must resort to a more violent attempt at erasure in book 6.

Milton's image of war as a form of debt servicing works because the early modern imagination easily elided coins and cannonballs. For example, in his *True and Briefe Relation of the Famous Siege of Breda*, Henry Hexham refers to the English "Cannoniers" as having "payd [the enemy] with their owne coine, as fast as ever they could discharge."[15] When the English artillerymen "discharge" their cannons, they throw metal balls that Hexham figures as "coine," a usage that tacitly equates military and financial exchanges. Similarly, James Mackenzie says that Irish cannoniers inside the city of Londonderry "repay" their besiegers "in the same coyn" by hurling cannonballs "of about ten pound weight each."[16] The coinage/cannonball metaphor was an apt one because both were in their own ways forms of currency: transactional objects passed back and forth between agents that thereby expressed human relationships (e.g., obligation, hatred, greed, etc.) in material terms. In sonnet 17, Milton glances at the idea of ammunition as a form of coinage and vice versa when he identifies the "two main nerves" of war as "iron and gold" (*CPEP* 8). The coinage/cannonball analogy was also reinforced by the fact that both were created by similar means from similar raw materials. When Satan imagines digging "Deep under ground" and smelting the hidden "materials dark and crude" to make "implements of mischief," he speaks the language of both the weapons maker and the coinage minter (*CPEP* 6.478, 488). This conjoining of the martial and financial is reinforced by the verb "to pay" in both Hexham's and Mackenzie's accounts. To "pay" someone could mean to remunerate in a monetary sense, but it could also mean to get even, in much the same way that to "quit" a debt could mean to satisfy it through repayment or revenge.

Satan's attempt to shift his debt out of a moral register is reflected in the legal puns in this section of the poem. For example, before he fires his cannons, Satan urges his opponents to listen to what he "propounds," and after the cannons have razed the ranks of good angels, he and Beelzebub congratulate themselves on having "propounded terms of composition" (*CPEP* 6.567, 612). Satan is enjoying a pun on "propound" as to bring forward an allegation or a pleading in a formal legal action.[17] The juridical overtones continue when

---

15. Hexham, *True and Briefe Relation*, 45.
16. Mackenzie, *Narrative*, 32.
17. *OED Online*, s.v. "propound," v., def. 1b.

Beelzebub answers in "like gamesome mood" (*CPEP* 6.620). Although there are no specifically legal definitions for "gamesome" in the *OED*, Milton's one other similar usage appears in *Doctrine and Discipline of Divorce* where he describes lawyers as "gamesters," suggesting that the word had a legal flavor for him. Satan adopts a similarly legal stance when he calls on heaven twice in succession to serve as a witness to his battlefield proceedings. He proclaims, "however witness Heaven, / Heav'n witness thou anon" (*CPEP* 6.563–64). This double stress on the need for a witness resonates with the important role witnesses played in early modern debt cases. Repeatedly, these cases turn on whether or not obligations have been repaid. At one end of the spectrum, a debtor might argue that he had fully discharged his debt but that the creditor was still forcing him to pay (a situation that could occur if the debtor had neglected to secure a written acquittance). At the other, a creditor might argue that the debtor had never paid a penny and that the written discharge was forged. And there were innumerable positions in between, usually involving evidentiary questions about who had paid how much to whom and under what circumstances. As a result, witnesses were of paramount importance when contracting and especially when acquitting debts. For instance, when the bond debt that Richard Powell owed Milton was finally repaid in full, the discharge had two witnesses: a Chancery clerk wrote that the obligation "is altogether Cancelled vacated and made voide" and then added, "I know the above named John Milton." Below this statement, the Lord Chamberlain wrote that the bond debt was "Discharged . . . because I saw the said Recognizance cancelled in [Milton's] hands" (*MC* 296). Standing before the massed armies, Satan impudently expects God to serve the same function as the Chancery clerk and the Lord Chamberlain and attest to the fact that he has come to pay what is owed.

Even denser legal associations surface when Satan describes himself as seeking "Peace and composure" (*CPEP* 6.560). He uses a cognate form when he mockingly tells Beelzebub that he offered "terms / Of composition" to the enemy forces who are writhing on the ground with joy, a sardonic description of the results of firing cannonballs into massed ranks of angels (*CPEP* 6.612-13). Editors of *Paradise Lost* have typically captured only one facet of these puns: to "compose" could mean to settle military differences, and so Satan sarcastically describes his weapons as a means to seek peaceful composure.[18]

---

18. For example, Roy Flannagan glosses this line as Satan's faux attempt to reach a military "peace and treaty": Flannagan, *Paradise Lost*, 524n173.

In the seventeenth century, the words "composition" and "composure" also had particularly intense legal and financial associations. Compositions usually involved the delivery of coinage from one party to another, as when Milton describes the inhabitants of Canterbury "coming to composition" with their enemies for £3,000 (*History of Britain, CPW* 5:343). The link between composition and money became more pronounced in 1643 when Parliament established the Committee for Compounding for the Estates of Royalists and Delinquents. The Commonwealth government sequestered the property of all those considered to be delinquents (virtually a synonym for royalists in Milton's day),[19] and those who wished to regain possession had to appear before the committee to compound for their estates. While this process typically included a pledge never again to take up the king's cause, the core component of almost all compositions was a fine. For example, Milton's royalist brother, Christopher, submitted a petition "to compound to free [his estate] out of Sequestracion," and he agreed to "satisfye and pay such ffine as by this Comtee. for Composicions with Delinquents shall be imposed" (*LR* 2:156).[20]

In book 6 of *Paradise Lost*, Milton presents a parody of this kind of compounding in which the good angels serve as a version of the committee and Satan as the compounding delinquent. Whereas Christopher Milton made his composition and paid his compounding fine in order to come to peace with his opponents, Satan does the opposite. His "terms of composition" are merely camouflage for a renewed offensive, and instead of literal money, he pays his compounding fine with a "hail / Of iron globes" (*CPEP* 6.589–90). These "iron globes" serve as a form of counterfeit currency. "Feit" comes from the French *fait* or "made," so Satan's ammunition is literally counter-feit in the sense of being made the wrong way, from cold metal instead of from the immaterial stirrings of the grateful heart. Milton reinforces this association in book 4 when Uriel looks down and sees that Satan is himself "counterfeit" (*CPEP* 4.117). Playing on the fact that coins had faces stamped onto them, Milton means that Satan's face has been disarranged by passion. Satan has "marred

---

19. *OED Online*, s.v. "delinquent," n., def. 2.

20. Ironically, Milton himself also had to sue for composition because he had an extent on Richard Powell's Wheatley property. In one of his Chancery bills, Milton explains that since Powell was a royalist and his property was sequestered, Milton was forced "to compound . . . for . . . Tithes lands Tenements and premisses for that the said Richard Powell in his life tyme was reputed A delinquent" (*MC* 307). See also W. R. Parker, *Milton*, 397. For more on the way that compounding for royalists' estates worked for creditors, see Habakkuk, "Public Finance."

his borrowed visage" in the sense that he no longer looks like the blooming cherub who approached Uriel in book 3 (*CPEP* 4.116), and Uriel can now see the "counterfeit." This image of Satan as himself a form of counterfeit currency simultaneously invokes the idea of Satan the counterfeiter in book 6 who delivers a corrupted, mismade coinage on the field of battle.

Words such as "composition," "compounding," and "composure" could be so readily used in the context of settling post–Civil War differences because they already had the more widespread and general meaning of negotiated agreements between creditors and debtors. The common lawyer Sir Thomas Blount gives a typical definition in his law dictionary, *Nomo-lexicon*: a composition is "an end or order set down between a Creditor and a Debtor."[21] Those who found themselves drowning in debt could approach their creditors with an offer to compound. For example, the debtor might offer pay through a substitute asset such as by signing over a mortgage or bond. Or he might describe the wasted state of his finances and then ask to have the debt reduced and the repayment period lengthened.[22] Creditors often accepted this kind of offer on the grounds that a lower return was better than the risk of no return at all. As a creditor himself and the son of a scrivener, Milton would have had ample experience with how these composition arrangements worked, all the more so as debt composition was the primary type of law that Christopher Milton practiced after the war.[23] In early modern financial terms, when Satan describes his artillery as a form of "composure" and as "terms of composition," he is offering to pay off his debt through alternative means. Since he owed a moral "debt . . . of gratitude," acts of reverence are the only appropriate form of coinage. However, Satan offers to "compose" his debt differently and to acquit it in a more material way.

The battlefield is a fitting location for Satan's attempt to compose and then to discharge his debt. Seneca describes the way that a consciousness of unpaid debts could give rise to hatred. For some people, "the more they owe, the more they hate," and they feel the "Mortal hatred, that . . . arises from the Shame of an abused Benefit." Satan's sense of an immense debt similarly leads him straight to an equally immense hatred of God. And as Seneca explains, this sense of indebtedness converts easily into aggression: when debtors are "Conscious of not paying the Debt," they "wish the Creditor out of

---

21. Blount, *Nomo-Lexicon*, s.v. "chevisance," n.

22. Debt composition functioned as an informal precursor to true bankruptcy laws, which did not enter English legal and financial culture until early in the eighteenth century.

23. Campbell, "Milton, Sir Christopher."

the way."²⁴ In Senecan terms, Satan wants simultaneously to cancel out his debt and to cancel out his creditor. His battlefield "balls / Of missive ruin" serve as a means to both ends (*CPEP* 6.518–19). In early modern English financial practices, debt instruments were often canceled by drawing crosshatched lines of ink over the face of the document. Sometimes, however, the acquittal was more literally incisive. When the 1627 Powell loan was finally repaid, the witness note in the Lord Chamberlain's book that the debt had been finally "Discharged" was accompanied by a physical defacement of the bond instrument itself. Someone—perhaps Powell, Milton, Milton's agent, or the Chancery clerk—took out a knife and in the presence of the Chancellor cut razor-thin slits in a crosshatched pattern across the surface of the document.²⁵ Appropriating and dialing up this means of marking debts as paid, Satan forges—literally "composes"—weapons that then serve to compose and acquit what he owes, in the process attempting to destroy his enemies and injure God.

THE TITHES OF WAR

Thus far, my discussion of debt has operated at the broad level of those obligations that people might owe to one another. However, when he shows a created being, Satan, misconceiving of his debt relationship to his creator in material terms, Milton also invokes the supercharged seventeenth-century legal issue of the tithe. For Milton, the basic problem with the canon law of tithes was that it turned what should have been a strictly moral debt into a legal one. In contrast, a pro-tithe writer such as Spelman agreed that tithes were a moral debt, but he also stressed their legally binding nature: they are owed in conscience, and they are owed under English canon law, which has the right to enforce them. Spelman even calls tithes "God's rent" in order to emphasize that tithes paid to one's parish priest are morally and legally binding in the same way as rent paid to one's landlord.²⁶ Because tithes were seen as legal debts, the tither's intention was of secondary importance, and tithes handed over in a spirit of resentment were almost as good as those paid in

---

24. Seneca, *Seneca's Morals Abstracted*, 158–59. Similarly, Aristotle writes, "debtors wish their creditors did not exist": *Nicomachean Ethics*, book 9, 1167b21.

25. See Recognizance of Statute Staple, 11 June 1627, National Archives C152/61. I am grateful to Susan Moore for assistance with this document.

26. Spelman, *Larger Treatise*, 89. Milton derisively quotes this phrase in *Likeliest Means* (*CPW* 7:292).

a spirit of cheerful willingness. William Prynne stresses this point when he writes that tithes should not be regarded in the manner of voluntary charity or alms, which are a "free Benevolence." They are instead a "just Debt and Duty" commanded by the Bible and enforceable at law.[27]

Milton had no patience with this view of tithing, and in *Likeliest Means* he sets out to refute it, arguing that ministers should be maintained solely by the voluntary donations of their congregations. Whereas the majority of anti-tithers concentrated on the pragmatic inequalities of the existing tithing system, Milton focuses instead on the fundamental harm that tithes do to Christian religion.[28] In *Likeliest Means*, he argues that to require tithes by law brings the corrupting power of lucre into the church. It creates "hirelings," men who become ministers to have comfortable benefices and to enjoy the pleasures of well-stocked libraries and barnyards. It also hurts parishioners, since men and women forced to pay tithes soon learn to grudge at religion as a whole. Milton's view of tithes crystallizes early in *Likeliest Means* in his discussion of Abraham and Melchizedek, a story that features as something of a biblical ur-text in early modern tithing debates. As Abraham and his army return home victorious from battle, the priest-king Melchizedek meets them in the field with gifts of food and drink, a passage that theologians had for centuries read typologically as the clergy administering the Eucharist to the laity. In return, Abraham gives Melchizedek "tithes of all" (Gen. 14:20). Most biblical references to tithing come from the later Mosaic law, and so anti-tithers used this fact to argue that tithing was part of the old covenant: Christ released believers from the duty to tithe when he released them from other restrictive ceremonies such as circumcision and dietary laws. However, pro-tithers used the Abraham and Melchizedek story to make a counterargument. Because this story predated the revelation on Mount Sinai, pro-tithers saw it as proof that the tithe mandate stretched back to the earliest days of the Israelites and is thus a binding moral obligation on all believers. In *Likeliest Means*, Milton offers two rebuttals. First, Abraham's motive for the tithe was "partly his gratitude to requite" Melchizedek for the gift of food and "partly his reverence to the person and his benediction" (*CPW* 7:285). His tithing was spontaneous and voluntary, and so this passage does not support an argument for forced tithes. Second, Abraham's tithes are simply a material expres-

---

27. Prynne, *Gospel Plea*, 9.
28. Woolrych, "Milton against Hirelings," 93. Milton's view of tithing has received relatively little critical attention. Other than Woolrych's introduction, the primary discussion is Hawkes, "Concept of the 'Hireling.'"

sion of a spiritual truth: they symbolize "that subjection, which all the faithful, both ministers and people owe to Christ, our high priest and king." They are a "signe of homage and subjection" and a "signe of allegiance due to our eternal king" (*CPW* 7:286, 287). As symbols, they should not be taken literally, and Milton argues that the only true tithe is subjection to God, not material gifts given to the clergy.

At various points in books 4 and 6 of *Paradise Lost*, Milton invokes the tithe debate. When Satan confesses in soliloquy that he owes God a "debt immense . . . of gratitude," Milton echoes his claim in *Likeliest Means* that Abraham gives tithes out of "gratitude" (*CPW* 7:285). Abraham has the "grateful mind" that Satan lacks, and whereas Abraham freely gave as an expression of that gratitude, Satan finds the debt of gratitude to be "burdensome" (*CPEP* 4.55, 53). In book 4, Satan admits that he refused to honor his obligation to God because he "'sdained subjection" (*CPEP* 4.50). This behavior contrasts with Milton's account in *Likeliest Means*, for unlike Satan, Abraham willingly gives tithes to express that "subjection" which he owed to God, the ultimate source of all good things (*CPW* 7:286). When Satan malevolently tries to pay his obligation to God through a coinage other than freely given submission and reverence, Milton creates a poetic enactment of what he saw as the debased logic of forced tithing. Milton's image of Satan as engaged in a militarized version of tithing also reprises his comments in *Likeliest Means*. The earliest biblical form of tithes occurred when "*Abram* and his whole armie" gave Melchizedek the "spoiles" of battle (*CPW* 7:285). But whereas Abraham renders gifts of thanksgiving in the wake of battle and in celebration of peace, Satan uses a skewed form of tithing in order to trigger more slaughter. In *Likeliest Means*, Milton uses the term "heave offering" to describe biblical tithes: for example, he calls them a "heave-offering to the Lord," and he writes that Jacob offered the Levites "first a heave-offering" (*CPW* 7:281, 288). The Hebrew word for heave offering is *terumah*, which itself comes from a verb stem meaning "to lift up." Satan makes his own ballistic version of the heave offering. In the process, Milton provides a poetic reenactment of the intensity and hostility associated with the seventeenth-century tithe debate, which in General Monck's memorable words had become an "issue of blood."[29]

Satan's offer to seek "composure" and "composition" with his enemies also takes us straight into the practice of tithe negotiations and early modern jurisdictional tensions. In the previous section, I discussed Satan's "terms

---

29. Quoted in James, "Political Importance," 18. Tithing disputes became even more heated after 1660 when many ejected ministers returned to their benefices.

of composition" only in a secular context as a settlement between a debtor and creditor. However, "composition" was also a widely used term in ecclesiastical tithing contexts. Like debt compositions, tithing compositions were the means through which laity and clergy agreed upon alternative forms of payment. The basic logic of tithing was that since God had caused gifts such as crops and cattle to multiply freely upon the earth, it was only just that people who benefited from this unearned bounty should render a tenth of it to God's clerical servants.[30] Thus, biblically speaking, tithes should be paid in kind: every tenth sheaf of wheat, every tenth piglet, etc. Even in a relatively traditional, agrarian economy, the idealized system of in-kind—or praedial—tithes presented a welter of complications (e.g., what if the farmer had only nine piglets?). Praedial tithes had eventually been supplemented by personal tithes, which were a percentage of the fruits of one's industry (e.g., tanning leather or weaving cloth).[31] Over the centuries, changing work habits, new forms of land use, and an increasingly mercantile economy had placed this system under increasing strain. To give an example, imagine a farmer who chose to let his fields lie fallow for two years and to support his family instead by agistment (pasturing someone else's sheep) and by cutting the trees on his land for lumber. He did not owe praedial tithes on the sheep since their wool and lambs were not his to give—although a priest could argue that he should pay personal tithes from his agistment revenue. Moreover, trees were not considered titheable at all, a fact that had led to many bitter disputes in the ecclesiastical courts.[32] In theory, then, this farmer's tithing obligations would be cut almost in half as a result of his changing occupation.

In cases such as this, the solution was for the farmer and the clergymen to work out what was known as a composition. For instance, the farmer could agree to pasture the vicar's sheep among the others under his care. Or he

30. For historical discussions of tithing in the seventeenth century, see Hill, *Economic Problems*, 77–131; James, "Political Importance"; Spaeth, *Church in an Age of Danger*; Shiels, "'Right of the Church'"; Simpson, "Continuum of Resistance."

31. This system was further complicated by the introduction of mixed tithes and by the division of praedial and personal tithes into great and small tithes that went, respectively, to the vicar and the rector. After the dissolution of the monasteries, the classification of tithes was entangled by the many lay owners of tithes, men who had impropriated tithe lands and who thus had a legal claim on the titheable produce of those lands. On the innumerable legal disputes resulting from tithes, see Helmholz, *Oxford History*, 433–73. Steve Hindle has traced one mid-century tithe dispute that shows how tithing expressed complex understandings of community and obligation: "Micro-Spatial Dynamics."

32. On tithes and trees, see Helmholz, *Oxford History*, 449–50.

could agree to repair the vicar's fences and outbuildings while his fields lay fallow. While compositions could take a variety of forms, the most common solution involved both parties agreeing to a monetary equivalent of in-kind tithes, and many people felt that the impersonal tithe of coins was less wrenching than handing over calves or haystacks.[33] In the instance above, in addition to personal tithes on his agistment revenue, the farmer might agree to pay a percentage of the income he received on his lumber sales. Understandably, these tithe compositions had to be constantly renegotiated as people changed their forms of work, purchased lands with different forms of yield, or relocated to new parishes. Especially since inflation had devalued long-standing arrangements, it is easy to see why Helmholz calls composition cases a "growth enterprise" in the early modern period.[34] For example, the first canon law case that the Civilian lawyer Sir Julius Caesar discusses in his legal notebook is *Ayers v. Crowe*, in which a priest, Ayers, had "compounded with the parishioners" but then sued one of them, Crowe, on the grounds that that composition was not being paid. Caesar records the varying testimony about the tithe agreement. One witness who "depose[d] of the composition" was ultimately contradicted by others, and the result was a great "diversitie touching the composition." The case was made more complicated by the fact that others besides Ayers had taken "benefite by the composition." In the end, Crowe could not prove that his *probatione compositionis* or "alleged composition" (for a lesser sum) was in fact what had been agreed upon, and the verdict went to the cleric-plaintiff, Ayers.[35] Caesar's observations about this case provide us with a reasonable indicator of how and why composition disagreements filled the church courts, a reminder of the fact that economic, legal, and theological matters were more mingled in the early modern worldview than in the modern one.

In *Likeliest Means*, Milton discusses the possibilities under which tithes—and, to clarify, he is talking about the "good" kind of purely voluntary tithes—could be converted into a monetary form. He quotes Deuteronomy 14:23: "Thou shalt eat before the Lord thy God, in the place which he shall chuse to place his name there, the tithe of thy corn, of thy wine, and of thy oyle, etc." (*CPW* 7:282). Imagining the predicament of one of the Israelites who "could not bring his tithe in kinde, by reason of his distant dwelling from the taber-

---

33. For a useful discussion of the varying circumstances involving compositions, see Blackstone, *Commentaries*, 2:29–32.
34. Helmholz, *Roman Canon Law*, 91.
35. Helmholz, *Three Civilian Notebooks*, 1.

nacle or temple," the author of Deuteronomy explains that this man could, in Milton's paraphrase, "turn [his tithe] into monie." In early modern practice, many parishioners stopped here. Having turned the praedial tithe into cash, they paid a tenth to the parish priest. However, Milton quotes this biblical passage to make a different point, and the conversion of material goods into coins is only half the story. Once the Israelite farmer arrives at the temple, the coins are to convert right back again. He was to "bestow that monie on whatsoever pleased him; oxen, sheep, wine, or strong drink" (*CPW* 7:282). This man does not tithe money directly to God or God's servants. Instead, he uses money solely as a transport device for conveying resources efficiently from one place to another. Once the farmer reaches the temple, the money should be reconstituted into its real form. As regards the Levite, or priest, the Israelite is commanded, "thou shalt not forsake him," meaning that the tithe bounty should be shared. Perhaps most importantly, Milton writes that this reconstituted praedial tithe—now in the form of oxen, wine, etc.—is not simply to be donated as a material gift. Instead, the author of Deuteronomy instructs his readers in how to use the purchased goods: they are to invite the priest and "eat and drink thereof then before the Lord both he and his household" (*CPW* 7:282, paraphrasing Deut. 14:24–26). The tithe bearer uses his money to procure a meal for himself, his household, and the Levite priest, so that all of them can join before the Lord in an act of communion and reverence.

When Satan comes before the good angels seeking "terms of composition" and asking for "peace and composure" in book 6 of *Paradise Lost* (*CPEP* 6.612-13, 560), Milton figures him as one of those many early modern parishioners who wanted to renegotiate their tithes into another form.[36] Satan is seeking to "compose" his tithe debt by paying it not in kind—i.e., not through an expression of love that mirrors the love poured out on him—but rather by flinging the debased equivalent of coins/cannonballs. Unlike the Israelite in the passage from Deuteronomy above, Satan by his act of mock tithing does not intend to foster community between himself, his peers, and his God. Satan's parodic composition also echoes the early modern complaint that compositions were typically not as good as the in-kind tithes they replaced. In his *Petition of Two Sisters*, the early modern rector Francis Trigge likens composition agreements to the "casting of metals." Just as resmelting

---

36. While the burden of enforcing tithes had passed from the canon courts to Parliament and the secular courts during the Interregnum, after the Restoration it passed right back again. By 1661, the canon courts were back in full swing, and tithe disputes formed a major portion of their business. See Hutton, *Restoration*, 173.

metals can adulterate their purity, similarly "summes of money . . . are not so good in value, as were heretofore tithes in kind."[37] Milton depicts Satan delivering a similarly vitiated composition on the battlefield. To be clear, Trigge and Milton disagree in all other respects about tithes since despite his wariness about compositions, Trigge thinks that praedial and personal tithes should be mandatory. In contrast, Milton creates a parody of composition in order to criticize tithing in all of its aspects and to show how it brings hostility and violence into Christian worship.

Milton's critique of the canon law of tithes is simultaneously a critique of common law practices. In my discussion of defamation in chapters 2 and 3, I argued that Milton looked to English common law because it provided an alternative to what he saw as the abuses of the prerogative courts. But just because he liked the common law's approach to defamation does not mean that he thought common law was above reproach in all matters. Instead, Milton's stance toward legal systems varies according to the subject at hand. For example, in *Pro Populo Anglicano Defensio*, he feels that the common law served England well by limiting "the legal rights of kings" and ensuring that the king is "subject to the laws" (*CPW* 4:340). But as I will argue in the next chapter, his ideas about the need for locally administered justice are tacit criticisms of the common law courts. Although he repeatedly uses terms and ideas drawn from different legal systems to articulate the interplay of constraint and freedom that lies at the core of his moral vision, Milton refuses to regard any human-made system of law as a perfect expression of God's will for humanity. With the exception of canon law, toward which he is implacably hostile, he feels that all forms of law have some advantages on some issues. And the corollary is that they all sometimes act unjustly. When he criticizes compositions in book 6, Milton takes a sideswipe at a trend in contemporary common law jurisprudence. When a tithing dispute involved compositions, common law judges were increasingly prone to issue a prohibition, an order that transferred the case out of the ecclesiastical courts' jurisdiction and brought it instead into the common law courtroom, often the Court of the Exchequer.[38] The reasoning was that when tithes converted into purely monetary transactions, the layman and clergyman involved had transferred their reciprocal obligations into the realm of debt and contract, matters cognizable at common law. However, Milton felt that tithing should lie outside the jurisdiction of both canon law

---

37. Trigge, *Petition of Two Sisters*, [E7].

38. Helmholz, *Oxford History*, 304–6. The standard early modern discussion of the common law's jurisdiction over compositions is Coke's *De Modo Decimandi*.

and common law. Thus compositions are fundamentally bankrupt regardless of the jurisdiction in question, and the common law courts' enforcement of tithing compositions is an example of precisely the kind of state meddling in ecclesiastical affairs against which Milton protests so vehemently in his *Treatise of Civil Power*. Milton's desire for all jurisdictions to keep their hands off tithes is a modulated version of his position on divorce. In his divorce tracts, Milton wants to move control over marriage entirely out of the reach of the canon law and mostly out of the reach of the common law. He allows that Parliament has a—limited—role to play in legislating marriage: "the law can only appoint the just and equall conditions of divorce" and should "take care that the conditions of divorce be not injurious," conditions that would presumably be regulated by common law judges (*Doctrine and Discipline*, *CPW* 2:349, 350). While he thinks that the decision to divorce should be left up to the individuals involved, he admits the need for statutory controls on divorce's material configurations, presumably because marriage was a crucial social institution that determined the transfer of property and the legitimation of children. In contrast, he regards tithes as an exclusively voluntary and private transaction between the individual believer and the minister, and so it should lie outside the boundaries of all temporal jurisdictions.

THE GOOD TITHE

In book 3 of *Paradise Lost*, Milton provides the poem's closest approximation of how tithes ought to work. After God and the Son make plans for humanity's salvation, Milton shows the angels bursting into song: "Heav'n rung / With jubilee and loud hosannas" (*CPEP* 3.348–50). In addition to their songs, the angels also give God material gifts: "With solemn adoration down they cast / Their crowns inwove with amarant and gold" (*CPEP* 3.351–52). This image of giving gifts to God meets the criteria of proper tithing that Milton lays out in *Likeliest Means*: the gifts are spontaneous expressions of gratitude, and they are symbols of the angels' subjection. In this sense, the community of heaven is a tithing community. Importantly, the gifts are both tangible and intangible. The angels give praise, but they also give their crowns, a description that epitomizes Milton's refusal to divide matter and spirit. Milton also stresses the botanical aspects of these tithes. This passage closely reprises John the Divine's vision in Revelation 4 of the heavenly throne surrounded by worshipful beings. Among these beings are the twenty-four elders, dressed in white robes, wearing "on their heads crowns of gold." The elders then "cast their crowns before the throne" of the Most High and sing hymns of praise

(Rev. 4:4, 10). Although he generally stays close to this depiction, Milton adjusts one key detail: his angels wear crowns of "amarant and gold." Pausing to stress the botanical addition, Milton describes the amaranth's history and geography: in heaven it "grows / And flow'rs aloft shading the fount of life / And where the river of bliss through midst of Heav'n / Rolls o'er Elisian flow'rs her amber stream" (*CPEP* 3.356–59). As if the image of angels casting crowns might seem too mercantile a practice in the polity of heaven (after all, a "crown" was also a term for a coin), Milton weaves amaranth into the crowns' fretwork. In fact, in the next few lines, the gold disappears entirely, and the angels cast not crowns at all but "loose garlands thick thrown off." As a result, the "bright / Pavement . . . / Impurpled with celestial roses smiled" (*CPEP* 3.362–64). Milton here reflects the primal logic of tithes as the first fruits of the land. Those who gave tithes were rendering back to God things that God himself had caused to flourish on the face of the earth. In giving their crowns of gold and amaranth to God, the angels are returning God's own gifts. This depiction of tithing in heaven provides a counterpoint to Satan's actions. Unlike the good angels, Satan wants to drain all of the joyful spiritual content out of the action of throwing things at God, one facet of what Fallon calls his "mechanistic descent."[39] Unlike their praedial and richly botanical gifts to God, Satan's offering is a debased form of currency. His imagination pierces through the "superficial" veneer of "plant, fruit, flower ambrosial, gems and gold" that covers the face of heaven, all the things that could be considered the first fruits of the land (*CPEP* 6.476, 475). He fixes instead on things "Deep under ground, materials dark and crude" (*CPEP* 6.477). Like early modern parishioners who used compositions to convert praedial tithes into their monetary equivalent, Satan offers "terms of composition" that substitute ammunition for the floral first fruits given by the good angels.

When he connects Satan's artillery to the contemporary tithe controversy, Milton gestures toward the homology between canons and cannons. As early as *Animadversions*, Milton began playing with the similarity of these two words, for he tells his ecclesiastical opponent, Bishop Joseph Hall, "your owne Canons shall be turn'd against you" (*CPW* 1.703). He transmutes the canon law of the Church of England into weapons that are then fired at Hall himself. The elision of canons and cannons is eased by the fact that neither Milton nor his compositors made a consistent lexical distinction between them. Thus it often looks like Milton is using the "wrong" word. For instance

---

39. Fallon, *Milton among the Philosophers*. The phrase comes from the title of chapter 7, "To Shadowy Types from Truth: Satan's Mechanistic Descent" (194).

in *Colasterion* he writes of what "*the Cannon law decrees*" when, to modern eyes, he should have written "*Canon law*." And in *Eikonoklastes*, he refers to "Canons, and other deadly Instruments of Warr" when we would expect him to use "Cannons" (*CPW* 2:736, 3:452). In book 6 of *Paradise Lost*, Milton experiments further with the way that one kind of cannonry could turn into the other.[40] Another conceptual pun connects Satan's work on the battlefield to early modern forced tithes. Because of roots in *deci*- or tenth, collecting tithes was often referred to as "decimation."[41] For example, in his *Christian Directory*, Richard Baxter discusses the need for all Christians to pay "the Tenth of our revenews or increase," and in justification, he argues that "Decimation was used" by Abraham, using "decimation" as a synonym for "Tythes." Similarly, Blount gives one meaning of decimation as "tithing, or paying the tenth part."[42] In *Likeliest Means*, Milton plays on the linked meaning of decimation as both tithing and destroying, for he ends his dedicatory epistle to Parliament with the hope that England can be delivered "from the oppressions of a Simonious decimating clergie" (*CPW* 7:275). In *Paradise Lost*, Milton folds both these senses of decimation into his depiction of Satan at war. The "iron globes" shot from the mouths of cannons are a means of decimation in that they are a demonic substitute for the proper tithe of gratitude (*CPEP* 6.590), and Satan uses them to decimate the ranks of God's true servants.

40. Milton might also be thinking of a related similarity between "ordinance" and "ordnance" as referring respectively to law and military equipment. As with canon/cannon, there was no consistent lexical distinction between them, and Milton writes both of a castle furnished with "short Ordinance" and of the "Ordnance of Marriage" (*History of Moscovia, CPW* 8:509; *Colasterion, CPW*, 2:749).

41. The word originally came out of a form of Roman military punishment in which every tenth man was executed.

42. Baxter, *Christian Directory*, 196; Blount, *Nomo-Lexicon, s.v.* "decimation."

CHAPTER 7

"Justice in Thir Own Hands": Local Courts in the Late Prose

Threaded throughout this book has been the idea that the enforcement of civil order should not simply be in the hands of state officials and that people themselves should be involved in regulating the societies they live in. As David Quint points out, one of the most consistent notes in Milton's writings is his resistance to centralizing projects and impulses.[1] This resistance is at the heart of Milton's argument in *Areopagitica* that the highly participatory processes of the common law provide the best means to control and punish injurious words, and it explains his arguments in the divorce tracts that husbands and wives, not canon lawyers, should decide the terms under which marriages are made and dissolved. As this chapter argues, a similar belief informs his later political tracts. Of the six pamphlets he wrote between 1659 and the Restoration in May 1660, five contain suggestions for reforming England's laws and judicial system: *A Letter to a Friend, Proposalls of Certaine Expedients*, the document known as *A Letter to General Monck*, and both editions of *A Readie and Easie Way*.[2] In all of these, Milton advocates for a decentralized

---

1. Quint, *Epic and Empire*, 324.
2. Milton's thoughts on the judiciary have been generally overlooked by critics. Blair Worden writes that the issue "does not seem to have been high among Milton's priorities," by which he means that Milton's suggestions about law consistently follow his suggestions about constitutional structure. However, Milton's comments about law also consistently precede his suggestions for reforming education, and few would argue that education was a low priority for him. See Worden, "John Milton and Oliver Cromwell," 262.

model of legal authority, one in which local communities assume more of the work of making and applying laws.

Milton's vision of England as a nation made up of multiple small jurisdictions is exactly contemporaneous with his congregational arguments. In *Likeliest Means*, written in 1659, he writes that Christ's church should not be "ti'd to nation, dioces or parish" but should instead consist of "many particular churches complete in themselves" (*CPW* 7:292). In *De Doctrina Christiana*, he offers a similar hope: Christians should have "no national church" but rather "a great number of particular churches, each absolute in itself" (*CPW* 6:602). In his *Aphorisms*, published the same year as *Likeliest Means*, James Harrington writes, "That there may be Liberty of Conscience, there must be a National Religion" (quoted in *CPW* 7:521). Milton felt exactly the opposite: the only way to achieve liberty of conscience was to sweep away the nationalized system of religion and allow local people to create and maintain congregations of their choosing. These "particular churches" will better serve the needs of their members, and people will participate more energetically and intelligently in churches that are not part of a nationwide franchise. Milton often pairs law and religion as the fundamental systems of human society, as when he says that Roman society was founded on "Religion and law" or that God gave two gifts to humanity, "Justice" (by which he means "temporal Law") and "Religion" (*Areopagitica, CPW* 2:497; *Tenure of Kings and Magistrates, CPW* 3:222). Together, religion and law foster inner and outer righteousness, so they are the twin axes along which God's grace works in the social world. As he watched the government disintegrate in 1659–60, Milton thought about ways to protect both religion and law from chaos. In *Likeliest Means*, he proposes "particular churches" as a means to protect religion. In the five political tracts studied here, he makes a parallel proposal for protecting the law. He argues for what we might think of as "particular courts," autonomous local courts empowered to do justice in response to the needs of each community, ones he hoped would help protect the nation against tyranny.[3]

This chapter offers a broad survey of the suggestions for judicial reform Milton offers in these five pamphlets. In section 1, I look at his call for a network of local courts staffed with elected officials, and in section 2, I examine his claim that these communities should even make their own laws. In these

---

3. Milton's interest in local courts runs in parallel with his indebtedness to the idea of the corporation, a virtuous collective that exists independently from any particular constitutional form. See Haydon, "*Paradise Lost* and the Politics of the Corporation." On corporations in early modern thought, see Turner, *Corporate Commonwealth*.

two sections, I contrast Milton's thinking with contemporary developments in common law jurisprudence. Whereas common law jurists such as Sir Matthew Hale and Sir Edward Coke wanted to centralize and standardize the administration of law, Milton wants to disperse it and preserve its local irregularities.[4] However, Milton's desire to put legal justice in the hands of local communities also had its limits. In previous chapters, we have seen Milton's support for the common law model of the jury trial. I argue in this chapter's third section that over the course of these pamphlets he drifts away from the jury and inclines instead toward a Civilian model in which verdicts were given by judges. Milton's faith in the jury was an extension of his faith in the English people. That faith was at a low ebb in 1659–60, and as it dwindled, his judicial views changed. In these five works, Milton appears to be feeling for an elusive middle ground: he wants to shift judicial authority more onto the shoulders of each village and township, but, with his darkening view of the "inconsiderate multitude" of the English populace (*Readie and Easie Way, CPW* 7:446), he seems newly skeptical about the idea that juries provide the straightest path to justice. I conclude by contrasting Milton's ideal of a jury-less courtroom with the trial that his contemporary John Bunyan received. Bunyan's conviction and twelve-year imprisonment at the hands of judges alone (i.e., no jury was present) illustrates the possible risks of Milton's imagined system.

LOCAL COURTS

Milton's ideas about localized justice first emerge in *A Letter to a Friend*, which he wrote in October 1659 in response to the constitutional deadlock between the Rump and the Army. Sketching his solutions for rescuing the commonwealth from growing political chaos, Milton includes a tentative plan for amending its legal system:

> As for the reformacion of lawes and the places of judicature, whether to be hyere, as at present, or in every county as hath been long aim'd, and many other such proposals, tending no doubt to publick good, they may be considered in due time, when we are passed these pernicious pangs in a hopefull way of health and firme constitution. (*CPW* 7:331–32)

---

4. In effect, Milton supports what legal historian Richard Ford describes as the "decentralized patchwork of local courts and courts of specific categorical jurisdiction" that was more typical of English jurisprudence in earlier centuries, a patchwork of courts that was steadily disappearing as the common law consolidated its legal monopoly: Ford, "Law's Territory," 883.

This passage combines two juridical reforms. First, he wants a substantive "reformacion" of the legal code, an indication that he agreed with those who wanted to regularize the nation's vast, disorganized body of statutes and to reconcile contradictions in its case law.[5] Second is a reconsideration of "the places of judicature." On this second point, he is as yet undecided whether the courts should remain "hyere [i.e., in London], as at present" or whether new courts should instead be established in "every county." Based on his claim that these local courts have been "long aim'd," we can infer that Milton was familiar with contemporary calls to restructure the nation's judicial system. Over the course of several centuries, the authority and vitality of many smaller, local courts (e.g., hundred courts, courts leet and baron, sheriffs' courts, wapentakes, etc.) had decreased and that of the centralized common law courts and Chancery had grown. But this shift had created judicial logjams that were further aggravated by the rising levels of litigation, the relatively short windows of the law terms, and the long roads to London. While common law and equity had developed ways to expedite the administration of justice (for example, Chancery used inquests of local men to help with fact finding, and common law judges traveled the assize circuits), neither approach solved the problems of delay and inefficiency.[6]

Milton was hardly the first to suggest that fully empowered local courts offered better alternatives to the judicial status quo. Mid-seventeenth-century pamphlets by James Freize and William Cole offer representative arguments for how law and equity courts, respectively, might be improved. In *A Moderate Inspection into the Corruption of the Pratique Part of the Common Law*, Freize reasons that the best way to "establish the ancient Law of *England* in its purity, grounded on the Judicial Law of *God*" is to install "Judges in every Province, County, Hondred, Wapentake, and Town corporate."[7] Instead of having central judges visit towns on their circuits, Freize wants to embed them permanently in each community. The resulting judiciary will more closely resemble the original "purity" of the common law, and so Freize imaginatively hearkens back to an idealized time before the Norman Conquest when law was believed to be more a form of communal self-regulation than an administration of the king's writ. Freize's plan was not mere idle dreaming. William

---

5. For more on Milton's affinity for the law reform movement, see Chapman, "Milton and Legal Reform."

6. Dawson, *History of Lay Judges*, 152–57. On Chancery's attempts to blend local and central concerns, see Jones, *Elizabethan Court*, 279.

7. Freize, *Moderate Inspection*, 3–4.

Sheppard, Cromwell's law reformer, actually drew up bills proposing a network of county courts throughout England, and these were read to Parliament in 1656 at the urging of Milton's friend John Desborough.[8] Freize's plan for reforming the common law courts resembles William Cole's proposals for equity courts. Arguing that "Countrey men, Clothiers, Weavers, etc are most competent Judges of Countrey affairs," Cole asks, "Can the people of London, or Masters of Chancery, judg the equity of things acted in *Cornwall* or *Wales*, better then the chief, able men of the Neighborhood?"[9] A common practice in equity proceedings was to have depositions administered in the counties and then sent to Chancery for a final decree. However, Cole thinks that the men of the neighborhood should themselves be the "Judges of Countrey affairs."

Although in *A Letter to a Friend* Milton still seems hazy about the way to improve England's courts, his thinking soon sharpened. In *Proposalls of Certaine Expedients*, written about a month after *A Letter*, he makes clearer and more detailed arguments in favor of local courts. Milton offers ten proposals for "the preventing of a civill war now feard, and the settling of a firme government" (*CPW* 7:336). His tenth proposal reads as follows:

> Lastly, that the administration of Civill Justice may be in the City or chief towne of every county without appeal, Judges and all such officers by themselves chosen, whereby they shall have no cause to clamour against the supreame Councell, nor can hope for more equall Justice in another place. (*CPW* 7:338)

Each "City" and "chief towne" should have its own place of justice, as clear a statement for local courts as we find anywhere in the seventeenth century. Recognizing that this plan might present jurisdictional problems in cases "of severall Countyes," Milton makes provision for "a common Judicature, as ther is here, in the Capitall citty" (*CPW* 7:338). In later works, he stresses the political and ideological value of this plan, but here he is more pragmatic: Litigants will not be able to move from one court to another in search of "more equall justice," a reference to the jurisdiction hopping that so bogged down early modern litigation. Moreover, those who receive justice at the local level "shall have no cause to clamour against the supreame Councell," Milton's solution to the fact that seventeenth-century Parliaments spent a disproportion-

---

8. Matthews, *William Sheppard*, 194–200.
9. Cole, *Rod for the Lawyers*, 9.

ate amount of time hearing cases on appeal from the lower courts.[10] It is not clear what Milton means when he says that these courts will administer "Civill Justice." The phrase could be a catchall term for legal justice as a whole—in other words, justice that applies to the *cives*, the body of citizens—in which case Milton's proposed courts would handle both criminal and civil suits. However, given comments in later treatises, it seems more likely he means that they will handle only civil cases, which made up the majority of England's legal traffic. If so, Milton presumably thinks that crimes above the level of misdemeanors should be heard by common law courts either at the assizes or at Westminster.

The most eye-opening element in this passage is Milton's claim that "Judges and all such officers" should be "by themselves [i.e., by the townsfolk] chosen."[11] This is the judicial corollary to his congregationalist claim in *Likeliest Means* that Christians should have "free consent" in "chusing both thir particular church and thir church-officers" (*CPW* 7:292). Both proposals push back against the status quo since neither Church of England ministers nor English judges were elected by their constituents. While some minor judicatures had elected officials (such as mayors of the courts staple, who administered the law merchant in key market towns), in most the flow of cases was supervised by assigned judges. The presence of professional, appointed judges became even more pronounced as one moved up the jurisdictional hierarchy. For example, in a court such as the palatine court of Chester, the Chancellor of Chester and the Justice of Chester (who had respective jurisdiction over questions of equity and law) were both appointed by either the earl or the duke.[12] As for judges in the main central courts, Sir Thomas Smith succinctly describes the selection process: those "most approved for learning, age, discretion, and exercise" among the common lawyers called to the bar are chosen by "the Prince."[13]

We see a sharp contrast between Milton's ideas about how to restructure the judiciary and those expressed by two major common law jurists of the seventeenth century: Sir Matthew Hale and Sir Edward Coke. In his *History of the Common Law of England*, Hale reasons that when all judges "have had

---

10. Chancery and Star Chamber also spent much of their time hearing cases that had first passed through other judicatures, and there was a high degree of duplication of judicial effort in the seventeenth century.

11. On the importance of local office holding, see Goldie, "Unacknowledged Republic."

12. See Coke, *Fourth Part of the Institutes*, 211–12.

13. T. Smith, *De Republica Anglorum*, 55.

a Common Education in the Study of the Law" and the benefits of shared discussion in the halls of Westminster, their judgments on the bench will "carry a Consonancy, Congruity, and Conformity to one another" that would be impossible to achieve otherwise. He explicitly contrasts the benefits of this system with the "Confusion and Disparity that would unavoidably ensue, if the Administration was by several incommunicating Hands, or by provincial Establishments."[14] Coke's legal outlook was similar, and he had even lost his position as chief justice because he argued that King James as a legal layman was incapable of reasoning like a judge. In Coke's view, only a professionally trained caste of lawyers could understand and apply the common law. Nicholas K. Blomley writes that Coke saw the law not as "a variegated and diverse system of localized practices" but as a "disembedded superstructure." The interpretation and application of that law should rest with the professional custodians of that superstructure, not with those who lived in "the multiple local sites in which law acquires meaning."[15] Milton's thinking pushes in exactly the opposite direction. He proposes the very "provincial Establishments" that Hale and Coke oppose, and he likes the idea that justice would be administered by what Hale calls "incommunicating Hands," or judges who do not necessarily share a common professional training or a common outlook.

Whereas Coke's goal was to do away with the possibility that "different courts might offer different remedies," Milton's plan actually makes these different remedies more likely.[16] His desire for elected judicial officials opens the door to lay judges, men more committed to communal justice as they understood it than to some overarching idea of "the law" as taught at the Inns of Court or recorded in Plowden's or Dyer's *Reports*.[17] In *Likeliest Means*, Milton rejects the idea of a "peculiar tribe of levites," or priests, and he would not

14. Hale, *History of the Common Law*, 162. For more on Hale's thinking, see Cromartie, *Sir Matthew Hale*.

15. Blomley, *Law, Space*, 75–76. Holdsworth writes, "Coke, more than any other single man, helped to secure the victory of the principle that the common law is supreme in the state": Holdsworth, *History of English Law*, 5:195.

16. Jones, "Crown and the Courts," 288. This is not to suggest that all common law courts in the provinces marched in lockstep with centralized ideologies. For example, historians have demonstrated how local courts adapted to local customs and communal norms even as they enforced parliamentary statutes and common law standards. See Rushton, "Local Laws, Local Principles"; McComish, "Defining Boundaries."

17. Milton here swims against the current, for the prevailing trend was to replace lay judges with professional ones. See Dawson, *History of Lay Judges*, 1. This trend was linked to the

have religion controlled by "a partie, a distinct order in the commonwealth" (*CPW* 7:319). In *Proposalls of Certaine Expedients*, written the same year, he effectively rejects any "peculiar tribe" of judges. Interestingly, Milton's plan for a judicial bench elected by each community conflicts with his constitutional plan. He calls for a "Grand Council" that would be composed of members for life, and, in the event of vacancies, only the "well affected people" should be allowed a role in choosing replacements (*CPW* 7:337).[18] Yet in the same document, he claims that at the county and town level all judicial officers should be "by themselves [i.e., by the populace] chosen" (*CPW* 7:338). When he wrote this treatise, Milton was fast abandoning any pretense that England could have a functionally representative government. His republican ideals seem to be increasingly focused onto the nation's judicial system, and he looks to the law as the place where the power of "good and lawful people of the . . . neighbourhood" could be preserved and perhaps even expanded.[19]

MAKING NEW LAWS

Milton's thinking about the English law and the English judiciary changes between *Proposalls of Certaine Expedients* and the first edition of *A Readie and Easie Way*, published four months later in February 1660. Now he imagines the English adopting a federal principle in which each county becomes an autonomously functioning state, and he introduces the idea that these federated counties will not only administer the law for themselves but actually make it too:

> Every county in the land [should be] made a little commonwealth, and thir chief town a city, if it be not so call'd already; where the nobilitie and chief gentry may build, houses or palaces, befitting their qualitie, may bear part in the government, make their own judicial lawes, and execute them by their own elected judicatures, without appeal, in all things of civil government between man and man. So they shall have justice in thir own hands, and none to blame but themselves, if it be not well administered. (*CPW* 7:383)

---

increasing professionalization among common lawyers: Prest, *Rise of the Barristers*; Brooks, *Pettyfoggers and Vipers*; Brooks, *Lawyers, Litigation*.

18. Zera Fink argues that Milton supported the model of a mixed state where sovereignty resides with the people but then is delegated to an aristocratic magistracy: Fink, *Classical Republicans*, 90–122.

19. This language appears in the 1641 Order for the Abolition of Star Chamber. See Gardiner, *Constitutional Documents*, 180.

In some ways, the juridical thinking in this passage simply reiterates and refines points that appear in the earlier two tracts. Milton makes it clearer than before that he is thinking about civil rather than criminal suits, for he says that his new courts will handle "all things of civil government between man and man." In civil matters, these courts will be "without appeal." However, serious crimes or transjurisdictional civil suits would be referred to centralized courts: "as for controversies that shall happen between men of several counties, they may repair, as they doe now, to the capital citie" (*CPW* 7:383). Whereas in the earlier tracts he was more focused on pragmatic reasons for localized justice, now he turns to the political and ideological benefits. England needs local courts staffed by elected judges because kings will try to "have all the benches of judicature annexd to the throne, as a gift of royal grace that we have justice don us" (*CPW* 7:384).[20] As in *Proposalls of Certaine Expedients*, Milton's transfer of judicial power to the localities coexists with a centralized state. For example, he writes, "I affirm that the Grand or General Councel being well chosen, should sit perpetual," and "I see not therefore how we can be advantag'd by successive Parlaments" (*CPW* 7:369). It may be that Milton can accept the idea of a perpetual, oligarchic central government so long as the English people's right to consent to and participate in their government is protected inside the high fences of an electoral judicial system. Admittedly, Milton's ideal judiciary can hardly be called democratic since, more than in the previous two treatises, he privileges the social elite—"the nobilitie and chief gentry"—who are to build houses and "palaces" in each county seat. These men are to do the lion's share of making the laws and administering them, a reminder of William Walker's and Blair Worden's point that by 1659 and 1660, Milton can be called a republican only in a very restricted sense.[21]

Unlike the earlier tracts that implied that local courts would administer the dominant common law, the first edition of *A Readie and Easie Way* opens up the possibility of actual local lawmaking. Milton writes that each town will "make their own judicial lawes, and execute them by their own elected judicatures." Recognizing the potential for chaos caused by conflicting sets of laws, Milton then clarifies that local laws must be "subordinate to the general power

---

20. Judicial independence was formally and permanently adopted in the 1701 Act of Settlement. For more on the politicization of the Stuart bench, see Brooks, *Law, Politics, and Society*, 9.

21. Walker, "Rhetoric, Passion"; Worden, "Milton's Republicanism." Corns makes a similar point that republicanism is more an idiom for Milton than an actual constitutional arrangement: "Milton and the Characteristics."

and union of the whole Republick," a claim that makes them more into bylaws (*CPW* 7:385). Yet despite the qualification, this is still a radical suggestion for dispersing legislative authority away from the nation's center. On the whole, Englishmen who lived in the provinces had an approach toward existing statutes and case law that probably appealed to Milton. They tended to regard the law not as an "unalterable score" but rather as "a theme upon which they could improvise."[22] By giving actual legislative power to different communities, Milton seems intent on increasing this kind of flexible, area-specific improvisation. He may have been modeling his proposal for local lawmaking on the manor courts, which even in the seventeenth century shouldered a surprising amount of the work of local governance. As Smith explains, the manor courts had the authority to "make orders and lawes amongest themselves," although these dealt only with "small matters where no great summe is in question."[23] Milton imagines a similar network of local courts but gives them a more robust jurisdiction. He sums up the critical importance of vesting each community with legislative and judicial authority: "nothing can be more essential to the freedom of a people, then to have the administration of justice and all publick ornaments in thir own election and within thir own bounds" (*CPW* 7:384).

Milton's ideas for a local judiciary appear in only slightly modified form in the manuscript known as *The Present Means, and Brief Delineation of a Free Commonwealth, Easy to Be Put in Practice and Without Delay. In a Letter to General Monck* (henceforth *A Letter to General Monck*), written in March 1660. He stresses again the need for independent county governments that are "to assume the judicial Laws, either these that are, or such as they themselves shall new make severally" (*CPW* 7:393). As in earlier works, he seems to be thinking only about civil litigation ("Justice between man and man"), and he makes provision for cases that cross jurisdictions: "Matters appertaining to men of several Counties, or Territories, may be determin'd, as they are here at *London*, or in some more convenient place, under equal judges" (*CPW* 7:393). The most noteworthy feature is Milton's reiterated stress on these courts' ability to "new make" their own laws, although he adds that the courts might choose to use existing laws as well. As in the first edition of *A Readie and*

---

22. Curtis, "Quarter Sessions Appearances," 154. For two recent, useful studies of local involvement in and influence over the law, see Sharpe, "Law Enforcement"; N. Landau, "Changing Persona."

23. T. Smith, *De Republica Anglorum*, 65. Further discussion of the early modern manor courts can be found in Waddell, "Governing England."

Easie Way, Milton is alert to the fact that local bylaws cannot address all of the nation's needs, and he imagines a "Grand or General Council of the Nation" that would have the power to "make all General Laws." But having imaginatively installed a supervisory central council, Milton immediately reverses the flow of power, for he provides that all central laws would need to have the "Assent of the standing Council in each City." Milton waxes eloquent on the effects of this system: the central council in London would have "so little matter in thir Hands, or power to endanger our Liberty; and the People so much in thirs, to prevent them, having all Judicial Laws in thir own choice" (*CPW* 7:394). We might usefully contrast this position with Coke's observations on the legislative authority of minor courts. Writing about the Court of Common Council that regulated civic affairs in London, Coke says that while this court "may make constitutions and lawes," these serve only to promote "the better execution of the lawes and statutes of the Realme."[24] Local courts are small cogs that exist to help turn larger common law gears. In contrast, Milton is much more committed to the autonomous functioning of minor, regional courts: "all Judicatures, all Magistracies, to the Administration of all Justice between man and man" should be in each community's "own hands" (*CPW* 7:393). Milton's repeated use of the word "all"—"all Judicial laws," "all Judicatures," "all Magistracies" and "all Justice"—proclaims that total legal sovereignty is vested in local communities. The fact that Milton can claim that "all" power resides at the margins even as he makes provision for a grand council that makes national laws indicates how powerful is his need to see the judiciary as embodying the consent of the governed. He concludes his discussion of law in *A Letter to General Monck* with a final plea for the necessity of law reform: "For the full and absolute Administration of Law in every County, which is the difficultest of these Proposals, hath bin of most long desired; and the not granting it, held a general Grievance" (*CPW* 7:395).

In his last treatise of this period, the second edition of *A Readie and Easie Way* published in April 1660, Milton expands upon his suggestions that local communities should make and administer law for themselves. He reiterates the claim from *A Letter to General Monck* that local legislators may either "make thir own judicial laws" or "use these that are." Again, the emphasis is on elected judges: the laws will be administered "by thir own elected judicatures" (*CPW* 7:459). He also reiterates his suggestion for a central court that will hear cases from overlapping jurisdictions. To his recommendation that a system of local courts will put "justice in thir [i.e., the people's] own hands,"

24. Coke, *Fourth Part of the Institutes*, 249.

he adds the clarifying and intensifying phrase, "law executed fully and finally in thir own counties and precincts, long wishd and spoken of, but never yet obtaind" (*CPW* 7:459). One of the advantages to such autonomous judiciaries is they will have "few laws to expect or fear from the supreme authoritie; or those that shall be made, of any great concernment to public libertie" (*CPW* 7:459). He is working to imagine each county and precinct as its own self-legislating entity, one where the creation of laws is so complete and so efficient that there will be "few laws to expect or fear" from above. Recognizing that laws are still likely to be handed down from the nation's capital, Milton clarifies that these will be of no "great concernment" because "public libertie" will be well protected by each region's autonomous laws and courts. Unlike Coke, who thought that the nation would be best served by standardized legal norms, Milton wants laws that are tailor-made for each community. In his study of Milton's nationalism, Paul Stevens argues that Milton's understanding of the nation makes room for "a genuine, vibrant multiculturalism."[25] The legal and judicial passages in these five political treatises suggest that we can extend his claim: Milton's view of the English nation also accommodates a genuine, vibrant multijurisdictionalism.

EQUALL JUDGES

While Milton wants to shift as much judicial power as possible away from the central courts and the royal authority that, after May 1660, they would be serving, he also seems uneasy about the democratic potential latent in the traditional grand and petit juries. As Worden points out, Milton increasingly felt that "virtue lay in the minority."[26] There are suggestions in these treatises that even as he advocates for autonomously functioning local courts, he inclines toward a Romanist system in which verdicts were rendered by judges.[27] This intellectual shift marks a break with his earlier works, for he previously used the jury as an emblem of equality and the people's right to hold rulers accountable. For example, in *Tenure of Kings and Magistrates*, he writes, "if our

25. Stevens, "How Milton's Nationalism Works," 293.
26. Worden, *Literature and Politics*, 201. For a broader survey of Milton's struggle to accommodate the views of the English people as a whole, see Hammond, *Milton and the People*.
27. This distinction was not always of the bright-line variety and has sometimes been overstated by historians. On the one hand, as we saw above, Chancery delegated some of its functions to laypeople, and the canon law courts also used inquest panels. On the other, common law offenses could sometimes be dealt with summarily by the justice of the peace without the help of a jury. But broadly speaking, the distinction holds.

Law judge all men to the lowest by thir Peers, it should in all equity ascend also, and judge the highest" (*CPW* 3:219). Here Milton uses "Peers" as a shortened version of the phrase "a jury of one's peers," and his abbreviation calls attention to the fact that the king's true peers were not the aristocratic peers of the realm but rather those ordinary Englishmen who regularly assembled in courtrooms across the nation. *Eikonoklastes* similarly associates juries with political equality. Milton celebrates the "Law of this Nation" because "Kings in receiving Justice, and undergoing due trial, are not differenc'd from the meanest subjects," and he stresses the justice of an "op'n trial" according to the law of England (conveniently asking readers to forget that Charles I was not, in fact, given a common law trial) (*CPW* 3:594). In *Animadversions*, the jury is the antithesis of social hierarchy. When his opponent refers to a "Diocesan *Bishop*" full of a sense of his own authority, Milton dismissively likens this imagined churchman to "the foreman of a Jury" who is "puffe[d] up" by a "speciall endorsement" from the bench (*CPW* 1:713). His point is that jury members are equals and jury foremen are simply elected spokesmen. While the smug foreman might congratulate himself on the judge's "endorsement," he gains no authority thereby and has no right to lord it over his fellow jurors. Similarly, bishops should not claim any preeminence above their lay peers. The image of the jury was important to Milton in the 1640s because being tried by a jury was understood as being tried by the country itself. Indeed, "country" and "jury" could be used as synonyms in court settings. As Smith writes, men and women in the courtroom would formally ask for a jury trial by requesting to be judged by "God and the Countrie." Smith explains the idiom by pointing out that "these honest men that . . . come here" as jurors serve "in the place and stead of the Countrie."[28]

Milton's earlier faith in the jury seems to have thinned out by the time he wrote the political works discussed in this chapter. In *Proposalls of Certaine Expedients*, he is silent on the question of the jury, referring only to the need for "Judges and all such officers" to be chosen by the community. Since jurors were not considered officers of the court, Milton neither affirms nor rejects them as part of his revised judicial system. In the first edition of *A Readie and Easie Way*, we see the first inklings that he might be edging away from the jury trial. He draws links between his imagined government and the Dutch Republic: "we shall also far exceed the United Provinces by having, not many sovranties in one Commonwealth, but many Commonwealths under one sovrantie" (*CPW* 7:385). Although Milton claims that England under his

28. T. Smith, *De Republica Anglorum*, 79.

imagined system would outdo the Dutch, the Dutch system is clearly serving as a model for him. The United Provinces subscribed to Roman-Dutch law, which was an amalgam of Roman law fundamentals and Germanic law elements, and as in most of Europe, verdicts there were rendered by professional judges. By likening his plan for England to the federated model of the United Provinces, Milton might be imagining that aspects of their legal procedures would apply in England as well.

His shift away from the jury trial becomes clearer in *A Letter to General Monck* and the second edition of *A Readie and Easie Way*. In both, Milton calls for cases to be heard by "equall judges." In *A Letter to General Monck*, he writes, "Matters appertaining to men of several Counties, or Territories, may be determin'd, as they are here at *London*, or in some more convenient place, under equal Judges" (*CPW* 7:385). He adopts the same phrasing in the second edition of *A Readie and Easie Way*: in the event that the capital city is inconvenient for cases that cross jurisdictions, any "more commodious, indifferent place and equall judges" will suffice. The phrase "equall judges" is ambiguous. He could mean "equall" in the sense of fair, in much the same way that giving local courts final jurisdiction will prevent people from searching for "more equal justice" elsewhere. If so, "equall judges" simply means judges who are upright and impartial. But there are two other relevant meanings of "equal," both of which point toward Civilian procedure. In judicial contexts, the phrase "equal judges" often means equitable in its technical sense, i.e., equity as opposed to law. Equity courts ran on loosely Civilian lines, meaning that "equall judges" did not share power in the courtroom with a lay jury. Milton had the most familiarity with this judicial format, for his various suits in Chancery were heard and decided by a single judge, either the Chancellor or the Master of the Rolls. The phrase "equall judges" could also denote a collegiate bench or tribunal system in which a panel of judges gathered to hear cases and determine verdicts, as was the case in prerogative courts such as the Council of Wales and the Marches and also Star Chamber. It could also be applied to Civilian judges. For example, in *Pseudodoxia Epidemica*, Sir Thomas Browne explains his choice of Latin over English in judicial terms: he wanted to write "unto the Latine republike and equall judges of Europe."[29] Milton had other experiences with "equall judges." He appeared before the private court of the Goldsmiths' Company eight times between 1649 and 1651 and once in 1659 about renewing leases on the property in Bread Street. While we moderns can have trouble grasping the concept of a private court because

---

29. Browne, *Pseudodoxia Epidemica*, A4v.

"our thinking has been pervaded by a political theory of the omnipresent state,"[30] courts such as the Goldsmiths' were regarded as legitimate centers of adjudication in the early modern period. This court in particular provides an example of how collective verdicts could work. Records from October 5, 1649, note that after Milton made an offer to lease property, "It was resolved by the Ballate box 11. against 5" that he should have the option of a new lease (*LR* 2:263). Although it is not fully clear what Milton has in mind when he recommends verdicts by "equall judges," the available meanings make little room for the involvement of a lay jury.

THE TRIAL OF JOHN BUNYAN

Milton's apparent desire to invest more authority in judges carries with it both rewards and risks. The rewards I have already glanced at: his proposed system would be more efficient, and he imagines it as having a freedom to enact forms of justice that would be impossible in the more standardized framework of the common law. However, the attendant risks come into view if we compare Milton's ideas with the trial of the period's most famous dissenting preacher, John Bunyan. According to his posthumously published *A Relation of the Imprisonment of Mr. John Bunyan*, Bunyan was arrested on November 12, 1660, in Lower Samsell, Bedfordshire, for having violated the Conventicles Act, an Elizabethan statute that banned unlicensed religious gatherings. He was first brought before Francis Wingate, justice of the peace in nearby Harlington, who offered to release him on bail with sureties provided that he promised to refrain from preaching.[31] When Bunyan refused, Wingate drew up a mittimus, a court order that committed him to the Bedford jail until the local quarter sessions. Seven weeks later, in early January 1661, Bunyan appeared before the quarter sessions judges Sir John Kelynge (presiding), Sir William Becher, Sir George Blundell, Sir Henry Chester, and Thomas Snagge. In the language of the bill of indictment, he had "devilishly and perniciously abstained from coming to church to hear divine service" and had proved himself to be "a common upholder of several unlawful meetings and conventicles, to the great disturbance and distraction of the good subjects of this kingdom, contrary to the laws of our sovereign lord the king."[32] Bunyan's biographer Richard L.

---

30. Dawson, *History of Lay Judges*, 5.

31. *A Relation of the Imprisonment of Mr. John Bunyan* was based on five letters that Bunyan wrote from the Bedford jail to his congregation, and it was first published in 1765.

32. Bunyan, *Relation*, 9.

Greaves observes that the ensuing trial was "less like the usual questioning of the accused"—since there were no witnesses and, as we shall see, no jury—and more like a theological "debate."[33] With various unsympathetic interjections from the other judges, Kelynge probed Bunyan about his determination to preach according to his sense of his divine calling; his refusal to attend the parish church; and his rejection of the Book of Common Prayer. Faced with Bunyan's biblically rooted defense of himself, Kelynge finally grew impatient, declaring that the judges "could not wait . . . any longer." He asked Bunyan, "you confess the indictment, do you not?" to which Bunyan replied that he had preached and prayed at "many meetings" with his flock. Hearing this admission, Kelynge gave judgment: "You must be had back again to prison, and there lie for three months following." At the end of that period Bunyan was either to submit to the Church of England or be banished. The penalty for defying the order of banishment would be capital: Bunyan would "stretch by the neck for it."[34] It is worth underlining the fact that these judges came from nearby Bedfordshire towns such as Southill, Howbury, Cardington Manor, Tilsworth, and Marston Manor, and they were also known for their royalist sympathies: Kelynge had been imprisoned at Windsor Castle from 1642 to 1660 for supporting the king; Becher and Blundell had been recently knighted; and within a few months of Bunyan's trial, Chester too would be knighted and Snagge would be appointed sheriff.[35] These facts belie Milton's hope in his 1659–60 political tracts that local men of the "better sort" would be less in thrall to central ideologies and thus more inclined to administer dispassionate, balanced forms of justice.

What is missing from Bunyan's account of the quarter sessions is any reference to a jury. Because his offense was a violation of an Elizabethan statute designed to protect the peace of the realm, it should have gone first to a grand jury that would determine if an indictment should be issued and then to a petty jury that would try the actual case. Records of county quarter sessions indicate just how much time was usually spent identifying, calling, impaneling, and instructing lay jurors, and thus the absence of the jury from Bunyan's *Relation* is all the more striking.[36] Admittedly, there was precedent for Kelynge's choice of summary procedure, for justices sometimes simply heard

33. Greaves, *Glimpses of Glory*, 136.
34. Bunyan, *Relation*, 27–28.
35. Greaves, *Glimpses of Glory*, 134–35.
36. For a thorough discussion of the practices of English quarter sessions, see Pritchard, *Jurisdiction, Practice, and Procedure*.

cases and issued verdicts themselves in an attempt to streamline court proceedings.[37] However, summary procedure was usually reserved for petty matters, so Bunyan's jury-less hearing and then twelve-year imprisonment on a criminal charge bear some signs of irregularity. At least, Bunyan himself soon came to think so. Having read some law books during the early months of his imprisonment, he asked his wife to petition to have his case heard at the assizes, when circuit judges and juries tried matters deemed too serious for the quarter sessions. After repeated attempts to win support for her husband's request, Mrs. Bunyan finally approached a group of judges and justices staying at the Swan Inn in Bedford.[38] The most important and sympathetic of these was Hale, and in response to her last-ditch plea for help, Hale explained why he could not simply order the case to be retried: "Woman, I told thee before that I could do thee no good; because they have taken that for a conviction which thy husband spoke at the sessions: and unless there be something done to undo that I can do thee no good."[39] He then repeated "very mildly" the essential legal fact: "they have taken what thy husband spake, for a conviction."[40] One detects a note of regret here from Hale, the careful jurist, that Bunyan's disputation with his judges should have been used as a substitute for the more formal processes of "conviction." Justice Chester gave a more brutal version of Hale's claim that he could not simply "undo" the earlier trial. Mrs. Bunyan had asserted that Kelynge's verdict was wrong because "it was but a word of discourse that they took for a conviction." Chester replied that Bunyan had been "lawfully convicted" because the verdict was "recorded" in the written proceedings of the court. In what might well strike us as specious reasoning, Chester meant that because the quarter sessions was a court of record where proceedings and decisions were given written form, the verdict was thereby impeachment-proof. Thus the matter was closed, and Mrs. Bunyan was being a nuisance.[41] Hale then concluded the exchange by offering Mrs. Bunyan what was in context some sound legal advice: either obtain an official writ of error (an order that sent a case to a higher court on appeal on the grounds of

37. For more on these proceedings, see P. King, "Summary Courts."
38. There is no record of Mrs. Bunyan's first name.
39. Bunyan, *Relation*, 42.
40. Bunyan, *Relation*, 46.
41. Bunyan, *Relation*, 43. We may see here evidence of Douglas Hay's argument about why assize judges were slow to overturn quarter sessions verdicts or to discipline the quarter sessions judges themselves: the state understood how much the nationwide mechanisms of enforcement and adjudication relied on the work of unpaid men at the county level: Hay, "Dread of the Crown Office."

procedural error) or sue out a pardon. We do not know why the Bunyans did not follow the first course, although poverty is a likely cause: obtaining a writ of error and then pushing it through the proper judicial channels was not inexpensive, and Mrs. Bunyan had four children to support. As for the second, Bunyan refused on principle since a pardon involved admitting that one had been in the wrong.[42]

Returning to Bunyan's quarter sessions trial, if we accept that Kelynge and his fellow judges saw Bunyan as a threat to the social order who needed to be imprisoned, they had reasons to want to avoid a jury trial, for contemporary events had thrown the respective power of judges and juries into contention. Before the sixteenth century, common law trials did not, as a rule, include in-court presentation of evidence or the testimony of witnesses. Instead, jury members were thought of as self-informing—i.e., either they already knew the persons and circumstances involved or it was assumed that they would go ask questions on their own. During a trial, juries heard statements from both plaintiff and defendant, and then they voted their consciences. They could acquit or convict even in the face of overwhelming evidence to the contrary since what the jury believed was, legally speaking, all that mattered. In other words, there was no higher standard of truth—such as what the evidence suggested—to which plaintiffs, defendants, or even judges could point as being more dispositive than the jury's conclusion. Beginning in the sixteenth century, however, a more pronounced division of labor arose in the common law courtroom.[43] Each case was divided into matters of law, which fell to the judge and lawyers, and matters of fact, which fell to the jury. Jurors became more passive spectators, and they shared power with the judge. Furthermore, in-court presentations of facts and testimony made the jury's assessments more open to question, and a jury could be even disciplined for finding against the evidence. However, by the middle of the seventeenth century, there were protests against this recent erosion of the jury's authority. For example, in his *Jurors Judges of Law and Fact*, John Jones argues that since historically juries weighed both fact and law, they should be empowered to dispense even with

---

42. Ironically, the fear that Bunyan would successfully sue out a pardon explains why, after his three-month imprisonment expired, Kelynge and his fellow judges did not move to enforce a sentence of banishment. As Bunyan explains, "they could not meddle with me, as touching the execution of their sentence; because of the liberty offered for the suing out of pardons." Presumably to avoid giving him the chance to sue for pardon, they opted instead to leave him in the limbo of imprisonment. Bunyan, *Relation*, 41.

43. The discussion in this paragraph is generally drawn from T. A. Green, *Verdict according to Conscience*.

statutory punishments. The extent of the jury's authority was a controversial issue in several high-profile cases. In 1653, the Leveller John Lilburne argued that while he had broken the law by returning from exile, the law itself was illegal. The jury evidently agreed, for they refused to convict despite Lilburne's frank admission of his guilt. Similarly, William Penn admitted to a jury in 1670 that since he had preached to a London crowd, he was guilty of a criminal offense under the Restoration's Clarendon Code. Again, the jury acquitted him in the face of the evidence. By acquitting both men, the juries were tacitly claiming they had the authority to override the law itself.[44] In *Pilgrim's Progress*, Bunyan shows Faithful being tried by a jury, and he clearly had no illusions that referring decisions to a jury of peers necessarily resulted in impartial justice: the jurors are Mr. Blind-man, Mr. No-good, Mr. Malice, Mr. Love-lust, Mr. Live-loose, Mr. Heady, Mr. High-mind, Mr. Enmity, Mr. Liar, Mr. Cruelty, Mr. Hate-light, and Mr. Implacable. On the other hand, we should remember that the jury was, in the words of one legal historian, "the most representative institution available to the English people" in the seventeenth century and that juries could, if they chose, override both judges and evidence.[45] Bedfordshire had been one of the main centers of parliamentary sympathy during the Civil War, and after the Restoration it teemed with religious dissent. Had Bunyan's case been heard at the 1661 assizes, he might have faced the kind of malevolent jury that condemned Faithful. On the other hand, he might have faced the kind that acquitted Lilburne and Penn. At the very least, we can surmise that having worked so hard and so unsuccessfully to have his case heard in a regular common law courtroom and having experienced the exactions of an irregular quarter sessions, Bunyan would not have shared Milton's confidence about the need for "equall judges."[46]

---

44. While the movement to give juries formal authority over both law and fact did not survive into the eighteenth century, the jury's power was secured another way. In the 1670 *Bushell's Case*, Judge Vaughan overturned the legality of disciplining a jury, holding that except in the case of provable corruption, a jury's decision was sacrosanct and could not be challenged by the judge, no matter how much it might seem to fly in the face of the evidence.

45. Roberts, "Juries and the Middling Sort," 182.

46. Several years later in his *A True and Impartial Narrative*, Bunyan would revisit the way that local judges could corrupt the law. In the words of his title page, his treatise describes "*Some Illegal and Arbitrary proceedings by certain Justices of the Peace.*"

Afterword: Justice in the Columbia Manuscript

I conclude this book by adopting an oblique approach to Milton's works. Instead of studying his writings directly, as I have done in the previous chapters, I look instead at the textual company some of them keep in the collection known as the Columbia Manuscript. A long, slender notebook, the Columbia Manuscript contains full transcriptions of *Proposalls of Certaine Expedients*, *A Letter to a Friend*—both discussed in the previous chapter—and 156 of the state letters Milton wrote as Secretary of Foreign Tongues. The man who assembled the notebook—whom I subsequently refer to as "the Transcriber"—presumably had privileged access to Milton since *A Letter to a Friend* and ten of the state letters are known from no other source, a fact that makes the Columbia Manuscript an important document in Milton studies. In addition to Milton's writings, the Transcriber also copied out excerpts from other early modern printed and manuscript works, some of which I identify here for the first time. Like so many early modern miscellanies, the excerpts in the Columbia Manuscript are varied. Treatises such as "Of Statues and Antiquities" and "A brief descripcion of Genoa" coexist with reflections on the authority of the Privy Council and the diplomatic immunity of foreign ambassadors. However, the Transcriber's overarching principle of selection seems to have been an interest in jurisdictional diversity. Repeatedly, he copies out works that discuss different forms of legal authority, and he seems particularly intrigued by the way that smaller judicatures such as Chancery and Requests maintained a fragile autonomy in a common law country. As the previous chapter argued, Milton's late political tracts display a similar interest. The fact that the Transcriber selected two of these works, *A Letter to a Friend* and *Proposalls*, for inclusion in his own miscellany suggests that when the Transcriber looked at Milton, he saw someone, like himself, interested in what legal historian Peter Goodrich calls "minor jurisprudences," smaller, independent enclaves of law that were more typical of English jurisprudence before the common law widened its monopoly.[1] Goodrich suggests that the multiple jurisdictions of the early modern period allowed for a more variegated understanding of what legal justice could be and the purposes it could serve. Based on the evidence of the Columbia Manuscript, both the Transcriber and Milton would have agreed.

THE INDEX LEGALIS

The generally juridical tenor of the Columbia Manuscript is epitomized by the section of the notebook known as the "Index Legalis." As is typical of early modern commonplace books, the Columbia Manuscript was used in different ways by more than one owner.[2] In 1921, Columbia University acquired the notebook, which at one point had belonged to the great nineteenth-century book collector Sir Thomas Phillipps, who jotted observations about Milton on the notebook's flyleaf. It is unclear who owned the notebook before Phillipps, but Bernard Gardiner, warden of All Souls College and keeper of Oxford University's archives in the early eighteenth century, clearly had possession at one point since he used some of the blank pages to record his accounts. Other than the notes by Phillipps and Gardiner, the majority of the notebook appears to have been written in the mid- to late seventeenth century. In terms of textual organization, the contents run in two different directions. Starting at the front of the book and working toward the back, we find transcriptions of various treatises—mostly on judicial subjects, as I explore in the following section—along with the known works by Milton. Most of these are in English and written in secretary hand. The second project appears when we flip the notebook around and work from the back toward the front. Here we find the "Index Legalis," which is a collection of notes about Romanist law and legal procedures, all written in Latin using italic hand. The editors of both the Columbia Prose and the Yale Prose assume that the two portions

---

1. Goodrich, *Law in the Courts of Love*.

2. A description of this work, including the attribution of the closing notes to Gardiner, appears in the catalog card affixed to the first verso of the manuscript opposite Phillipps's inscription on the flyleaf recto. The "Index" appears at pages 144–49. I have relied on the transcription and translation provided in *CPW*.

(or "directions") of the notebook were written by different men. However, it seems also possible that one man wrote both and simply used English secretary hand for one and Latin italic hand for the other, a possibility supported by resemblances in some of the letterforms. (For the sake of simplicity and because the question of the notebook's authorship is tangential to my argument, I will assume that one man copied out both portions.) The "Index Legalis" participates in the tradition of commonplacing practiced by lawyers and law students on both sides of the Channel.[3] The Transcriber evidently had some familiarity with the tradition of Civilian commonplacing since he follows the standard Civilian organizational approach: he took several pages of his notebook, assigned each a legal subject heading—e.g., *Judicium, Materia et Materiatum, Sententia*, etc.—and then recorded relevant notes from his reading in the legal texts of the *ius commune*.[4] In contrast, legal commonplace books written by English common lawyers were organized by cases since the common law did not lend itself to this kind of thematic categorization. While the Transcriber's citations show that he had access to a variety of Civilian books, the "Index Legalis" barely skims the surface of even the basic elements of Civil law. Each page has only a few notes clustered at the top with ample blank space below, and so if the Transcriber initially envisioned a plan of intensive study, he did not follow through.

Only two scholars have glanced at the "Index Legalis," and they have done so strictly out of an interest in Milton's possible authorship. In 1938, the editorial team of the Columbia edition of *The Works of John Milton* led by Frank Allen Patterson included the "Index" in volume 18 under the category of "Additions to the Commonplace Book." Patterson is sure that Milton either wrote the "Index" or directed his amanuensis to do so. In his introduction, Patterson writes that this "unfinished collection of notes on legal matters . . . exactly parallels the entries on other subjects in the *Commonplace Book*," and "Milton prepared an elaborate page with twenty capital letters for the Index, but apparently abandoned the project after a short time." For Patterson, the "Index" provides "an interesting sidelight on [Milton's] interest in law," although he

---

3. Boyer, *Sir Edward Coke*, 31–33. The seventeenth-century judge Roger North urges his lawyer-readers to practice commonplacing: R. North, *Discourse on The Study of the Laws*, 24–29. For discussion of notebooks kept by Civilians, see Helmholz, *Three Civilian Notebooks*, xxx–xxxi. See also Ibbetson, "Common Law and *Ius Commune*."

4. Since the Transcriber must have had privileged access to Milton and to his papers, the "Index" offers a useful reminder that Milton's familial and social networks were largely made up of men who made their living at the law. For more on these legal networks, see Chapman, *Legal Epic*, 16–25.

does not further elaborate.[5] However, two decades later the editors of the *Complete Prose Works* published by Yale University Press disputed Patterson's claim. In Appendix A, the Yale editors include a description of the Columbia Manuscript, a listing of the contents of the front half (i.e., the various treatises transcribed in the notebook's "front to back" orientation), and a full copy of the "Index" accompanied by a translation. In his preface to Appendix A, Maurice Kelley argues that the handwriting in the "Index" does not match that of any of Milton's known amanuenses and that "the form of the notes and table ... differs markedly from that of Milton's authentic *Commonplace Book*" (*CPW* 1:956), a direct refutation of Patterson's claim for exact parallels.

I tend to agree with Kelley, although whereas his skepticism about Milton's authorship rests on paleography and formatting, my own is based on subject matter. The entries in the "Index" simply seem out of step with the uses that Milton made of Romanist law. As I argued in chapter 5, Milton relied on the Civil law of *iniuria* to write *Pro Se Defensio*. However, the entries listed under the heading "*Iniuria*" in the "Index Legalis" display an attention to courtroom technicalities that is inconsistent with Milton's interests. For example, the Transcriber notes that a plea entered in an *iniuria* action must include an "added statement as to place and time" and that in the event of judgment for the plaintiff, the judge "assigns a third part" of the damages "to the plaintiff and two thirds to the court" (*CPW* 1:960). Had Milton been directing the selection of materials, we would expect to find instead excerpts about the circumstances under which *fama* was admissible and the legal liabilities attached to *infames* rather than the procedural formalities that occupy the Transcriber. Milton was also deeply interested in Civilian ideas of equity (the subject of chapter 4), but none of the excerpts in the "Index Legalis" mention equity or even operate at this higher jurisprudential plane. The mismatch between the "Index" and Milton's other works springs more fully into view if we compare it to his commonplace book. Ruth Mohl demonstrates the tailored fit between most of the entries Milton made in his commonplace book and the contents of his prose works.[6] In contrast, none of the questions or procedures of law copied into the "Index" seem immediately germane to Milton's thinking. Moreover, Milton's knowledge of Civil law was more extensive and sophisticated than the rough fundamentals seen in the "Index," and so it seems unlikely that he would have selected these excerpts for transcription.

The "Index Legalis" feels instead like the work of someone employed

---

5. F. A. Patterson et al., *Works of John Milton*, 18:509–10.
6. Mohl, *John Milton and His Commonplace Book*.

by an English judicature (the options are many, ranging from major courts such as the Exchequer and King's Bench through smaller venues such as the Lord Mayor's Court) who had some occasion to rub shoulders with the Civil law now and then. This shoulder-rubbing could have come in various ways: through conversation with a colleague, through a formal consultation on some aspect of law, through a personal suit in a court such as Chancery that had a Civilian procedure, etc. Motivated to learn more about the *ius commune*, the Transcriber provides entries on a range of pragmatic issues that probably touched on or provided a different perspective on some real-world legal problems that he might have encountered: whether Civil laws about raw materials (e.g., flour) apply also to manufactured products (e.g., bread); the right of exiles to make a legally valid will; the Civil law's statute of limitations on different kinds of cases; whether criminal and civil suits about the same issue should be filed concurrently or sequentially; the way that verdicts are written in Civilian courts as opposed to canonical ones. While the Transcriber did not get very far in his educational program, the existence of the notebook offers a useful reminder that there were still Civil law enclaves in England (e.g., the Admiralty, the university courts, etc.) and that even those who worked outside those enclaves were often intrigued by Civilian approaches. The fact that the Transcriber also had access to Milton's state papers (many of which take up issues germane to Roman-based international law) reminds us that Milton lived in a social milieu that was deeply interested in questions of comparative law.

"THE DIVERSITY OF COURTS"

I turn now to the other portion of the Columbia Manuscript (its "front to back" orientation, as opposed to the "Index" which runs "back to front"), which has received more critical attention. This portion of the notebook contains (1) transcriptions of treatises on various subjects; (2) Milton's *Proposalls of Certaine Expedients* and *Letter to a Friend*; and (3) his state letters. Edward Jones argues that during the chaotic days around the Restoration, Milton ordered an additional copy made of the letters he had written on behalf of the Commonwealth, since his originals were likely to be seized by the new government.[7] The Transcriber took the notebook—into which he had previously copied treatises, including Milton's—and added hurried transcriptions of the letters. The state letters have been studied by editors and scholars, as have the

---

7. Personal communication, October 19, 2019.

copies of *Proposalls of Certaine Expedients* and *Letter to a Friend*. The preceding treatises, however, have received only the briefest of scholarly glances, and these have been motivated by a narrow interest in Milton's possible authorship. Patterson writes that the Columbia Manuscript as a whole "was obviously prepared for the poet himself," but this bare assertion is not otherwise supported (*CPW* 18:501). More recently, the Columbia Rare Book and Manuscript Library says in its online catalog that these treatises "seem to be materials [Milton] used in his official duties."[8] These claims are hard to square with the nature of the treatises. For example, the Transcriber has copied out a treatise by Thomas Sherer, a late-sixteenth-century clerk in the Council of Wales and the Marches, about the fine gradations of hierarchy within the English peerage. Sherer carefully describes the ladder of social privilege, noting that a duke's son has "the upr hand" of an earl and a "Vicountesse daughtr unmarried hath the upr hand of a Kts. [Knight's] wife" (*CM* 5). After Sherer's work, the Transcriber copies a treatise by Jasper Tudor, duke of Bedford, that classifies England's various peers (dukes, marquesses, earls, viscounts, barons, etc.) in terms of their proximity to the monarch and that specifies the ceremonial formalities appropriate to each. Milton was skeptical about hereditary rank and privilege, and his job as Latin Secretary did not require him to organize state events. Thus it is difficult to imagine the circumstances under which he would have needed to know that viscounts and barons are served at table without "kneeling, or wth coverd Basons, when they wash" or that "a Dutchesse may have her Traine borne by none above the degree of a Baronesse" (*CM* 6). The ideological gap between Milton and the Transcriber actually sharpens the interest of the Columbia Manuscript. The Transcriber's politics and Milton's politics were apparently at odds, and yet despite their fundamental disagreement about matters such as the centrality of the monarch in English society, the Transcriber still spent time and ink copying out works such as *Proposalls of Certaine Expedients* and *A Letter to a Friend*.[9]

The deeper we move into the notebook, the more we can see the connective tissue that binds together the treatises and that explains why Milton's tracts are paired with them. Near the beginning of the excerpt titled "The office and jurisdicion of the Constable and Marshall of Engl. and their Antiquity," the Transcriber refers approvingly to the "diversity of courts" in England (*CM* 9).

---

8. Columbia University Libraries, "John Milton Letters, 1649–1659."

9. The Transcriber's access to Milton's state papers supports John Shawcross's argument that Milton lived in a milieu of friends and relations that mingled Royalists and Parliamentarians. Shawcross, *Arms of the Family*.

This phrase epitomizes his interests, for he repeatedly copies out works about the various ways in which legal authority existed outside the structures of the common law. For example, the excerpt "Sr Rob. Cotton touching the Spanish Ambassadr" is a copy of a letter of advice that Cotton wrote to the duke of Buckingham in 1624 after the Spanish ambassadors had gone to the king and accused Buckingham of treason.[10] In the section transcribed in the Columbia Manuscript, Cotton reflects upon the degree to which ambassadors "by reprsenti[n]g the p[er]son of a Soveraigne pri[n]ce" are "by the law of Nacons exe[m]pt from legal tryall" (*CM* 17). The issue is a jurisdictional one. International law was newly emerging in early modern Europe as a result of work by jurists such as Grotius in the Netherlands and Gentili and Zouch in England,[11] and the question raised here is whether or not ambassadors were immune from prosecution at common law. Cotton concludes that they are. He then offers advice to Buckingham about how to handle the treason charge. Since Parliament is "the highest court of Justice" in the land, a select group of members from Commons and Lords should go to the ambassadors to hear the "charge and proofs" against Buckingham. Then the matter should receive "a fair and legall tryall in tht high court" of Parliament (*CM* 18–19). Whereas foreign ambassadors were exempt from all forms of domestic trial, an English peer such as Buckingham should stand to the legal justice administered by Parliament, the nation's highest court. There is a similar jurisdictional interest in the transcribed excerpt from *The State and Dignitie of a Secretary of Estates Place* by the earl of Salisbury, first printed in 1643. The excerpt in the Columbia Manuscript explains the circumstances under which the Secretary of State can make executive decisions that depart from established rules and laws. For instance, Salisbury writes that while "All Officers and Councellors or Princes have a prescribed Authoritie by Patent, by Custome or by oath," the Secretary of State has a "libertie to negotiate at discretion at home and abroad, wth friends and enemies, in all mattrs of search and intelligences" (*CM* 6).[12] As in Cotton's discussion of the legal status of Buckingham, this

---

10. It appears under the title "A Relation of the Proceedings against Ambassadors who Have Miscarried Themselves" (1–9) in the collection *Cottoni Posthuma: Divers Choice Pieces of that Renowned Antiquary Sir Robert Cotton*, which was compiled and published by James Howell in 1651. For discussion of Howell's collection and the contexts of Cotton's treatises, see Parry, "Cotton's Counsels."

11. On Milton's awareness of the immunities of ambassadors under international law, see Warren, *Literature and the Law of Nations*, 210–16.

12. Cecil (Earl of Salisbury), *State and Dignitie*, 1.

excerpt reflects on the extralegal powers of those at the top of the political hierarchy.

Further along in the notebook, we encounter other treatises with a similarly jurisdictional tilt. In "Some p[ar]ticulrs settled by the wisdom of former times and ratified by long custome concern[in]g the office of Requests," the Transcriber copies out a letter of unknown provenance addressed to King James arguing that the number of judges in the Court of Requests should not be reduced. Requests was an equity court that served as a judicial extension of the Privy Council to handle private petitions, in contradistinction to Star Chamber, which mostly handled public matters.[13] It was called the "poor man's court" because it provided cheap and speedy remedies (although by the seventeenth century it was not limited to the poor, and Milton's father had at least one appearance there). While Elizabeth I had had only two Masters of Requests, James I had increased the Masters to four, with a corresponding increase in the volume of suits. This increase triggered an attack from the common law courts, which issued a flood of prohibitions designed to block Requests' jurisdiction and thereby to route cases back into courts such as Common Pleas and King's Bench. The excerpts in the Columbia Manuscript provide a snapshot of this struggle. As recorded in the Acts of the Privy Council, James said that while he was willing for the time being "to have fowre Masters of the Requests in ordinary togeather," it was "not his Majesties purpose that number should bee continued, or bee a precedent for the future."[14] Instead, the king said he planned to reduce the Masterships back down to two. The letter that the Transcriber has copied into his notebook quotes the king and offers counterarguments for leaving the number of Masters at four. In addition to the harm it would do to the Masters themselves and those in training for these positions,[15] the proposed reduction would be "very hurtfll

---

13. While the historical orthodoxy was once that the Court of Requests vanished as a result of the Long Parliament, I. S. Leadam showed that it continued to hear cases during the Commonwealth period and even had a modest resurgence after the Restoration: Leadam, *Select Cases*. For further discussion of the history of the Court of Requests, see A. T. Carter, *History of English Legal Institutions*, 170–84; Hoyle, "Masters of Requests"; Stretton, *Marital Litigation*, 1–24.

14. Lyle, *Acts of the Privy Council*, 6. See also Baker, *Oxford History*, 204.

15. Masters of Requests Ordinary were those who accompanied the king on his progresses to handle the flood of private petitions. Since this left the main Requests court in London understaffed, the position of Masters of Requests Extraordinary had been developed to handle cases. Masters Extraordinary were not paid and served only with the expectancy of an appointment when an Ordinary position became vacant.

to ths publick" by causing long delays that would "breed much grief to the subj[ec]ts." The letter's author reminds the king that Requests is "erected and upholden by prerogative," and so "uncertainty" on the Requests bench will make it "become a publick scorn that canot stand wth the honr of his M[ajes]ties service" (*CM* 8). The Transcriber, like the author of the letter, thinks that a healthy Court of Requests staffed with four Masters will lead to much "publick good and satisfacon" (*CM* 8).

The Transcriber also provides two treatises on the court of the Constable and Earl Marshal, also known as the High Court of Chivalry. Here again we see his interest in bolstering the authority of a court that often conflicted with the common law. In the first of these treatises, "of the office of a Constable of England," the Transcriber explains that "the jurisdicion of the Constable is the exercise of the Martial law," and he describes the scope of the Constable's authority: the Constable has "enclosed in his office a Creditt for conservacion of the peace over all the land" (*CM* 8). The next treatise, "The office and jurisdicion of the Constable and Marshall of Engl. and their Antiquity," continues in this same vein (*CM* 9). The proper scope of martial law was a subject of intense concern in early modern England. Since martial law was essentially a form of Civil law, excessive enforcement could be regarded as threatening the proper jurisdiction of the common law. In 1622, common lawyers challenged the legality of the Constable's court, and although its authority was reaffirmed by the Privy Council, the court's jurisdiction remained a contested subject.[16] The Transcriber is clearly on the side of the Constable. He traces the antiquity of the Constable's office, specifies that the Constable and Earl Marshal's court is "declard by Act of Parliamt," rehearses the statutes that support the court's legitimacy, and then describes its jurisdiction: the Constable can try "deeds of armes and of war donn" and also "things wch cant be determind nor discussd by the comon law" (*CM* 9). However, he is also careful to describe the point at which the Constable's jurisdiction ends: whereas "any thing done wthin the realme shalbe tried and determind by the good lawes of the realme, . . . all apeales to be done of thi[n]gs out of the realme shalbe before the Constable and marshall" (*CM* 9). Although he focuses primarily on the Constable's court, the Transcriber is also thinking about the jurisdiction of the Admiralty, another court based on Civil law that was also subject to encroachments from

---

16. Squibb, *High Court of Chivalry*, 57. On the history of martial law in England, see Capua, "Early History of Martial Law." In a 1628 speech before the House of Commons, Selden argued for limiting the Constable's ability to use martial law and for the higher authority of the common law: Johnson and Cole, *Commons Debates 1628*, 462–65.

the common law. He writes that if "the Admirall, Constable, or Marshall do ag[ains]t the law," the Council "by p[ar]liam[en]ty authority to them grantd may redresse or limit the same" (*CM* 9).[17]

The Transcriber's jurisdictional interests are most clearly on display in his extensive borrowings from William Lambarde's 1635 *Archeion, or A Discourse upon the High Courts of Justice in England*. A common lawyer and justice of the peace in Kent, Lambarde wrote several influential legal works, and *Archeion* is his survey of the different key jurisdictions in early modern England. The Transcriber relies heavily on Lambarde. For example, he derives the word "constable" from two Saxon words and then acknowledges his source: "as saith Lambard" (*CM* 9). Similarly, he paraphrases Lambarde in his jurisdictional argument that the authority of the Privy Council exists independently of Parliament (*CM* 10).[18] The Transcriber's biggest debt to *Archeion* appears in his discussion of Chancery and the jurisdiction of the Chancellor, for the long discussion "Of the Ld chancellrs originall, his powr etc. and how his Authority in the chancery hath bin diverse times exte[n]dd by p[ar]liamts" is a verbatim transcription (*CM* 13).[19] The choice of Lambarde is especially noteworthy in view of Lambarde's stance on the relationship of law and equity. Contemporary common law jurists such as Christopher St. German and Edward Hake regarded equity as contained within the common law itself. However, Lambarde saw equity and law as "essentially and from their beginnings, at odds with one another," although he felt that that opposition could be "harmonious and productive."[20] This law/equity distinction appears in Lambarde's discussion of the etymology of the word "chancellor," a discussion transcribed in the Columbia Manuscript. "Chancellor" comes from the Latin *cancellarius*, meaning the one who cancels out. Lambarde explains that the Chancellor's role is to "make void a record" by "drawing certaine crosse lines lettice-wise wth his pen over it on it," a reference to the lattice-like strokes of ink that annulled documents in equity proceedings. Lambarde explains that this textual cancellation mirrors the authority of the Chancellor "in his court of equity" to "shut up the rigr of the ge[n]erall law, th[a]t it

---

17. For discussion of the contest between the Admiralty and the common law, see Zouch, *Jurisdiction of the Admiralty*. Zouch was a Civil lawyer who sat on the Admiralty bench, and like Gentili, he was one of the earliest English writers on international law.

18. See Lambarde, *Archeion*, 103–6.

19. Beginning on page 13 of the notebook, the Transcriber begins copying out Lambarde's discussion of Chancery. With only a few minor omissions, pages 45–58 of *Archeion* are reproduced directly in the Columbia MS.

20. Fortier, *Culture of Equity*, 69.

shall not break forth to the hurt of some one singular p[er]son" (*CM* 13). For Lambarde and implicitly for the Transcriber who copies his words, the power of the common law (the "ge[n]erall law") must coexist with other pockets of judicial authority, such as Chancery, so that people who are denied justice in one forum might find it in another.

Overall, the selection of treatises in this portion of the Columbia Manuscript indicates that the Transcriber agreed with that influential minority of voices in seventeenth-century England who were not happy about the growing hegemony of the common law. Coke was the architect of the common law's legal monopoly, and his jurisprudence inclined strongly toward the position that the best way to reduce corruption and improve the administration of law was to digest all legal systems into one. In his "Observacions upon Cookes Reports," Lord Ellesmere (the earl of Bridgewater's father) identifies the tenor of Coke's thinking: the Chief Justice sought to "cutt short the Jurisdiccion of all other Courts but of that Court wherein himselfe doth sitt."[21] Much of Ellesmere's career as Lord Chancellor was spent protecting Chancery's jurisdiction from being eroded by the rising common law tide. Across the early modern period, we can find others who agreed with Ellesmere. For example, the prominent Civilian Thomas Ridley deplores the fact that different jurisdictions fought over cases "as in a batable ground lying betweene two Kingdomes." Ridley argues that if jurisdictional lines are simply delineated more carefully, each jurisprudence can "reteine their owne right, and not the one be overtopt by the other."[22] From the distance of several centuries, all this can seem like mere technicalities relevant only to those who had a professional stake in the viability of different courts. However, as Goodrich argues, legal monopolies make a nuanced application of justice more difficult. Broad legal norms are blunt instruments that are intrinsically insensitive to local and individual variations. As Lambarde puts it in the excerpt transcribed in the Columbia Manuscript, if left unchecked, the "ge[n]erall law" inflicts harm, and so juridical forums such as equity must be available to provide more responsive and elastic forms of relief.

The Transcriber's discussions of equity are the last treatises in the Columbia Manuscript before we come to "Proposalls of certaine expedients for the p[re]venting of a civill war now feard, and the settling of a firme governmt. by J. M." Milton's last recommendation in *Proposalls* sits comfortably with the notebook's overall tenor: "10. and lastly, th[a]t the administration of Civill Jus-

---

21. Quoted in Knafla, *Law and Politics*, 297.
22. Ridley, *View*, [printer's flower]3, [printer's flower]4r.

tice may be in the City of chief towns of every county wthout appeal, Judges and all such officers by themselves chosen, whereby they shall have no cause to clam[o]r ag[ains]t the supreme Counsell, nor can hope for more equall Justice in any othr place" (*CM* 21). Then comes Milton's *Letter to a Friend* (untitled in the Columbia Manuscript), where he touches on the need to reform the "places of judicature" (*CM* 23) so that justice can be less standardized and more granular. Even his state letters, copied out in the Columbia Manuscript, are also about preserving jurisdictional variety since most of them are attempts to solve jurisdictional problems arising in international contexts, such as whether English merchant ships can be held or confiscated by foreign powers. The various forms of law presented in the Columbia Manuscript are the juridical equivalent to the "brotherly dissimilitudes" that Milton celebrates in *Areopagitica*, forms of difference that strengthened the nation's social and political fabric (*CPW* 2:555). On subjects ranging from books to England's diversity of courts, Milton expresses a consistent fundamental belief: blanket prescriptions flatten out the rich variety of civil and religious life, and people should be left as free as possible to make choices for themselves.

ACKNOWLEDGMENTS

One happy consequence of writing about the many different kinds of law that surrounded John Milton and his peers in early modern England is that it has prompted me to reflect on the many different voices that surround me. I do not inhabit a jurisdictional patchwork in the way that Milton did, but I am grateful to inhabit a social and intellectual one. I have an exceptional group of scholar colleagues, including Rebecca Ann Bach, who brought her incisiveness and intelligence to bear on the whole manuscript, and John Rumrich and Margaret Jay Jessee, who offered helpful suggestions on individual chapters. Eddie Luster, Delores Carlito, and Jeff Graveline provided help on various research questions, and two anonymous readers at the University of Chicago Press identified weak points in an earlier iteration of the manuscript. Simon Stern steered me straight on some technical legal questions and provided helpful comments on an earlier version of chapter 4, which appeared in *Contemporary Analysis of Law*, which he edits. I am grateful to Edward Jones and *Milton Quarterly* for permission to reprint "Defending Milton's *Pro Se Defensio*: A Legal Reading," *Milton Quarterly* 51 (2017): 75–96, © 2017 John Wiley and Sons Ltd., as chapter 5; and to *Renaissance Quarterly* for allowing me to use a portion of "Milton and Legal Reform," *Renaissance Quarterly* 69 (2016): 529–65, © 2016 Renaissance Society of America, in chapter 7. I cannot write anything without thinking of the debt I owe to two exceptional mentors, Margreta de Grazia and Cynthia L. Lewis. Mimi Fenton has been the most constant and generous of friends. Above all, Karen, Gordon, Ian, Angus, and Lucian make my life worthwhile.

BIBLIOGRAPHY

Achinstein, Sharon. "'A Law in This Matter to Himself': Contextualizing Milton's Divorce Tracts." In *The Oxford Handbook of Milton*, edited by Nicholas McDowell and Nigel Smith, 174–84. Oxford: Oxford University Press, 2009.
———. *Milton and the Revolutionary Reader*. Princeton: Princeton University Press, 1994.
Ainsworth, David. *Milton and the Spiritual Reader: Reading and Religion in Seventeenth-Century England*. New York: Routledge, 2008.
Ames, William. *Conscience with the Power and Cases Thereof*. N.p., 1639.
Aquinas, Thomas. *Summa Theologica*. Translated by Fathers of the English Dominican Province. 5 vols. Westminster, MD: Christian Classics, 1981.
Aristotle. *Nicomachean Ethics*. In *The Complete Works of Aristotle: Revised Oxford Translation*, edited by Jonathan Barnes. Vol. 2. Princeton: Princeton University Press, 1984.
Baker, John. *The Oxford History of the Laws of England, vol. 6: 1483–1558*. Oxford: Oxford University Press, 2003.
Barker, Arthur Edward. *Milton and the Puritan Dilemma*. Toronto: University of Toronto Press, 1942.
Barnes, Thomas G. "Star Chamber Mythology." *American Journal of Legal History* 5 (1961): 1–11.
Bartolus of Sassoferrato. *Omnium Iuris Interpretum Antesignani Commentaria*. Venice, 1544.
Baxter, Richard. *A Christian Directory, or A Summ of Practical Theologie and Cases of Conscience*. London, 1673.
Bellany, Alastair. "A Poem on the Archbishop's Hearse: Puritanism, Libel, and Sedition after the Hampton Court Conference." *Journal of British Studies* 34 (1995): 137–64.
———. *The Politics of Court Scandal in Early Modern England: News Culture and the Overbury Affair, 1603–1660*. Cambridge: Cambridge University Press, 2007.
———. "'Rayling Rymes and Vaunting Verse': Libellous Politics in Early Stuart England." In *Culture and Politics in Early Stuart England*, edited by Kevin Sharpe, 285–310. Stanford: Stanford University Press, 1993.

Bellany, Alastair, and Andrew McRae. "Early Stuart Libels: An Edition of Poetry from Manuscript Sources." Early Modern Literary Studies Text Series I, 2005. http://www.earlystuartlibels.net/htdocs/introduction/ii.html.

Belsey, Catherine. *John Milton: Language, Gender, Power*. New York: Basil Blackwell, 1988.

Berman, Harold J. *Faith and Order: The Reconciliation of Law and Religion*. Atlanta: Scholars Press, 1993.

———. *Law and Revolution: The Formation of the Western Legal Tradition*. Cambridge, MA: Harvard University Press, 1985.

———. *Law and Revolution II: The Impact of the Protestant Reformation on the Western Legal Tradition*. Cambridge, MA: Belknap Press of Harvard University Press, 2003.

Blackstone, William. *Commentaries on the Laws of England*. 4 vols. Oxford, 1766.

Blomley, Nicholas K. *Law, Space, and the Geographies of Power*. New York: Guilford, 1994.

Blount, Thomas. *Glossographia: Or, A Dictionary*. London, 1656.

———. *Nomo-Lexicon, A Law Dictionary*. London, 1670.

Blum, Abbe. "The Author's Authority: *Areopagitica* and the Labour of Licensing." In *Remembering Milton: Essays on the Texts and Traditions*, edited by Mary Nyquist and Margaret W. Ferguson. New York: Methuen, 1987.

Bobbio, Norberto. *Thomas Hobbes and the Natural Law Tradition*. Translated by Daniela Gobetti. Chicago: University of Chicago Press, 1993.

Bowman, Jeffrey A. "Infamy and Proof in Medieval Spain." In *Fama: The Politics of Talk and Reputation in Medieval Europe*, edited by Thelma Fenster and Daniel Lord Smail, 95–117. Ithaca, NY: Cornell University Press, 2003.

Boyer, Allen D. *Sir Edward Coke and the Elizabethan Age*. Stanford: Stanford University Press, 2003.

Brand, Paul. "The Equity of the Common Law Courts." In *Law and Equity: Approaches in Roman Law and Common Law*, edited by Egbert Koops and Willem J. Zwalve, 39–54. Leiden: Martinus Nijhoff, 2014.

Breasted, Barbara. "*Comus* and the Castlehaven Scandal." *Milton Studies* 3 (1971): 201–24.

Brittan, Jillisa, and Richard A. Posner. "Penal Theory in *Paradise Lost*." *Michigan Law Review* 105 (2007): 1049–66.

Brooks, Christopher W. *Law, Politics, and Society in Early Modern England*. Cambridge: Cambridge University Press, 2008.

———. *Lawyers, Litigation and English Society since 1450*. London: Hambledon Press, 1998.

———. *Pettyfoggers and Vipers of the Commonwealth: The "Lower Branch" of the Legal Profession in Early Modern England*. Cambridge: Cambridge University Press, 1986.

Brown, James C. "Revealed Law in Salmasius." In *Milton, Rights, and Liberties*, edited by Christophe Tournu and Neil Forsyth. Bern: Peter Lang, 2007.

Browne, Thomas. *Pseudodoxia Epidemica, or, Enquiries into Very Many Received Tenents and Commonly Presumed Truths*. London, 1646.

Brundage, James A. *The Medieval Origins of the Legal Profession: Canonists, Civilians, and Courts*. Chicago: University of Chicago Press, 2008.

Bunyan, John. *A Relation of the Imprisonment of Mr. John Bunyan*. London, 1765.

———. *A True and Impartial Narrative*. London, 1670.

Burgess, Glenn. *The Politics of the Ancient Constitution: An Introduction to English Political Thought, 1603–1642*. University Park: Pennsylvania State University Press, 1992.
Butler, Todd. "Milton, Deliberative Liberty, and the Law of Spousal Privileges." *Milton Studies* 59 (2017): 231–58.
Cable, Lana. "Coupling Logic and Milton's Doctrine of Divorce." *Milton Studies* 15 (1981): 143–59.
Cairns, John W., and Grant McLeod, eds. *The Dearest Birthright of the People of England: The Jury in the History of Common Law*. Oxford: Hart, 2002.
Campbell, Gordon. "Milton, Sir Christopher (1615–1693)." In *Oxford Dictionary of National Biography*, edited by H. C. G. Matthew and Brian Harrison. Online ed., ed. Lawrence Goldman, January 2008. Oxford: Oxford University Press, 2004. http://www.oxforddnb.com/view/article/18798.
Capua, J. V. "The Early History of Martial Law in England from the Fourteenth Century to the Petition of Right." *Cambridge Law Journal* 36 (April 1977): 152–73.
Carter, Albert Thomas. *A History of English Legal Institutions*. London: Butterworths, 1906.
Carter, John. *Vindiciae Decimarum. Of Tithes, A Plea for the Ius Divinum*. London, 1640.
Cecil, Robert (Earl of Salisbury). *The State and Dignitie of a Secretarie of Estates Place*. London, 1643.
Chapman, Alison A. "The Lay Reader's Guide to *Milton v. Cope*: Trust, Debt, and Loss in Chancery." *Milton Quarterly* 52 (2018): 113–27.
———. *The Legal Epic: Paradise Lost and the Early Modern Law*. Chicago: University of Chicago Press, 2017.
———. "Milton and Legal Reform." *Renaissance Quarterly* 69 (2016): 529–65.
Chroust, Anton-Hermann. "Aristotle's Conception of Equity." *Notre Dame Law Review* 18 (1942): 119–28.
Chroust, Anton-Hermann, and John Richard Murphy. "Lex Acilia and the Rise of Trial by Jury in the Roman World." *Notre Dame Law Review* 24 (1948): 1–40.
Cicero. *De Officiis/On Duties*. Indianapolis: Bobbs-Merrill, 1974.
Coke, Edward. *An Exact Abridgment in English of the Eleven Books of Reports of the Learned Sir Edward Coke*. London, 1651.
———. *The Fourth Part of the Institutes of the Laws of England*. London, 1644.
———. *The Selected Writings of Sir Edward Coke*. Edited by Steve Sheppard. 3 vols. Indianapolis: Liberty Fund, 2003.
———. *The Third Part of the Institutes of the Laws of England*. London, 1644.
Cole, William. *A Rod for the Lawyers*. London, 1659.
Columbia University Libraries. "John Milton Letters, 1649–1659." CLIO online catalog entry. Accessed September 20, 2019. https://clio.columbia.edu/catalog/4079110.
Cormack, Bradin. *A Power to Do Justice: Jurisdiction, English Literature, and the Rise of Common Law, 1509–1625*. Chicago: University of Chicago Press, 2007.
Corns, Thomas N. "Milton and the Characteristics of a Free Commonwealth." In *Milton and Republicanism*, edited by David Armitage, Armand Himy, and Quentin Skinner, 25–42. Cambridge: Cambridge University Press, 1995.

Coughlin, John J. *Canon Law: A Comparative Study with Anglo-American Legal Theory*. Oxford: Oxford University Press, 2011.

———. *Law, Person, and Community: Philosophical, Theological, and Comparative Perspectives on Canon Law*. Oxford: Oxford University Press, 2012.

Cover, Robert. *Narrative, Violence, and the Law: The Essays of Robert Cover*. Edited by Martha Minow, Michael Ryan, and Austin Sarat. Ann Arbor: University of Michigan Press, 1992.

Creaser, John. "Milton's *Comus*: The Irrelevance of the Castlehaven Scandal." *Milton Quarterly* 21 (1987): 24–34.

Cressy, David. *Dangerous Talk: Scandalous, Seditious, and Treasonable Speech in Pre-modern England*. Oxford: Oxford University Press, 2010.

Croft, Pauline. "Libels, Popular Literacy and Public Opinion in Early Modern England." *Historical Research* 68 (1995): 266–85.

Cromartie, Alan. *Sir Matthew Hale, 1609–1676: Law, Religion and Natural Philosophy*. Cambridge: Cambridge University Press, 1995.

Curtis, T. C. "Quarter Sessions Appearances and Their Background: A Seventeenth-Century Regional Study." In *Crime in England 1550–1800*, edited by J. S. Cockburn, 135–54. Princeton: Princeton University Press, 1977.

Damaska, Mirjan R. "Of Hearsay and Its Analogues." *Minnesota Law Review* 56 (1992): 425–58.

Darbishire, Helen, ed. *The Early Lives of Milton*. New York: Barnes and Noble, 1932.

Dawson, John P. *A History of Lay Judges*. Union, N.J.: Lawbook Exchange, 1999.

Dean, David. *Law-Making and Society in Late Elizabethan England: The Parliament of England, 1584–1601*. Cambridge: Cambridge University Press, 1996.

Dering, Edward. *A Collection of Speeches Made by Sir Edward Dering*. London, 1642.

D'Ewes, Simonds. "Journal of the House of Commons: April 1571." In *Journals of All the Parliaments during the Reign of Queene Elizabeth*, 155–80. Shannon, Ireland, 1682. British History Online. www.british-history.ac.uk/no-series/jrnl-parliament-eliz1/pp155-80.

Dobranski, Stephen B. *Milton, Authorship, and the Book Trade*. Cambridge: Cambridge University Press, 1999.

———. *Readers and Authorship in Early Modern England*. Cambridge: Cambridge University Press, 2005.

Donne, John. "Preached at Lincoln's Inne [January 30, 1619/20]." In *John Donne Sermons*. Digital Collections, BYU Library. Provo, UT: Brigham Young University, 2019. https://lib.byu.edu/collections/john-donne-sermons/.

Dzelzainis, Martin. "'In These Western Parts of the Empire': Milton and Roman Law." In *Milton and the Terms of Liberty*, edited by Graham Parry and Joad Raymond, 57–68. Cambridge: D. S. Brewer, 2002.

———. "Liberty and the Law." In *Milton, Rights, and Liberties*, edited by Christophe Tournu and Neil Forsyth, 57–67. Bern: Peter Lang, 2007.

———. "Managing the Later Stuart Press, 1662–1696." In *The Oxford Handbook of English Law and Literature, 1500–1700*, edited by Lorna Hutson, 529–47. Oxford: Oxford University Press, 2017.

———. "Republicanism." In *A Companion to Milton*, edited by Thomas N. Corns, 294–308. Malden, MA: Blackwell, 2001.
Eden, Kathy. *Hermeneutics and the Rhetorical Tradition: Chapters in the Ancient Legacy and Its Humanist Reception*. New Haven: Yale University Press, 1997.
Edgerton, Samuel Y., Jr. *Pictures and Punishment: Art and Criminal Prosecution during the Florentine Renaissance*. Ithaca, NY: Cornell University Press, 1985.
Fallon, Stephen M. *Milton among the Philosophers: Poetry and Materialism in Seventeenth-Century England*. Ithaca, NY: Cornell University Press, 1991.
Fink, Zera S. *The Classical Republicans: An Essay in the Recovery of a Pattern of Thought in Seventeenth-Century England*. Evanston, IL: Northwestern University Press, 1962.
Fish, Stanley. *How Milton Works*. Cambridge, MA: Harvard University Press, 2001.
Flannagan, Roy, ed. *Paradise Lost*. In *The Riverside Milton*. Boston: Houghton Mifflin, 1998.
Fletcher, H. F. *The Intellectual Development of John Milton*. 2 vols. Urbana: University of Illinois Press, 1956.
Ford, Richard T. "Law's Territory (A History of Jurisdiction)." *Michigan Law Review* 97 (1999): 843–930.
Fortier, Mark. *The Culture of Equity in Early Modern England*. Burlington, VT: Ashgate, 2005.
Fraher, Richard M. "Conviction according to Conscience: The Medieval Jurists' Debate concerning Judicial Discretion and the Law of Proof." *Law and History Review* 7 (1989): 23–88.
———. "Preventing Crime in the High Middle Ages." In *Popes, Teachers, and Canon Law in the Middle Ages*, edited by James Ross Sweeney, 212–33. Ithaca, NY: Cornell University Press, 1989.
Freeman, James A. *Milton and the Martial Muse: Paradise Lost and European Traditions of War*. Princeton: Princeton University Press, 1980.
Freize, James. *A Moderate Inspection into the Corruption of the Pratique Part of the Common Law*. London, 1656.
French, Joseph Milton, ed. *The Life Records of John Milton*. 5 vols. New Brunswick, NJ: Rutgers University Press, 1966.
———. *Milton in Chancery: New Chapters in the Lives of the Poet and His Father*. New York: Modern Language Association, 1939.
Fuller, Thomas. *A Sermon of Reformation Preached at the Church of Savoy*. London, 1643.
Fulton, Thomas. *Historical Milton: Manuscript, Print, and Political Culture in Revolutionary England*. Amherst: University of Massachusetts Press, 2010.
Gardiner, Samuel Rawson, ed. *The Constitutional Documents of the Puritan Revolution*. 3rd ed. Oxford: Clarendon Press, 1906.
Goldie, Mark. "The Unacknowledged Republic: Officeholding in Early Modern England." In *The Politics of the Excluded, c. 1500–1800*, edited by Tim Harris, 153–94. London: Palgrave, 2001.
Goodrich, Peter. *Law in the Courts of Love: Literature and Other Minor Jurisprudences*. London: Routledge, 1996.
Gordon, Andrew. "The Act of Libel: Conscripting Civic Space in Early Modern England." *Journal of Medieval and Early Modern Studies* 32 (2002): 375–98.

Gordon, Robert W. "Critical Legal Histories." *Stanford Law Review* 36 (1984): 57–125.
Gray, Charles M. *The Writ of Prohibition: Jurisdiction in Early Modern English Law*. 2 vols. New York: Oceana, 1994.
Greaves, Richard L. *Glimpses of Glory: John Bunyan and English Dissent*. Stanford: Stanford University Press, 2002.
Green, Adrian. "Law and Architecture in Early Modern Durham." In *Law, Lawyers, and Litigants in Early Modern England: Essays in Memory of Christopher W. Brooks*, edited by Michael Lobban, Joanne Begiato, and Adrian Green, 265–91. Cambridge: Cambridge University Press, 2019.
Green, Thomas Andrew. *Verdict according to Conscience: Perspectives on the English Criminal Trial Jury, 1200–1800*. Chicago: University of Chicago Press, 1985.
Greenberg, Lynne. "Dalila's 'Feminine Assaults': The Gendering and Engendering of Crime in *Samson Agonistes*." In *Altering Eyes: New Perspectives on Samson Agonistes*, edited by Mark R. Kelley and Joseph Wittreich, 192–218. Newark: University of Delaware Press, 2002.
———. "Law." In *Milton in Context*, edited by Stephen B. Dobranski, 328–37. Cambridge: Cambridge University Press, 2010.
———. "Milton's Figure of the Whore: Criminal Prosecution and Law Reform." Unpublished manuscript, consulted November 5, 2019.
———. "'A Peal of Words': Criminal Speech in *Samson Agonistes*." In *Reassembling Truth: Twenty-First-Century Milton*, edited by Charles W. Durham and Kristin Pruitt, 189–200. Susquehanna, PA: Susquehanna University Press, 2003.
Greene, Jody. *The Trouble with Ownership: Literary Property and Authorial Liability in England, 1660–1730*. Philadelphia: University of Pennsylvania Press, 2005.
Greenfield, Matthew. "Trial by Theater: Jonson, Marston, and Dekker in the Court of Parnassus." In *Solon and Thespis: Law and Theater in the English Renaissance*, edited by Dennis Kezar, 19–39. Notre Dame, IN: University of Notre Dame Press, 2007.
Gregerson, Linda. *The Reformation of the Subject: Spenser, Milton, and the English Protestant Epic*. Cambridge: Cambridge University Press, 1995.
Gregory, Tobias. "Did Milton Have an Erastian Phase?" *Milton Quarterly* 49 (2015): 159–66.
Habakkuk, H. J. "Public Finance and the Sale of Confiscated Property during the Interregnum." *Economic History Review* 15 (1962): 70–88.
Hale, Matthew. *The History of the Common Law of England*. Edited by Charles M. Gray. Chicago: University of Chicago Press, 1971.
Halkett, John. *Milton and the Idea of Matrimony: A Study of the Divorce Tracts and Paradise Lost*. New Haven: Yale University Press, 1970.
Hall, John. *An Humble Motion to the Parliament of England Concerning the Advancement of Learning, and Reformation of the Universities*. London, 1649.
Hall, Joseph. *A Defense of the Humble Remonstrance, against the Frivolous and False Exceptions of Smectymnuus*. London, 1641.
———. *An Humble Remonstrance to the High Court of Parliament*. London, 1640.
Haller, William. "Two Early Allusions to Milton's *Areopagitica*." *Huntington Library Quarterly* 12 (1949): 207–12.

Halliday, Paul D. "Birthrights and the Due Course of Law." In *The Oxford Handbook of English Law and Literature, 1500–1700*, edited by Lorna Hutson, 587–603. Oxford: Oxford University Press, 2017.

Hamburger, Philip. "The Development of the Law of Seditious Libel and the Control of the Press." *Stanford Law Review* 37 (1985): 661–765.

Hammond, Paul. *Milton and the People*. Oxford: Oxford University Press, 2014.

Haskin, Dayton. *Milton's Burden of Interpretation*. Philadelphia: University of Pennsylvania Press, 1994.

Hawkes, David. "The Concept of the 'Hireling' in Milton's Theology." *Milton Studies* 43 (2004): 64–85.

———. *The Culture of Usury in Renaissance England*. New York: Palgrave, 2010.

———. *John Milton: A Hero of Our Time*. Berkeley: Counterpoint, 2009.

Hay, Douglas. "Dread of the Crown Office: The English Magistracy and King's Bench, 1740–1800." In *Law, Crime and English Society, 1660–1830*, edited by Norma Landau, 19–45. Cambridge: Cambridge University Press, 2002.

Haydon, Liam D. "*Paradise Lost* and the Politics of the Corporation." *SEL Studies in English Literature 1500–1900* 57 (2017): 135–55.

Helmholz, R. H. *The Oxford History of the Laws of England, vol. 1: The Canon Law and Ecclesiastical Jurisdiction from 591 to the 1640s*. Oxford: Oxford University Press, 2004.

———. *Roman Canon Law in Reformation England*. Cambridge: Cambridge University Press, 1990.

———, ed. *Select Cases on Defamation to 1600*. London: Selden Society, 1985.

———, ed. *Three Civilian Notebooks, 1580–1640*. London: Selden Society, 2011.

Herbert, George. *A Priest to the Temple, or The Country Parson*. London, 1652.

Herrup, Cynthia. *The Common Peace: Participation and the Criminal Law in Seventeenth-Century England*. Cambridge: Cambridge University Press, 1987.

Hexham, Henry. *A True and Briefe Relation of the Famous Siege of Breda*. London, 1637.

Hill, Christopher. *Economic Problems of the Church, from Archbishop Whitgift to the Long Parliament*. Oxford: Clarendon Press, 1968.

Hindle, Steve. "The Micro-Spatial Dynamics of Litigation: The Chilvers Coton Tithe Dispute, *Barrows vs. Archer* (1657)." In *Law, Lawyers, and Litigants in Early Modern England: Essays in Memory of Christopher W. Brooks*, edited by Michael Lobban, Joanne Begiato, and Adrian Green, 140–63. Cambridge: Cambridge University Press, 2019.

———. *The State and Social Change in Early Modern England, c. 1550–1640*. New York: St. Martin's Press, 2000.

Hinds, Peter. "Roger L'Estrange, the Rye House Plot, and the Regulation of Political Discourse in Late-Seventeenth-Century London." *Library* 3 (2002): 3–31.

Holdsworth, Sir William. *A History of English Law*. 17 vols. London: Methuen, 1924.

Howard, W. Scott. "Milton's 'Divorcive' Liberties: Ecclesiastical, Domestic, or Private, Civil and Cosmological." *Early Modern Literary Studies* 10 (May 2004): 5.1–12.

Hoxby, Blair. *Mammon's Music: Literature and Economics in the Age of Milton*. New Haven: Yale University Press, 2002.

Hoyle, R. W. "The Masters of Requests and the Small Change of Jacobean Patronage." *English Historical Review* 126 (2011): 544–81.

Hudson, William. *A Treatise of the Court of Star Chamber by William Hudson as Taken from Collecteana Juridica*. Edited by Francis Hargrave. Birmingham: Legal Classics Library, 1986.

Hughes, Ann. "Milton, *Areopagitica*, and the Parliamentary Cause." In *The Oxford Handbook of Milton*, edited by Nicholas McDowell and Nigel Smith, 200–217. Oxford: Oxford University Press, 2009.

Hutson, Lorna. *The Invention of Suspicion: Law and Mimesis in Shakespeare and Renaissance Drama*. Oxford: Oxford University Press, 2007.

———, ed. *The Oxford Handbook of English Law and Literature, 1500–1700*. Oxford: Oxford University Press, 2017.

Hutton, Ronald. *The Restoration: A Political and Religious History of England and Wales 1658–1667*. Oxford: Clarendon Press, 1985.

Ibbetson, David. "Common Law and *Ius Commune*." In *The Selden Society Lectures 1952–2001*, 673–705. Buffalo, NY: William S. Hein, 2003.

———. "The Earl of Oxford's Case (1615)." In *Landmark Cases in Equity*, edited by Charles Mitchell and Paul Mitchell, 1–32. Oxford: Hart, 2012.

———. "Edward Coke, Roman Law, and the Law of Libel." In *The Oxford Handbook of English Law and Literature, 1500–1700*, edited by Lorna Hutson, 487–506. Oxford: Oxford University Press, 2017.

Illo, John. "*Areopagiticas* Mythic and Real." *Prose Studies* 11 (1988): 3–23.

Im, Seo Hee. "Between Habbakuk and Locke: Pain, Debt, and Economic Subjectivation in *Paradise Lost*." *Modern Language Quarterly* 78 (2017): 1–25.

Ingram, Martin. *Church Courts, Sex, and Marriage in England, 1570–1640*. Past and Present Publications. Cambridge: Cambridge University Press, 1987.

———. "Law, Litigants, and the Construction of 'Honor': Slander Suits in Early Modern England." In *The Moral World of the Law*, edited by Peter Coss, 134–60. Cambridge: Cambridge University Press, 2000.

James, Margaret. "The Political Importance of the Tithe Controversy in the English Revolution, 1640–1660." *History* 26 (1941): 1–18.

Jansson, Maija. *Proceedings in the Opening Session of the Long Parliament: House of Commons, vol. 1: 3 November–19 December 1640 (Proceedings of the English Parliament)*. Rochester: University of Rochester Press, 2000.

Jenkins, Joseph S. *Inheritance Law and Political Theology in Shakespeare and Milton: Election and Grace as Constitutional in Early Modern Literature and Beyond*. New York: Routledge, 2016.

Jenks, Susanne. "Picking Up the Pieces: Cases Presented to the London Sheriffs' Courts between Michaelmas 1461 and Michaelmas 1462." *Journal of Legal History* 29 (2008): 99–145.

Johns, Adrian. *The Nature of the Book: Print and Knowledge in the Making*. Chicago: University of Chicago Press, 2009.

Johnson, Andrew. "Music Critic's Book Is Pulped as Penguin Loses Defamation Case." *Inde-

pendent, October 27, 2007. http://www.independent.co.uk/news/uk/crime/music-critics-book-is-pulped-as-penguin-loses-defamation-case-398144.html.

Johnson, Robert C., and Maija Jansson Cole, eds. *Commons Debates 1628, vol. 2: 17 March–19 April 1628*. New Haven: Yale University Press, 1977.

Jones, W. J. "The Crown and the Courts in England, 1603–1625." In *Law, Liberty, and Parliament: Selected Essays on the Writings of Sir Edward Coke*, edited by Allen D. Boyer, 282–301. Indianapolis: Liberty Fund, 2004.

———. *The Elizabethan Court of Chancery*. Oxford: Clarendon Press, 1967.

Jonson, Ben. *Poetaster*. Edited by Tom Cain. Manchester: Manchester University Press, 1995.

Justinian. *The Digest of Justinian*. Edited by Theodor Mommsen. Translated by Alan Watson. 4 vols. Philadelphia: University of Pennsylvania Press, 1985.

Kahn, Victoria. *Wayward Contracts: The Crisis of Political Obligation in England, 1640–1670*. Princeton: Princeton University Press, 2004.

King, John N. *Milton and Religious Controversy: Satire and Polemic in Paradise Lost*. Cambridge: Cambridge University Press, 2000.

King, Peter. "The Summary Courts and Social Relations in Eighteenth-Century England." *Past and Present* 183 (2004): 125–72.

Klinck, Dennis R. *Conscience, Equity and the Court of Chancery in Early Modern England*. Farnham, Surrey: Ashgate, 2010.

Klotz, Lisa. "Ben Jonson's Legal Imagination in *Volpone*." *Studies in English Literature, 1500–1900* 51 (2011): 385–408.

Knafla, Louis A. *Law and Politics in Jacobean England: The Tracts of Lord Chancellor Ellesmere*. Cambridge: Cambridge University Press, 1977.

Kneidel, Gregory. *John Donne and Early Modern Legal Culture: The End of Equity in the Satyres*. Pittsburgh, PA: Duquesne University Press, 2015.

Kolbrener, William. *Milton's Warring Angels: A Study of Critical Engagements*. Cambridge: Cambridge University Press, 1997.

Kranidas, Thomas. "Style and Rectitude in Seventeenth-Century Prose: Hall, Smectymnuus, and Milton." *Huntington Library Quarterly* 46 (1983): 237–69.

Kuehn, Thomas. "*Fama* as a Legal Status in Renaissance Florence." In *Fama: The Politics of Talk in Medieval Europe*, edited by Thelma Fenster and Daniel Lord Smail, 27–46. Ithaca, NY: Cornell University Press, 2003.

Kuttner, Stephan. "Natural Law and Canon Law." *University of Notre Dame Natural Law Institute Proceedings* 3 (1949): 85–116.

LaBreche, Ben. "*Areopagitica* and the Limits of Pluralism." *Milton Studies* 54 (2013): 139–60.

Lambarde, William. *Archeion, or, A Discourse upon the High Courts of Justice in England*. London, 1635.

Landau, Norma. "The Changing Persona of the Justices and Their Quarter Sessions." In *The Oxford Handbook of English Law and Literature, 1500–1700*, edited by Lorna Hutson, 239–56. Oxford: Oxford University Press, 2017.

Landau, Peter. "*Aequitas* in the 'Corpus Iuris Canonici.'" *Syracuse Journal of International Law and Commerce* 20 (1994): 95–104.

Leadam, I. S., ed. *Select Cases in the Court of Requests*. London: Selden Society, 1898.

Lee, Daniel. *Popular Sovereignty in Early Modern Constitutional Thought*. Oxford: Oxford University Press, 2016.

Lefebvre, Charles. "Natural Equity and Canonical Equity." *American Journal of Jurisprudence* 8 (1963): 122–36.

Lemmings, David. *Law and Government in England during the Long Eighteenth Century: From Consent to Command*. Basingstoke: Palgrave, 2011.

Leonard, John. *The Value of Milton*. Cambridge: Cambridge University Press, 2016.

L'Estrange, Roger. *An Answer to the Appeal from the Country to the City*. London, 1679.

———. *Considerations and Proposals in Order to the Regulation of the Press*. London, 1663.

Levack, Brian. *The Civil Lawyers in England, 1603–1641: A Political Study*. Oxford: Oxford University Press, 1973.

Levy, Leonard W. *Emergence of a Free Press*. New York: Oxford University Press, 1985.

Lewalski, Barbara K. *The Life of John Milton: A Critical Biography*. Oxford: Blackwell, 2000.

Lieb, Michael. *Milton and the Culture of Violence*. Ithaca: Cornell University Press, 1994.

Lilburne, John. *Londons Liberty in Chains Discovered*. London, 1646.

Lobis, Seth. "Satan and the Problem of Gratitude." Exeter, U.K.: International Milton Symposium, 2015.

Loewenstein, David. "Milton and the Poetics of Defense." In *Politics, Poetics, and Hermeneutics in Milton's Prose*, edited by David Loewenstein and James Grantham Turner, 171–92. Cambridge: Cambridge University Press, 1990.

———. "Treason against God and State: Blasphemy in Milton's Culture and *Paradise Lost*." In *Milton and Heresy*, edited by Stephen B. Dobranski and John P. Rumrich, 176–98. Cambridge: Cambridge University Press, 1998.

Loewenstein, Joseph F. *The Author's Due: Printing and the Prehistory of Copyright*. Chicago: University of Chicago Press, 2002.

Lyle, J. V., ed. *Acts of the Privy Council of England, vol. 36: 1618–1619*. London: His Majesty's Stationery Office, 1929. www.british-history.ac.uk/acts-privy-council/vol36.

Mackenzie, James. *A Narrative of the Siege of London-Derry*. London, 1690.

Macnair, Michael R. T. "Equity and Conscience." *Oxford Journal of Legal Studies* 27 (2007): 659–81.

———. *The Law of Proof in Early Modern Equity*. Berlin: Duncker and Humblot, 1999.

Maltzahn, Nicholas von. "Naming the Author: Some Seventeenth-Century Milton Allusions." *Milton Quarterly* 27 (1993): 1–19.

Manning, Roger B. "The Origins of the Doctrine of Sedition." *Albion: A Quarterly Journal concerned with British Studies* 12 (1980): 99–121.

March, John. *Actions for Slaunder*. London, 1647.

Marchant, Ronald A. *The Church under the Law: Justice, Administration, and Discipline in the Diocese of York, 1560–1640*. Cambridge: Cambridge University Press, 1969.

Marcus, Leah S. "The Milieu of Milton's *Comus*: Judicial Reform at Ludlow and the Problem of Sexual Assault." *Criticism* 25 (1983): 293–327.

Masson, David. *The Life of John Milton*. 7 vols. New York: Peter Smith, 1946.

Matthews, Nancy L. *William Sheppard, Cromwell's Law Reformer*. Cambridge: Cambridge University Press, 1984.

Maus, Katherine Eisaman. *Being and Having in Shakespeare*. Oxford: Oxford University Press, 2013.

McComish, James. "Defining Boundaries: Law, Justice, and Community in Sixteenth-Century England." In *Legalism, Community, and Justice*, edited by Fernanda Pirie and Judith Scheele, 125–50. Oxford: Oxford University Press, 2014.

McIlwain, Charles Howard. *The High Court of Parliament and Its Supremacy: An Historical Essay on the Boundaries between Legislation and Adjudication in England*. New Haven: Yale University Press, 1910.

McRae, Andrew. *Literature, Satire, and the Early Stuart State*. Cambridge: Cambridge University Press, 2004.

———, ed. *"Railing Rhymes": Politics and Poetry in Early Stuart England*. Vol. 69. Themed Issue of *Huntington Library Quarterly*, 2006.

Medine, Peter E. "Gratitude and *Paradise Lost*: A Neglected Context." In *Milton and the Grounds of Contention*, edited by Mark R. Kelley, Michael Lieb, and John T. Shawcross, 115–49. Pittsburgh, PA: Duquesne University Press, 2003.

Mercurius Aulicus (for King Charles II). 1649.

Meyjes, G. H. M. Posthumus. *Jean Gerson Apostle of Unity: His Church Politics and Ecclesiology*. Translated by J. C. Grayson. Leiden: Brill, 1999.

Milton, John. *The Complete Poetry and Essential Prose of John Milton*. Ed. William Kerrigan, John P. Rumrich, and Stephen M. Fallon. New York: Modern Library, 2007.

———. *The Complete Prose Works of John Milton*. Ed. Don Wolfe et al. 8 vols. New Haven: Yale University Press, 1953–82.

———. *Joannis Miltoni Angli Pro Se Defensio*. London, 1655.

———. "John Milton Letters, 1649–1659." Columbia Rare Books Library X823M64 S62. Columbia University, New York.

A Modest Confutation of a Slanderous and Scurrilous Libell. London, 1641.

Mohamed, Feisal G. *Milton and the Post-secular Present: Ethics, Politics, Toleration*. Stanford: Stanford University Press, 2011.

Mohl, Ruth. *John Milton and His Commonplace Book*. New York: Frederick Ungar, 1969.

Mukherji, Subha. *Law and Representation in Early Modern Drama*. Cambridge: Cambridge University Press, 2006.

Muldrew, Craig. *The Economy of Obligation: The Culture of Credit and Social Relations in Early Modern England*. New York: St. Martin's Press, 1998.

Nevitt, Marcus. "Women in the Business of Revolutionary News: Elizabeth Atkin, 'Parliament Joan,' and the Commonwealth Newsbook." In *News, Newspapers, and Society in Early Modern Britain*, edited by Joad Raymond, 84–108. London: Frank Cass, 1999.

North, Marcy L. *The Anonymous Renaissance: Cultures of Discretion in Tudor-Stuart England*. Chicago: University of Chicago Press, 2003.

North, Roger. *Discourse on The Study of the Laws*. Reprint of MS in Hargrave Collection. London: Baldwyn, 1824.

Oakley, Francis. *Natural Law, Laws of Nature, Natural Rights*. New York: Continuum, 2005.

Orr, D. Alan. "March, John (1611/12?–1657), Barrister and Legal Writer." In *Dictionary of National Biography*, September 23, 2004. www.oxforddnb.com.

Ovid. *Metamorphoses*. Translated by Rolfe Humphries. Bloomington: Indiana University Press, 1955.
Parker, Alice. "Tobias Smollett and the Law." *Studies in Philology* 39 (1942): 545–58.
Parker, William Riley. *Milton: A Biography*. Edited by Gordon Campbell. 2nd ed. 2 vols. Oxford: Clarendon Press, 1996.
Parliament, England and Wales. *An Act against Several Atheistical, Blasphemous and Execrable Opinions Derogatory to the Honor of God, and Destructive to Human Society*. London, 1650.
Parry, Graham. "Cotton's Counsels: The Contexts of *Cottoni Posthuma*." *British Library Journal* 18 (1992): 29–43.
Patterson, Annabel. *Censorship and Interpretation: The Conditions of Writing and Reading in Early Modern England*. Madison: University of Wisconsin Press, 1984.
Patterson, Frank Allen, et al., eds. *The Works of John Milton*. 18 vols. New York: Columbia University Press, 1938.
Perkins, William. *Hepieikeia: Or, a Treatise of Christian Equitie and Moderation*. London, 1604.
Peters, Edward. "Wounded Names: The Medieval Doctrine of Infamy." In *Law in Mediaeval Life and Thought*, 43–89. Sewanee, TN: Press of the University of the South, 1990.
Peters, Julie Stone. "A 'Bridge over Chaos': *De Jure Belli*, *Paradise Lost*, Terror, Sovereignty, Globalism, and the Modern Law of Nations." *Comparative Literature* 57 (2005): 273–93.
Phillips, Henry E. I. "The Last Years of the Court of Star Chamber, 1630–4." *Transactions of the Royal Historical Society* 21 (1939): 103–31.
Pidd, Helen. "Rushdie Wins Apology—and Spurns Cash—in Libel Case." *Guardian*, August 26, 2008. https://www.theguardian.com/books/2008/aug/27/salmanrushdie.law.
Plowden, Edmund. *La Second Part de Les Reports, Ou Commentaries*. London, 1610.
———. *The Second Part of the Commentaries or Reports*. 2 vols. London: Brooke, 1816.
Plucknett, Theodore F. T. *A Concise History of the Common Law*. 5th ed. Boston: Little, Brown, 1956.
Pocock, J. G. A. *The Ancient Constitution and the Feudal Law: A Study of English Historical Thought in the Seventeenth Century*. Cambridge: Cambridge University Press, 1987.
Post, Robert. "Reconciling Theory and Doctrine in First Amendment Jurisprudence." *California Law Review* 88 (2000): 2355–74.
Prest, Wilfrid. *The Rise of the Barristers: A Social History of the English Bar, 1590–1640*. Oxford Studies in Social History. Oxford: Oxford University Press, 1991.
Pritchard, Thomas Sirrell. *The Jurisdiction, Practice, and Procedure of the Quarter Sessions in Judicial Matters, Criminal, Civil, and Appellate*. London: Sweet and Maxwell, 1904.
Prynne, William. *A Gospel Plea (Interwoven with a Rational and Legal) for the Lawfulness and Continuance of the Ancient Setled Maintenance and Tenthes of the Ministers of the Gospel*. London, 1653.
———. *A New Discovery of the Prelates Tyranny*. London, 1641.
Quint, David. *Epic and Empire*. Princeton: Princeton University Press, 1993.
Raymond, Joad. "Censorship in Law and Practice in Seventeenth-Century England: Milton's *Areopagitica*." In *The Oxford Handbook of English Law and Literature, 1500–1700*, edited by Lorna Hutson, 507–28. Oxford: Oxford University Press, 2017.

———. *The Invention of the Newspaper: English Newsbooks, 1641–1640*. Oxford: Clarendon Press, 2005.

———. "The Rhetoric of Milton's Defenses." In *The Oxford Handbook of Milton*, edited by Nicholas McDowell and Nigel Smith, 272–90. Oxford: Oxford University Press, 2009.

Reports, or, New Cases with Divers Resolutions and Judgements Given upon Solemn Arguments [Court of King's Bench]. London, 1648.

Revard, Stella P. *The War in Heaven: Paradise Lost and the Tradition of Satan's Rebellion*. Ithaca: Cornell University Press, 1980.

Ridley, Thomas. *A View of the Civile and Ecclesiastical Law*. London, 1607.

Roberts, Stephen K. "Juries and the Middling Sort: Recruitment and Performance at Devon Quarter Sessions." In *Twelve Good Men and True: The Criminal Trial Jury in England, 1200–1800*, edited by J. S. Cockburn and Thomas A. Green, 182–213. Princeton: Princeton University Press, 1988.

Robertson, Randy. *Censorship and Conflict in Seventeenth-Century England: The Subtle Art of Division*. University Park: Pennsylvania State University Press, 2009.

Rogers, Pat, and Paul Baines. "The Prosecutions of Edmund Curll, 1725–1728." *Library* 5 (2004): 176–94.

Rosenblatt, Jason P. *Torah and Law in Paradise Lost*. Princeton: Princeton University Press, 1994.

Rushton, Peter. "Local Laws, Local Principles: The Paradoxes of Local Legal Processes in Early Modern England." In *Law, Lawyers, and Litigants in Early Modern England: Essays in Memory of Christopher W. Brooks*, edited by Michael Lobban, Joanne Begiato, and Adrian Green, 185–206. Cambridge: Cambridge University Press, 2019.

Russell, Conrad. *Parliaments and English Politics, 1621–1629*. Oxford: Clarendon Press, 1979.

Sauer, Elizabeth. *Milton, Toleration, and Nationhood*. Cambridge: Cambridge University Press, 2014.

———. *"Paper-Contestations" and Textual Communities in England, 1640–1685*. Toronto: University of Toronto Press, 2005.

Scofield, Cora L. *A Study of the Court of Star Chamber*. New York: Burt Franklin, 1969.

Sellin, Paul R. "Alexander More before the Synod of Utrecht." *Huntington Library Quarterly* 58 (1995): 239–48.

Seneca. *Seneca's Morals Abstracted: In Three Parts*. Edited by Roger L'Estrange. London, 1679.

Sharpe, J. A. *Defamation and Sexual Slander in Early Modern England: The Church Courts at York*. Borthwick Papers, no. 58, 1980.

———. "Law Enforcement and the Local Community." In *The Oxford Handbook of English Law and Literature, 1500–1700*, edited by Lorna Hutson, 221–38. Oxford: Oxford University Press, 2017.

Shawcross, John T. *The Arms of the Family: The Significance of John Milton's Relatives and Associates*. Lexington: University Press of Kentucky, 2004.

———. *The Development of Milton's Thought: Law, Government, and Religion*. Pittsburgh, PA: Duquesne University Press, 2008.

Shiels, W. J. "'The Right of the Church': The Clergy, Tithe, and the Courts at York, 1540–

1640." In *The Church and Wealth*, edited by W. J. Shiels and Diana Wood, 231–55. Oxford: Oxford University Press, 1987.

Shuger, Debora. *Censorship and Cultural Sensibility: The Regulation of Language in Tudor-Stuart England*. Philadelphia: University of Pennsylvania Press, 2006.

———. "The Prison Diaries of Archbishop Laud." In *Taking Exception to the Law: Materializing Injustice in Early Modern English Literature*, edited by Donald Beecher, Travis Decook, Andrew Wallace, and Grant Williams, 120–36. Toronto: University of Toronto Press, 2015.

———. *The Renaissance Bible: Scholarship, Sacrifice and Subjectivity*. Berkeley: University of California Press, 1994.

Silver, Victoria. "'A Taken Scandal Not a Given': Milton's Equitable Grounds of Toleration." In *Milton and Toleration*, edited by Sharon Achinstein and Elizabeth Sauer, 144–70. Oxford: Oxford University Press, 2007.

Simpson, Paula. "The Continuum of Resistance to Tithe, c. 1400–1600." In *Pieties in Transition: Religious Practices and Experiences, c. 1400–1600*, edited by Robert Lutton and Elizabeth Salter, 93–108. Aldershot, UK: Routledge, 2007.

Skinner, Quentin. *Foundations of Modern Political Thought*. 2 vols. Cambridge: Cambridge University Press, 1978.

———. "Milton and the Politics of Slavery." In *Milton and the Terms of Liberty*, edited by Graham Parry and Joad Raymond, 1–22. Cambridge: D. S. Brewer, 2002.

Smith, Nigel. "*Areopagitica*: Voicing Contexts, 1643–5." In *Politics, Poetics, and Hermeneutics in Milton's Prose*, edited by David Loewenstein and James Grantham Turner, 103–22. Cambridge: Cambridge University Press, 1990.

———. "Legal Agency as Literature in the English Revolution." In *The Oxford Handbook of English Law and Literature, 1500–1700*, edited by Lorna Hutson, 604–23. Oxford: Oxford University Press, 2017.

Smith, Sir Thomas. *De Republica Anglorum*. London, 1583.

Smollett, Tobias. "The Frederician Code." *The Critical Review: Or, Annals of Literature* 13 (1762): 1–12.

Smuts, R. Malcolm. "Jonson's *Poetaster* and the Politics of Detraction." *English Literary Renaissance* 49 (2019): 224–47.

Spaeth, Donald. *The Church in an Age of Danger: Parsons and Parishioners, 1660–1740*. Cambridge: Cambridge University Press, 2000.

Spelman, Sir Henry. *The Larger Treatise Concerning Tithes*. London, 1647.

Squibb, G. D. *The High Court of Chivalry: A Study of the Civil Law in England*. Oxford: Clarendon Press, 1959.

Stein, Peter. *Roman Law in European History*. Cambridge: Cambridge University Press, 1999.

Stevens, Paul. "How Milton's Nationalism Works: Globalization and the Possibilities of Positive Nationalism." In *Early Modern Nationalism and Milton's England*, edited by David Loewenstein and Paul Stevens, 273–301. Toronto: University of Toronto Press, 2008.

Stewart, Douglas. "Speaking to the World: The Ad Hominem Logic of Milton's Polemics." *Seventeenth Century* 11 (1996): 35–60.

St. German, Christopher. *The Dialoges in English, Betwene a Doctour of Divinitye, and a Student in the Lawes of England.* London, 1569.
Strain, Virginia Lee. "Legal Reform and 2 *Henry IV*." In *The Oxford Handbook of English Law and Literature, 1500–1700*, edited by Lorna Hutson, 277–97. Oxford: Oxford University Press, 2017.
Straumann, Benjamin. *Roman Law in the State of Nature.* Translated by Belinda Cooper. Cambridge: Cambridge University Press, 2015.
Stretton, Tim, ed. *Marital Litigation in the Court of Requests, 1542–1642.* Cambridge: Cambridge University Press, 2008.
Strier, Richard, ed. *Shakespeare and the Law: A Conversation among Disciplines and Professions.* Chicago: University of Chicago Press, 2013.
Svendsen, Kester. "Milton's *Pro Se Defensio* and Alexander More." *Texas Studies in Literature and Language* 1 (1959): 11–29.
Syme, Holger Schott. "(Mis)Representing Justice on the Early Modern Stage." *Studies in Philology* 109 (2012): 63–85.
Tatarczuk, Vincent A. *Infamy of Law: A Historical Synopsis and a Commentary.* Catholic University of America Canon Law Studies. Washington, D.C.: Catholic University of America Press, 1954.
Thorne, Samuel E. "Sir Edward Coke: 1552–1952." In *The Selden Society Lectures, 1952–2001*, 3–18. Buffalo, NY: William S. Hein, 2003.
Trigge, Francis. *To the Kings Most Excellent Majestie. The Humble Petition of Two Sisters the Church and Common-Wealth.* London, 1604.
Tubbs, J. W. *The Common Law Mind: Medieval and Early Modern Conceptions.* Baltimore: Johns Hopkins University Press, 2000.
Tuck, Richard. *Natural Rights Theories: Their Origin and Development.* Cambridge: Cambridge University Press, 1979.
Turner, Henry S. *The Corporate Commonwealth: Pluralism and Political Fictions in England, 1516–1651.* Chicago: University of Chicago Press, 2016.
Vinogradoff, Sir Paul. *Roman Law in Mediaeval Europe.* London: Harper, 1909.
Visconsi, Elliott. *Lines of Equity: Literature and the Origins of Law in Later Stuart England.* Ithaca: Cornell University Press, 2008.
Waddell, Brodie. "Governing England through the Manor Courts, 1550–1850." *Historical Journal* 55 (2012): 279–315.
Walker, William. "Rhetoric, Passion, and Belief in *The Readie and Easie Way*." *Milton Studies* 52 (2011): 23–57.
Walter, John. "'Law-Mindedness': Crowds, Courts, and Popular Knowledge of the Law in Early Modern England." In *Law, Lawyers, and Litigants in Early Modern England: Essays in Memory of Christopher W. Brooks*, edited by Michael Lobban, Joanne Begiato, and Adrian Green, 164–84. Cambridge: Cambridge University Press, 2019.
———. "'The Pooremans Joy and the Gentlemans Plague': A Lincolnshire Libel and the Politics of Sedition in Early Modern England." *Past and Present* 203 (2009): 29–67.
Walterscheid, Edward C. "The Early Evolution of the United States Patent Law: Antecedents." *Journal of the Patent and Trademark Office Society* 77 (October 1995): 771–802.

Warren, Christopher N. *Literature and the Law of Nations, 1580–1680.* Oxford: Oxford University Press, 2015.

———. "Milton and the Epochs of International Law." *European Journal of International Law* 24 (2013): 557–81.

Wennerlind, Carl. *Casualties of Credit: The English Financial Revolution, 1620–1720.* Cambridge, MA: Harvard University Press, 2011.

White, R. S. *Natural Law in English Renaissance Literature.* Cambridge: Cambridge University Press, 1996.

Wiiffels, Alain. "*Ius Gentium* in the Practice of the Court of the Admiralty around 1600." In *The Roman Law Tradition*, edited by A. D. E. Lewis and David Ibbetson, 119–29. Cambridge: Cambridge University Press, 1994.

Wilson, Luke. "Ben Jonson and the Law of Contract." In *Rhetoric and Law in Early Modern Europe*, edited by Victoria Kahn and Lorna Hutson, 143–65. New Haven: Yale University Press, 2001.

Witte, John. *God's Joust, God's Justice: Law and Religion in the Western Tradition.* Grand Rapids, MI: William B. Eerdmans, 2006.

Woolrych, Austin. "Milton against Hirelings." In *Complete Prose Works of John Milton*, rev. ed., 7: 75–95. New Haven: Yale University Press, 1980.

Worden, Blair. "John Milton and Oliver Cromwell." In *Soldiers, Writers and Statesmen of the English Revolution*, edited by Ian Gentles, John Morrill, and Blair Worden, 243–64. Cambridge: Cambridge University Press, 1998.

———. *Literature and Politics in Cromwellian England: John Milton, Andrew Marvell, Marchamont Nedham.* Oxford: Oxford University Press, 2007.

———. "Milton's Republicanism and the Tyranny of Heaven." In *Machiavelli and Republicanism*, edited by Gisela Bock, Quentin Skinner, and Maurizio Viroli, 225–45. Cambridge: Cambridge University Press, 1990.

Zouch, Richard. *The Jurisdiction of the Admiralty of England Asserted against Sir Edward Coke's Articuli Admiralitatis.* London, 1663.

INDEX

Abraham, 150
    and Melchizedek, in OT, 142–43
    See also tithes/tithing
Achinstein, Sharon, 49
Act of Anne (1710)
    protects copyrights, 115
    See also author(s)
Act of Oblivion, 15–16
ad hominem attack(s), 48, 59–60
    Milton opposes, 54
    Pro Se Defensio as, 128–29
    See also calumny; defamation; *fama*; *infamia*; libel
adultery, 90, 91
aequitas (internal equity), 88–89, 91, 93, 94–95, 97. *See also* equity; law, Roman
aequum, legal term for "just," 125
Ames, William, 35–36
ammunition
    metaphors for (Satan's), 137, 139–40, 149
    See also debt; Satan; violence; war
angels
    good, in *Paradise Lost*, 136–39
        re-enact tithing, 148–49

animus corrigenda, 44
anonymity
    and libel, 116
    protects authors, 67–72
    See also libel
Answer to a Book, Intituled. . . , 68. *See also* anonymity
Answerer, the, 68. *See also* anonymity
Aquinas, Thomas
    on legal vs. moral debt, 134–35
    See also debt
Arcadices Charisius, 124
Aristophanes
    as defamer, not libeller, 56
Aristotle, 94
    on equity (*epikeia*), 86–87
Athens, ancient
    on blasphemy/libel, 53
Augustus Caesar
    punished defamation, 53
author(s)
    booksellers/printers/publishers as liable as, 114–16
    as "contrivers" (Coke), 115
    early modern vs. modern definitions of, 114–18

author(s) (*continued*)
  Milton expands definition of, 113–14 (*see also* More, Alexander)
  should avoid anonymity, 67–68
  See also individual names; books/treatises; libel
Ayloffe, James
  Milton's lawsuit against, 11
Ayres v. Crowe, 145

Bacon, Sir Francis, 32, 79
"bail and surety"
  as metaphoric penalty for licensed book, 64
  See also punishment
Barker, Arthur, 18
Bartolus (Roman jurist), 36
Bastwick, John, 28, 29
Baxter, Richard
  on tithing, 150
Beelzebub, 137–38
Bible, Christian, 13
  on divorce, 80
  on external/internal equity (Milton), 89–93, 95–98
  on tithing, 132
  See also individual books and names; theology
bishops, English
  as equal to lay peers, 163
  slander against, 29–32, 46
Blackstone, William
  on libel, 115–16
  See also libel
blasphemy
  Greeks and Romans didn't tolerate, 53
  intolerable (Milton), 75–77
  redefined, 76
  See also libel; theology
Blasphemy Act (1650), 75, 76–77
Blomley, Nicholas K.
  on Coke on law as superstructure, 157
Blount, Thomas
  Glossographia, 64
  Nomo-Lexicon, 150

books/treatises
  as courtrooms (Milton), 36–38, 41–42, 45, 47, 55
  and defamation
    must avoid, 56–57
    punishment for, 57, 62–65
  licensed, 64–65
  licensing of, 70–72
    worse than defamation, 74–75
  manners important in, 58–59
  Milton's ambivalence about, 50–51
  "mischievous," 65
  readers of as jury, 61
  and truth, 58 (*see also* truth)
  unlicensed, 70
  value of offensive (Milton), 52
  See also individual titles; defamation; speech, freedom of
Browne, Sir Thomas, 164
Buckingham, duke of, 176
Bunyan, John, 153
  Relation of the Imprisonment of Mr. John Bunyan (account of travails), 165–69
  trial of, 165–69
Bunyan, Mrs. John
  intervenes with judges, 167–68
Burton, Henry, 28, 29

Cable, Lana, 97
Cadmus
  Ovid's rendition of myth of, 58
Caesar, Sir Julius, 84
  on composition, 145
Callistratus, 124
calumny (*calumnia*), 6, 111
  Donne's use of term, 40
capias ad satisfaciendum, writ of, 64
Carter, John, 133
Catholic Church, xiv
  hierarchy of, 24
censorship, 24–25
  inuria suits as, 55
  Milton on, 50–51, 54, 62–63, 67
  in Plato's *Republic* and Roman Empire, 53

centralization
    Milton allows for, 159, 160–62
    See also courts, common law
champerty
    seriousness of, 6–7
Chancellor's Court of the University of Oxford, 12
    jurisdiction of (Lambarde), 179
Chancery. *See* Court of Chancery
charity
    importance of, 59
    and internal equity, 95–96 (*see also* equity)
Charles I, king, 66
Charles II, king, 113
Chester, Henry
    on judgment against Bunyan, 165, 167
    See also Bunyan, John
Church of England
    Bunyan and, 166 (*see also* Bunyan, John)
    Milton attacks, 24, 69
    protection of prelates of, 28
churches
    on localization of (Milton), 152
Cicero, Marcus Tullius, 93
    De Inventione, 82
    on internal equity, 88–89
    See also equity
Civil War, English, 71
coinage
    and composition, 139
    as metaphor for ammunition, 137, 143
    See also debt; war
Coke, Sir Edward, 65, 83, 119, 162
    "The Case *de Libellis Famosis*," 28
    champions common law, 157, 180
    on Justinian, 82
    on libel, 29, 115–16 (*see also* libel)
Cole, William
    proposals for equity courts, 154–55
Columbia Manuscript, 170–81
Columbia Rare Book and Manuscript Library
    on "Index Legalis," 175

commonplacing, Civilian
    in "Index Legalis," 172
composition
    debt, defined, 140
    Satan mocks, 149
    in tithing contexts, 144–45
    See also debt; tithes/tithing
Confuter, the
    defends Hall against Milton, 45–49
    guilty of defamation, 55
    guilty of libel (Milton), 49
    See also calumny; defamation; libel
Constable
    jurisdiction of, 178
contumelia
    iniuria and, 26, 111
    See also *iniuria*
Cope, Sir John
    Milton sues estate of, 79–80
copyright, 115
    vs. anonymity, 68
Corpus Juris Civilis (corpus juris), xiii–xv, 8, 84, 86, 92–93, 107
    Pandects (*Digest*), 82, 124, 127
Cotton, Sir Robert, 176
Council of Wales and the Marches, 14, 164
counties
    as functioning states, federated, 158, 163–64
court, conciliar, 34, 66
court, King's Bench, 12, 65, 177
    compared to Court of the Admiralty, 1–2
Court of Chancery, 11–12, 154, 155, 164, 170, 179, 180
    and Civil law, 107–8
    equity suit brought to, 79–80
Court of Common Pleas, 11, 12, 177
Court of High Commission, 34
Court of Requests, 14, 170
    Masters of, 177–78, 177n15
Court of the Exchequer, 12, 147
Court of the Goldsmiths, 12
Court-libell
    term used once by Milton, 63–64

courts, civil
  "without appeal," non-criminal, 159
courts, Civilian, 83, 84, 164
courts, common law, 27–28, 57n13, 177
  should be local, autonomous (Milton), 153–57, 153n4
courts, Continental Civil, 104
courts, ecclesiastical, 26–27, 34
courts, English secular, 27
courts, equity, 164, 177
courts, manor
  as local, 160
courts, modern
  and hearsay evidence, 118, 119
  on libel in electronic media, 67
courts, prerogative, 164
  and common law, 25–29, 147
courts, private, 164–65
courts, university, 83, 107
Cover, Robert
  on *nomos*, 8, 10
creation, God's
  Satan fixated on, 136–37
  See also God
Cressy, David, 113
crime
  civil law and, xv
  More guilty of, 123
  seditious libel as, 29–32, 34
  vocabulary connoting (March), 72–73
  See also libel
Cromwell, Oliver, 68
Curll, Edmund
  tried for lewd publication, 114–15
Cyprian, Saint, 89

debt
  of gratitude, 134–35, 140, 143, 150 (*see also* Satan; tithes/tithing)
  imprisonment for
  as metaphoric penalty for licensed book, 64, 65
  legal procedures re, 138
  legal vs. moral, 133–36
  See also punishment; tithes/tithing
decimation
  double meaning of, 150
  See also tithes/tithing
defamation, 112n30
  against malefactors justified, 43–45
  oral vs. written, 43–44
  anonymous, 67–72
  and common law, 52, 71–75
  conditions required for charging, 27, 37, 38
  of professional competence, 48–49
  successful argument for (Milton), 38
  compared to libel (Milton), 48–49, 56
  components of legal (March), 72–75
  "how-to" book on (March), 74
  intolerable (Milton), 51
  lawsuits concerning, excessive (March), 73
  Milton on (*Areopagitica*), 50–77
  as private matter, 55–56
  punishable in court (Milton), 57
  See also censorship; libel
Dering, Sir Edward, 23
detecting
  as legal term, 35–36
detraction
  public vs. private (Herbert), 43–44
  See also libel
Deuteronomy
  on defamation and divorce, 96
  on divorce, 87, 89–92
  on tithing, 145–46
  See also Bible, Christian
D'Ewes, Sir Simonds, 83
dispensation/concession
  divorce as, 90–92
  See also divorce
"diversity of courts"
  Transcriber interested in, 175–81
divorce
  and defamation, 96

Deuteronomy on, 89–92, 96
Milton's tracts on, 6, 9–10, 18, 23, 68–69, 79–98 passim, 103–4, 148
See also marriage; Milton, John: works of
Dobranski, Stephen B., 114
Donne, John
  on informants, 41–42
  on law and divinity, 11
  sermon at Inns of Court, 39–42
Drury, John, 123
du Moulin, Peter
  actual author of *Regii Sanguinis Clamor (Clamor)*, 113
due process
  for judging books, 62–63
  violated, 47, 64–65
Dutch Republic
  compared to Milton's federated plan, 163–64
Dzelzainis, Martin, 10

Eden, Kathy, 93–94
Edgerton, Samuel
  on *pittura infamandi*, 128–29
education
  Hall criticizes England's system of, 60
Elizabeth I, queen, 177
Ellesmere, Lord
  protects Chancery, 180
enfranchisement
  limitations to (Milton), 62–63
equity
  court of (Chancery), 11
  definition ambiguous, xv–xvi, 79–80, 87, 88n30
  and divorce, 80
  and law, 85–93, 154, 179
  two principles of, 88–93
    internal, 95–96
error, writ of, 5–6
evidence
  Milton uses hearsay, 118–20
  See also testimony

existimatio
  in *iniuria* suit, 111

Fallon, Steve, 136, 149
fama
  about More, 119–20, 120n52, 121–22 (see also *Regii Sanguinis Clamor [Clamor]*)
  defined, 119
  See also infamia; infamy
Fish, Stanley, 12
Fraher, Richard M., 119
Freize, James
  on reforming common-law courts, 154–55
Fuller, Thomas
  on divorce, 90
  See also divorce

Gardiner, Bernard, 171
Genesis, 90
  Abraham and Melchizedek episode in, 142–43
  See also Bible, Christian
God
  and blasphemy, 76–77
  and divorce, 91–93
  and marriage, 95
  Satan's hatred of, 140–41
  and tithes, 133, 148–49
  See also divorce; law, Mosaic; marriage; theology
gold
  gifts to God made of, 148–49
  See also tithes/tithing
Goldsmiths' Company, private court of, 164–65
Goodrich, Peter, 171, 180
gossip
  Herbert defends oral, 42–44
  See also *ad hominem*; defamation; slander
government
  Milton redesigns English to localize, 150–69, 180–81
  See also individual categories

Greaves, Richard L., 165–66
Greeks, ancient
  on heresy, 75
Greene, Jody, 115
Grotius, Hugo, 81–82, 81n5
Guerret, Elisabeth
  More's assignation with, 126

Hale, Sir Matthew, 85
  favors judges schooled in common law, 157
  on judgment against Bunyan, 167–68
  See also Bunyan, John
Halkett, John, 97
Hall, Bishop Joseph
  Defense of the Humble Remonstrance, A, 31, 46
  Humble Remonstrance, An, 29–32, 46
  Milton's enmity toward, 149
  and seditious libel, 29–32, 33–34, 46
Hall, John
  on English education system, 60
  Humble Motion to the Parliament..., 60
Haller, William, 60
Halliday, Paul, 17
Harrington, James, 152
Haskin, Dayton
  on understanding the Bible, 93
Helmholz, Richard, 26–27
  on Civil and canon law, 85
  on composition, 145
  on *iniuria*, 118 (see also *iniuria*)
Herbert, George
  Country Parson, The, 42–45
  on language of infamy, 129
  on licit vs. illicit speech, 42–45
heresy
  tolerable (Milton), 75–77
Hermoginian, 82, 86
Hexham, Henry, 137
High Court of the Admiralty, 84, 107
  compared to King's Bench, 1–2

High Court of Chivalry, 178
Hindle, Steve, 27
Horace (Quintus Horatius Flaccus)
  satirized in Jonson, *Poetaster*, 99–102
Hostiensis, 89
House of Lords
  and authorship, 116
  See also Parliament, English
Howard, W. Scott, 97
Hoxby, Blair, 66
Hudson, William, 29
Hutson, Lorna, 74

Ibbetson, David, 48–49
Illo, John, 66
"Index Legalis"
  of Columbia Manuscript, 171–81
infamia
  defined, 122
  legal, 122–25, 128
  See also infamy
infamy
  diminishes legal rights, 62
  public duty to spread (Herbert, Milton), 43–44, 129
  punishment against "malefactors," 43
  See also *fama*; *infamia*; libel; malefactors
iniuria
  according to *Institutes*, 117–18
  and *contumelia/calumnia*, 26, 111–12
  in "Index Legalis," 173
  jurisprudential language of, 109–12
  law of, 36–37, 55, 99, 128
  libel as, 11, 33, 110–12
  See also libel
Institutes Iustiniani, 107
  importance of, 117–18
ius commune, xiv, 33, 78, 104, 113, 174
  areas punished, 108, 117
  components of, 84
  on equity, 88
  fama in, 119, 126, 127 (see also *fama*)
  requires eyewitnesses, 121

ius patronatus, xiii
ius privatum/ius publicum distinction, 111

James I, king, 177
Janus, 52
Jesus Christ, 34, 39–40, 76
    and equity, 92
    tithes paid to, and to God, 133
    See also Bible, Christian; equity; God
Jews
    divorce permitted to, 90
    tithes required of, 132
John, gospel of, 39–40, 61. *See also* Bible, Christian
John the Divine, 148
Jones, Edward, 174
Jones, John, 168–69
Jonson, Ben
    Poetaster of, 99–102
judge(s), 14
    of Bunyan's case, 165–68
    Civilian, 164
    Confuter as, wrongfully (Milton), 47–48
    "equall," 164–65
    should be elected, not appointed (Milton), 156, 157, 159
    See also various categories of courts; jury(ies); justice
jury, grand
    authors' role as (Milton), 38
    See also books/treatises; readers
jury(ies)
    authority of fluctuates, 168–69
    composed of equals, 163
    early modern, 13–14
    metaphorical vs. literal (Milton), 37–38
    Milton's views on, 61–62, 153, 163–65
    missing from Bunyan's trial, 166–69
    readers as, 38n43, 47, 49, 61–62
    See also books/treatises; courts; judge(s); trial, legal
justice
    and common law, 60–67
    equity part of, 87–88, 89
    kings not immune to, 163
    localized, 151–69, 180–81
    and mercy, 89
    as truth (Milton), 19
    See also various categories of courts; equity; judges; juries; law
Justinian, emperor, xiii, 82, 84. See also *Corpus Iuris Civilis*

Kelley, Maurice
    on handwriting in "Index Legalis," 173
Kelynge, Sir John
    prosecutes Bunyan, 165–68
Klinck, Dennis R.
    on equity, 88
Kranidas, Thomas, 35

laesus (Latin adjective)
    form of *iniuria*, 110
    See also *iniuria*
Lamb, John
    tried for libel, 115
    See also libel
Lambarde, William
    Archeion, or A Discourse upon the High Courts..., 179–80
    on common law, 180
Latin
    as judicial *lingua franca*, 164
    in Milton's writing, 3, 4, 17, 20–21, 99, 104, 110–11
Laud, William, Archbishop, 28
law
    basis of Milton's tracts on divorce, 79–98 (*see also* Milton, John: works of)
    as chaos, 12
    due processes of, 47, 62–65
    Edenic vs. Deuteronimic, 90, 91, 92
    equity and, 85–93, 95, 179 (*see also* equity)
    interpreting God's (Milton), 93–98 (*see also* law, Mosaic)
    and judiciary changes (Milton), 158–62

law *(continued)*
  and manners (civility), 59
  many kinds of, 12–16
    Milton draws on, 18–19, 45, 78–79, 147–48
    Milton's knowledge of, 106–9, 173
    public knowledge of, 74
    and religion gird society (Milton), 152
    and theology, 10–11, 12–13, 18 (*see also* blasphemy; heresy)
  See also individual categories
law, canon, 16
  and Civil law, 84–85
  vs. common law, 80–85
  defined, xiii–xiv
  and external equity, 89 (*see also* equity)
  Milton attacks, 17, 79, 80–81, 131–32, 147
  and Roman law, 83–85, 107
  on tithing 132, 140–41 (*see also* tithes/tithing)
  as too literalist, 131–32
law, case, xv, 82. *See also* law, common
law, civil
  and canon law, 80–85
  defined, xv
  exemplified, 5–8, 15–16, 64–66, 118
  See also law, common
law, Civil, 18, 33, 93, 178
  as Continental, 55, 78
  defined, xiv
  deprives *infames* of rights, 123–24
  English wary of, 82–83
  on *fama*, 119, 120
  "Index Legalis" and, 170–81 passim
  Milton and, 83, 85–93, 104–12
  and Roman law, 107
  unnecessary to study (North), 82–83
  used by Court of the Admiralty, 1–2
  See also law, Roman
law, common (early modern English), xv, 15, 16, 18, 154
  authority of questioned, 178
  vs. Chancery, on equity, 79–80n4
  on character, 126–27
  and defamation, 37–38, 44–45, 46–49, 52, 68, 71–75
  defined, xiv–xv, 60–61
  as divine, 13
  exemption from of internationals, 176–77
  "frivolous," 64
  juries consist of laymen, 61
  and justice, 60–67 (*see also* justice)
  Lilburne champions, 66
  Milton criticizes, 147–48
  and prerogative courts, 25–29
  and Roman law, 82, 101–2
  threat to other law categories, 180
  used by King's Bench, 1–2
  See also law, civil
law, Continental, 100–101
law, criminal, 14–16
law, divine, 13
law, international, 17, xv
  newly emerging, 176
law, martial, 178
law, Mosaic, 79, 89–93, 95
  and tithing, 142–43
  See also Bible, Christian; equity; tithes/tithing
law, natural
  defined, xv
  Milton and, 16–19, 79
  and Roman law, 81–82
law, positive, 12
  defined, xv, 8
law, public
  compared to private (common) law, 7–8
law, Roman, 10, 26–27, 55n7, 79
  and canon law, 83–85, 107
  and Civil law, 107
  and common law, 82, 162, 162n27
  defined, xiii, xiv
  on divorce, 80–85, 92–93 (*see also* divorce)
  on equity, 80, 81–86, 87, 92–93 (*see also* equity)
  Jonson's use of, 99–102
  and natural law, 81–82
  See also law, canon; law, Civil

law, Roman-Dutch, 163-64
law, "Romano-canon," 81
law, statutory, 9. *See also* law, common
law, temporal, 13
lawsuits, 6-7, 7n10, 11-12, 130
  analogy in *Pro Se Defensio*, 105
  how to avoid excess of (March), 73-75
  infamia and, 123-24
  See also individual titles; law; litigation; More, Alexander; trial, legal
lawyers, 77, 105n12, 138
  audience to Donne's sermon, 39, 41
  See also law; lawsuits
legislation. *See* law; Parliament, English
Leonard, John, 9
L'Estrange, Roger
  on "authors'" accountability, 114, 116
  on libel, 56
  See also author(s); libel
Lewalski, K.
  criticizes *Pro Se Defensio*, 106
liability, legal
  for defamation, 62-64
  defined, 115-16
  See also books/treatises; defamation; libel
libel, 25
  Areopagitica and, 50-77
  Ben Jonson suffers, 99, 102
  blasphemy as, 53, 75-77
  Civil law of, 105-6
  common law and (Milton), 45-49, 104
  and defamation (Milton), 48-49, 54, 56-58
  many meanings of, 26
  Milton's accusation against More, 109 (*see also* More, Alexander)
  Roman law and, 100-101, 110
  seditious, 26, 28, 29-32, 56
    Star Chamber guilty of, 33
  See also calumny; defamation
liberty
  Areopagitica and, 72
  and legal systems, 3, 8, 10, 17-18, 78, 162

Milton and, 90, 152, 181
  See also speech, freedom of
licensing. *See under* books/treatises
Lieb, Michael, 128, 129
Lilburne, John, 169
litigation
  anxiety about, 72, 73
  civil, 155-56
  See also law; lawsuits; libel; trial, legal
Livy (Titus Livius), 32-33
Lobis, Seth
  on repaying debt with gratitude, 134
Loewenstein, Joseph F., 67-68
London
  fight for literary justice in, 58
Long Parliament, xiv, 33, 34-35, 79. *See also* Parliament, English
Lord Mayor's Court, 11
Luther, Martin, 84n15

Mabbott, Gilbert
  opposes licensing, 70-71
  See also anonymity; books/treatises
Mackenzie, James, 137
malefactor
  defined, 56-57
manners
  and morality, 58-59
  See also books/treatises
March, John
  Actions for Slaunder, 64, 72-75, 72n49
Mark, gospel of, 76. *See also* Bible, Christian
marriage
  Bible enigmatic on, 86, 93-94
  laws on, 82, 86
  Edenic law on, 90-92
  Milton's views on, 95, 97, 148
  not a sacrament, 90
  See also divorce
Marston, Jon
  ridicules Jonson, 99, 102
Marten, Henry, 64
Matthew, gospel of, 89-90. *See also* Bible, Christian

McNair, Michael, 83
Medine, Peter
  on moral debt, 133, 135
Mercurius Aulicus, 63–64
mercy
  and justice, 89
  See also equity; justice
metaphors
  for ammunition, 137, 139–40, 149
  for juries, 37–38
  for licensed book, 64–65
Milton, Christopher, 18–19, 105n12, 139, 140
Milton, John
  as blind, 55
  champions decentralizing juridical authority, 151–64, 180–81
  champions localizing legislative process, 158–62
  defendant against More, 108–9 (*see also* More, Alexander)
  defends freedom of speech, 20, 24–25, 32–35, 37, 46
  on Donne's take on calumny, 40–42
  on election vs. appointment of governing officials, 156–58
  as elitist, 158, 159
  enmity toward Hall, 31–32, 33–39, 46
  familiarity with law, 3, 4, 106–9
  fights with Confuter, 45–49, 59 (*see also* Confuter, the)
  and Herbert's take on calumny, 42–45
  on his own *fama*, 127–28
  and "Index Legalis," 173–81
  on informants about defamation, 41–42, 45, 129
  juridical language of in *Apology*, 46–49
  leans on common law, 46–47
  as moneylender, 64, 140
  and natural law, 16–19
  oppressed by anonymous authors, 68–70
  prose of, 4–5 and passim
  signs work, 69
  uninterested in fine points of aristocracy, 175

  use of term *libel*, 26 (*see also* libel)
  uses multiple categories of law, 18–19, 45, 78–80
  works of, 131–32n1
    Animadversions upon the Remonstrants . . . (Animadversions), 24, 25, 29, 32–39, 40, 42, 47, 52, 53, 163
    Apology against a Pamphlet, An . . . (An Apology), 24, 25, 45–49, 52, 53, 55, 56, 59, 61
    Areopagitica, 8–9, 19, 25, 49, 50–78, 136, 151, 181
    Colasterion, 5–6, 9, 68, 149–50
    Commonplace Book, 172, 173
    Considerations Touching the Likeliest Means . . . (Likeliest Means), 131–32, 133, 142, 143, 150, 152, 156, 157–58
    De Doctrina Christiana, 76, 152
    De Jure Belli ac Pacis, 81–82
    Defensio Secunda, 17, 62, 67–70, 102–5, 108, 112–13, 125–26
    Doctrine and Discipline of Divorce, 5, 6, 9, 10, 17, 59–60, 69, 71, 79–98 passim, 131, 138, 148
    Eikonoklastes, 57, 150, 163
    Judgment of Martin Bucer, The, 5–6, 23
    Letter to a Friend, A, 151–55, 170, 174, 175, 181
    Letter to a General Monck, A, 151–52, 160, 164
    Masque, A, 10
    Masque Performed at Ludlow Castle, 14
    Modest Confutation, A, 52
    "ownership" of, 69–70
    Paradise Lost, 10, 14, 25, 71, 132–50
    Present Means, and Brief Delineation. . . , 160
    Pro Populo Anglicano Defensio, 147
    Pro Se Defensio, 55, 102–30 passim, 173
    Proposalls of Certaine Expedients, 151–52, 155, 158, 159, 163, 170, 174, 175, 180–81
    Readie and Easie Way, A, 16, 23, 151–52, 158–60, 163–64

Reason of Church-Government and of Reformation, 24
Reason of Church-Government Urged..., 69
Samson Agonistes, 14
sonnet 7, 10
sonnet 12, 23
sonnet 16, 23
sonnet 17, 137
state letters, 174–75, 181
Tenure of Kings and Magistrates, 56, 57, 65, 152, 162–63
Tetrachordon, 59–60, 69, 79–98 passim, 131
Treatise of Civil Power, 75–77, 148
See also calumny; libel; More, Alexander; speech, freedom of

Milton, John, Sr.
  lawsuit against James Ayloffe, 11
Milton v. Cope, 16
Modest Confutation of a Slanderous and Scurrilous Libell, A, 26
  Milton fights back against, 45–49, 56, 68
  See also Confuter, the
Mohl, Ruth, 173
monopoly(ies)
  Goodrich on, 180
  licensing as, 70–71
  Milton wary of, 66
monsters
  people and books as (Milton), 57–58, 62, 65
  See also books/treatises
More, Alexander, 70
  aware of own guilt, 116n42
  fama about, 119–20, 120n52, 121–22, 126–27
  as Milton's adversary, 102–6, 108–30
  Milton's evidence against, 119–22
  as Protestant minister, 129–30
  role in publishing *Regii Sanguinis Clamor (Clamor)*, 113–14, 119–22, 125
  salacious *infamia* of, 122–23, 125–27, 129–30

works of
  Alexandri Mori Fides Publica (Fides Publica), 103, 108, 109, 113
  See also *Regii Sanguinis Clamor (Clamor)*
Moses
  allows divorce, 90–93
  See also Bible, Christian; law, Mosaic
mythology, Greek, 61. See also individual names

Naevius
  punished for attacking Metelli, 53
nomos
  defined, 8
  Milton and, 8–9
North, Roger, 82

Palmer, Herbert, 59–60, 69
Papinian (jurist), 124
pardon, legal
  Bunyan refuses, 167–68, 168n42
Parker, William Riley
  criticizes *Pro Se Defensio*, 103
Parliament, English, xv, 131
  administers justice to peerage, 176
  and debt delinquency, 139
  defamed, 63–64
  dismantles monopolies, 66
  as judiciary also, 54
  legislates against anonymity, 68
  Milton's works address, 9, 82, 91
pasquin/pasquil
  as libel, 31, 60, 112
  See also libel
Patterson, Frank Allen
  on "Index Legalis," 172–73, 175
Paul (Roman jurist), 124
Paul, Saint, 43
Peers
  Milton defines as ordinary men, 162–63
Pelletta, Claudia
  More's assignation with, 121–22, 126

Penn, William
    acquitted by jury, 169
Petrus Rebuffus, 84
Phillipps, Sir Thomas, 171
Pickering, Lewis, 31–32
Pilgrim's Progress, 169. *See also* Bunyan, John
Plato
    Gorgias, 17
    Republic, 53
Plowden, Edmund
    on equitable reading, 94–95
Pocock, J. G. A., 82
Post, Robert, 28
Powell, Richard, 12, 65n32, 138, 139n20, 141
prelates. *See* bishops
printers
    as liable as authors, 114–16
    See also author(s)
prison, King's Bench, 115. *See also* court, King's Bench
Protestants
    on marriage, 90
    More shames by promiscuity (Milton), 129–30
    See also More, Alexander; Smectimnuans
Prynne, William, 28, 29
    in *Colasterion*, 6, 7
    on tithes, 142
pun(s)
    on decimation, 150
    on "discharge," 136
    on indebtedness, 132–33
    legal (Satan's), 137
    on ordinance/ordnance, 150n40
punishment
    of authors via common law (Raymond), 63
    blasphemy merits (Milton), 75–77, 75–76n58
    capital, 66–67, 166
    physical
        against author unwarranted (Milton), 46
    fantasized (More/du Moulin), 111–12
    for public defamation/"faults," 27–28, 43, 72
    via pictures of *infamis*, 128–29
    See also crime; debt
Puritans, 81. *See also* Smectymnuans

qui tam proceedings, 27n10
Quint, David
    on Milton and decentralization, 151

Raymond, Joad, 63
    on Milton's knowledge of law, 106–7
readers (of books/treatises)
    as juries, 38n43, 47, 49, 61–62
    See also books/treatises
reading
    equitable, 93–97
    See also readers (of books/treatises); law
Reformation, English, xiv, 58
Regii Sanguinis Clamor (*Clamor*)
    attributed to More, 103, 104, 105, 108, 110–13
    du Moulin actual author of, 113
    More wrote preface of, 121
    See also More, Alexander
religion
    Bunyan's rejection of conventional, 165–69
    and law gird society (Milton), 152
    See also Bible, Christian; Smectymnuans; theology
Renaissance, Bolognese, 84
Revelation, 148–49. *See also* Bible, Christian
Rhadamanthus, 61
Ridley, Thomas, 84–85, 180
Romans, ancient
    intolerant of libel and blasphemy, 53, 76
    law/religion supports society of, 152
Romans, epistle to, 91. *See also* Bible, Christian
Russell, Conrad, 83

Salisbury, earl of, 176–77
Salmasius ("Claude"), 70n45, 112, 113, 120, 120n52, 126
Satan (in *Paradise Lost*)
  as counterfeit, 139–40
  hates God as debtor, 140–41
  legal/financial language of, 134–35, 138–41
  on tithing, 131–33
Sauer, Elizabeth, 66
  on juries, 13–14, 49
Selden, John
  on common law vs. Civil/canon law, 85
Sellin, Paul R., 129
Seneca the Younger, 134
  on debt and hatred, 140–41
Sherer
  in "Index Legalis," 175
Shuger, Debora, 24–25, 107
  on *Areopagitica*, 51–52n4
  on *inuria* law, 36–37
silence
  question of when appropriate, 25, 33, 41
Skinner, Cyriack, 117n45
slander
  ambiguity of term, 26
  criminal when aimed against bishops (Hall), 29–32
  synonym for *libel*, 39
  See also libel
slaves, Roman, 32–33, 86, 93
Smectymnuans, 40, 69
  Hall considers libelous, 29–32, 33–34, 36, 46
Smith, Nigel, 9
Smith, Sir Thomas, 160, 163
Smollett, Tobias, 12
Solon, 45, 129–30
Spanheim, Ezekiel, 123
speech, freedom of, 20, 24–25, 32–35, 37, 46, 50, 51. *See also* liberty
speech, injurious. *See* defamation; libel
Spelman, Henry, 133, 141
Star Chamber, 14, 66, 164, 177
  dissolved, 33, 35
  and seditious libel, 28, 28n11, 30, 31, 33–34, 39, 115 (*see also* libel)
  threatens free speech, 52
  See also other court categories
Stevens, Paul, 162
Stewart, Douglas, 103
  criticizes Milton's reliance on *fama*, 120, 128
Svendsen, Kester
  criticizes *Pro Se Defensio*, 102, 103, 114, 117–18, 122, 128
  on More's assignations, 126

testimony
  eyewitness and *ius commune*, 120–21
  infames can't give in trials, 124
Theodosius, Emperor, 84
theology
  law and, 10–11, 17, 18
  See also Bible, Christian; blasphemy; God; Jesus Christ
Thurloe, John, 124–25
tithes/tithing
  "good" (Milton), 143, 145–46, 148–50
  hybridized, 149
  in kind or coinage, 144–45, 144n31
  Milton opposes, 131–48
  Satan mocks, 146–47
  of war, 141–48
  See also Satan
Toland, John, 45
tort
  as "civil defamation," 26
  "monstrous" behavior as, 65
  See also defamation; libel
Transcriber, the, 173
  on Constable's jurisdiction, 178–79
  on "diversity of courts," 175–81
  and *ius commune*, 174
  on "minor jurisprudences," 170–71
  politics at odds with Milton's, 175
  relies on Lambarde, 179–80

trial, legal
  by jury, 13–14, 101, 165–66
  satirized in Jonson, *Poetaster*, 99–102
  See also various categories of courts;
    jury(ies); justice; law, civil; law, common
Trigge, Francis, 146–47
trust
  denied to three human categories, 62–63
truth
  as defense in defamation suits, 27, 46–47
  and free speech, 35
  must be heard (Milton), 38, 129
  and seditious libel cases, 28–29

Ulpian, 82, 86
Uriel, 139–40
usury
  1571 debates on and common law, 83

violence
  debt breeds, 136–37

tithing breeds (Milton), 132–33, 146–47, 149
  See also debt; Satan; tithes/tithing; war
Vlacq, Adrian, 113, 116n42

war
  as debt servicing, 137
  in heaven *(Paradise Lost)*, 131–32, 136–41
  tithes of, 141–48
  See also tithes/tithing; violence
Wars of the Poets, 99
Watson, Richard
  on Milton's three Latin defenses, 112
Wingate, Francis, 165
witnesses
  importance of, in debt proceedings, 138
  not used in early common-law trials, 168
  See also evidence; testimony; trial, legal
Worden, Blair, 162
wordplay
  canon/cannon, 149–50
  See also pun(s)
Wordsworth, William, 59

www.ingramcontent.com/pod-product-compliance
Lightning Source LLC
Chambersburg PA
CBHW051356290426
44108CB00015B/2036